Dr Mary MacLeod Rivett worked as the Western Isles Archaeologist and as an archaeology lecturer in the University of the Highlands and Islands for many years. Born in London, England, to a Scottish-Canadian family, she studied archaeology, anthropology and mediaeval studies at Cambridge, York and Glasgow. Her research and publications focus on the archaeology of the Viking Age and of the north of Scotland. She lives between Edinburgh, where she presently works for Historic Environment Scotland, and the Outer Hebrides.

The Outer Hebrides

A HISTORICAL GUIDE

Mary MacLeod Rivett

BIRLINN

First published in 2021 by
Birlinn Ltd
West Newington House
10 Newington Road
Edinburgh
EH9 1QS

www.birlinn.co.uk

ISBN: 978 1 78027 367 9

British Library Cataloguing-in-Publication Data
A catalogue record for this book is available on request
from the British Library

Typeset by Mark Blackadder, Edinburgh

Printed and Bound by Clays Ltd, Elcograf, S.p.A.

Contents

List of Illustrations

List of Plates

Acknowledgements

This book is the result of the generous input of many people's time and knowledge. All those who I have lived and worked with in the Hebrides should be acknowledged as contributors – the people who've taken the time to show me sites, to talk about the history of their areas, and who have got involved with recording and researching sites. Crofters, fishermen, archaeologists, historians, school children, teachers – it's hard to think who hasn't been involved in one way and another. Thank you. The heritage of the islands is all our heritage.

The staff at Birlinn, particularly Andrew, Deborah and Barbara, have been unbelievably patient, as the book has dragged on and on, from one deadline to another, through family crises, two house moves, two job changes. I hope that you feel that we have something worthwhile at the end of this long haul.

At the last minute, lots of people pulled together to sort out the illustrations, saving the whole effort. Jamie Barnes is owed particular thanks for the maps, Alan Braby for the use of images from earlier projects as well as the fantastic reconstruction drawing, and Simon Rivett for redrawing many of the photographs he'd taken.

In particular, though, this book wouldn't have happened without my family, immediate and extended, all of whom learned very early on not to ask how the book was going! Especially Simon. Thanks, my loves.

I'm sure there are many mistakes in the book – they're all mine, and not the responsibility of anyone else, and I apologise for them. I have tried to trace copyright holders for images, but if there are any missing, please let me know and if there are future editions, we will correct them. If I've missed out your favourite site, I'm really sorry – please let me know about that, too, and I'll do my best to include it if there is a next time.

Introduction

Failte gu na h-Eileannan Siar – Welcome to the Western Isles. The Outer Hebrides, as they are also known, seem like a remote and exotic place on the edge of the British Isles to modern visitors, a place where the language and culture are different to that of the mainland, often seen as preserving older ways of life and ideas. Visitors are startled by hearing Gaelic spoken on the ferry or aeroplane as they arrive, and disconcerted by the quiet of a *Leodhas* (Lewis) Sunday morning. The long, white nights of the summer and the dark storminess of winter emphasise this distance and difference, tropes which shape the modern identity of islanders.

But what are the islands? Where are they, and what was their history really like? Was it separate from the rest of Scotland, or was the culture of the islands shaped, as that of the mainland, by national and international social changes and events? How did the islands come to be the place they are today?

This guide is an introduction to the history and archaeology of the islands, chronologically arranged, with a gazetteer of sites for each section. You can use it as a reference book and follow up more detailed reading from the list at the end, or you can use it as a guidebook. Equally, it may be helpful to provide a picture of the islands to the armchair visitor who may never make it to the islands themselves. The guide is not comprehensive – that would be the work of decades. It includes, however, many of the sites which I think, after studying and working in the islands, are typical and relevant to understanding the development of the islands and their role in national and international history. Much more information about the islands' sites can be found in the National Record of the Historic Environment online (https://canmore.org.uk), and the Western Isles Sites and Monuments Record, also available online (smr.cne-siar.gov.uk/smr).

If you are using this as a guidebook, make sure that you understand the Scottish Outdoor Access Code. You can find details of this

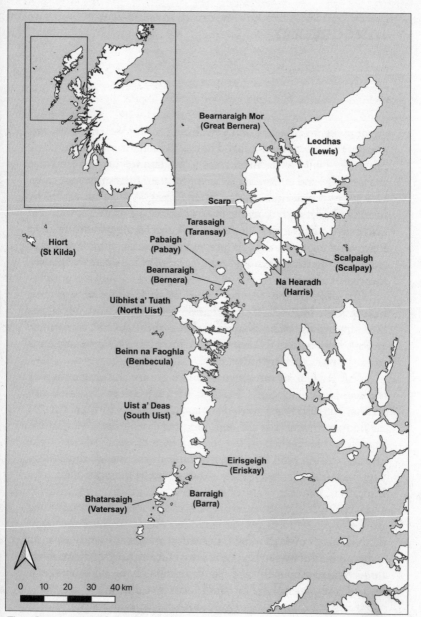

Fig. 1. Location map of islands in the Outer Hebrides

here: https://www.outdooraccess-scotland.scot/. In Scotland you may walk over land, other than private gardens, but you have a responsibility not to cause damage. Just because a site is included in this book does not guarantee access to the site. A note about how to find each site is included in the gazetteer, and many sites have paths and interpretation boards. However, some sites will require significant effort to reach them, for an appropriately equipped walker, and it is your responsibility to consider your level of fitness, the weather, your equipment and safety arrangements. Other sites may be shut off for agricultural or land management reasons, for example during lambing, or shooting seasons, or when burning heather. I have tried to ensure that there are descriptions of a variety of sites, of different levels of accessibility, for each chronological period.

A word on place names: the first language of the islands is Gaelic, and the visitor will find signs everywhere in Gaelic with, sometimes but not always, English following. To make the book as user friendly as possible, I have, in general, given Gaelic place names first in italics with English in brackets and subsequent place names in Gaelic, in each section. The exception to this is island names – after the first mention they are in English, to make it easier for the reader to follow. The spellings used in this book are the modern Gaelic spellings used by the most recent Ordnance Survey maps. These may differ a little from earlier Gaelic and English spellings, and where the earlier spellings are in common use, they will be included in brackets along with the English name. Similarly, metric measurements are used in the book, with few exceptions, but imperial measurements may also be included for convenience.

Geography

The Outer Hebrides are an archipelago of over 100 islands, 11 of which are now inhabited, lying off the western coast of Scotland. The island chain stretches over 200km from north to south, and is 47km at its widest point. Many perceive the islands as remote and rural, but they are just over an hour from the cities of Glasgow and Edinburgh by air, and easily reached by road and ferry, and this is reflected in the increasing numbers of visitors who make the trip each year.

Most of the Outer Hebrides is formed of Lewisian gneiss,

complex, impermeable, metamorphic rocks as much as 3 billion years old, some of the oldest rocks in Europe. These were formed when sedimentary rocks and igneous rocks were subject to tremendous heat and pressure as the earth's continents moved. The resulting stone is very hard, with many folds and fractures, variable in colour and texture, and sometimes containing crystals of garnet or sapphire, but it never contains fossils, having been formed before there was life on earth.

Some of the scattered offshore islands, such as the *Hiort* (St Kilda) archipelago to the west of the Outer Hebrides, and *Na h-Eileanan Seunta* (the Shiants) to the east, are based on hard igneous rocks formed in the cores of extinct volcanoes. On the Shiants, for example, you can see basalt columns like those of Staffa in the Inner Hebrides and the Giant's Causeway in Ireland. Patches of these igneous rocks are found throughout the islands, where volcanoes broke through the ancient gneiss.

There is a small area around *Steornabhagh* (Stornoway) where the geology is sedimentary rocks, soft, red conglomerates formed of sand and pebbles washed down and redeposited in rivers and streams between 200 million and 300 million years ago. Over these rocks, limestone and sandstone were laid down about 200 million years ago, when the area was beneath a warm sea. Little remains of these later sedimentary rocks on the Outer Hebrides, though they can be found on the western coast of the Inner Hebrides, particularly in Skye.

The geology of the islands is important because it shapes the landscape and its natural history. The southern part of *Leodhas* (Lewis), *Na Hearadh* (Harris), and the eastern sides of *Uibhist a' Tuath* (North Uist) and *Uibhist a' Deas* (South Uist) are relatively low, ancient mountains, ground down to their present height by glaciation, which are covered by very thin, acid soils. Where the underlying rock is more level, huge areas of blanket peat bog have built up because the stone does not drain well, and peat deposits cover much of the northern part of Lewis and the interior of North Uist. This peat has largely developed since the end of the last Ice Age, around 10,000 years ago, and people have been living on the islands for nearly that long, so peat has been developing and spreading to cover areas where our earliest ancestors lived. This process is discussed further later in the book, particularly in the chapters about the Neolithic and Bronze Ages.

Along the western coasts of the islands are areas of machair, fine, white sand beaches with dune systems behind them, formed of ancient shells washed up by the rising sea levels from the bottom of the Atlantic Ocean. As the sea level has risen around the islands over the last 10 millennia, these sand habitats have been pushed inland, covering earlier landscapes and overlapping peat deposits. This mixture of sand and peat is very fertile and made the western coasts desirable places to live in prehistory.

The islands have always had a fragile ecology. They are as far north as Hudson Bay in Canada and the southern part of Norway, but their natural northern climate is mitigated by the warmth of the North Atlantic Drift, part of the Gulf Stream current which carries warm water across the northern parts of the Atlantic. As a result, the climate is moderate; prolonged frosts are rare in the winter, but the summer temperatures are low, averaging about 13–14°C in July and August. The temperature of the sea also affects the prevailing winds, which come from the south-west, bringing rain from the ocean. Rainfall in the western side of Harris can be over 2,000mm per year, and this high rainfall, with cool temperatures, is part of the reason for the development of peat. The strength of the south-westerly winds is also a limiting factor in the environment; although winter temperatures are mild, storms are frequent, and the salt-laden winds inhibit plant growth. As a result, although the landscape was wooded in the earliest years after the retreat of the glaciers, as this woodland was gradually cleared by people, it was slow to regenerate. In recent decades, more and more natural regeneration of woodland has been occurring on the islands, a result of very low numbers of grazing animals and a changing climate.

Who are the islanders?

After many years of decline, the islands' population has stabilised at around 27,000. The majority lives in the largest and most northerly island, Lewis, with smaller populations on the islands to the south. The number of occupied islands varies from census to census, as smaller islands shift in and out of permanent occupation.

As the population of the islands has decreased over the last 100 years, it has also aged. Emigrants have tended to be younger, economically active people, and with improved healthcare older people have lived longer. At each census, the proportion of the elderly in the population increases, and the population of school-age children decreases. Some islands also have disproportionate gender ratios, with either more men or more women working away from home. However, immigration to the islands is also a significant factor, as it has been throughout history, and there have always been a wide variety of ethnicities and cultures on the islands.

This diversity means that, although the main languages spoken on the islands are Gaelic and English, other European, African and Asian languages are also widely spoken. Religious belief is also diverse, with a variety of Christian denominations, and organised Moslem and Baha'i communities. A higher proportion of the islands' population are observant believers than is the case elsewhere in the British Isles, and as a result, particularly in the northern islands of Lewis and Harris, Sunday is still a day of rest, with most shops and public services shut.

What do people do here?

One of the commonest questions asked by visitors to the islands is 'What do people do here?'. How does the economic life of the islands work? During the last 50 years, the major employer in the islands has been the local council, *Comhairle nan Eilean Siar*, followed closely by the Western Isles Health Board. Between the two bodies, they provide schools, public services, medical services, care for the young, needy and elderly, infrastructure development, and support for development projects. National and European government support for agriculture, infrastructure, development and projects has also contributed very significantly to the economy. The usual trades, such as building, plumbing and electricity, are also required, and the service economy, providing food, drinks, accommodation, guiding, and entertainment for visitors and locals, is of growing importance. There is a high rate of self-employment, or partial self-employment and, given the small local market, many people combine part-time work with self-employment or a small business.

Famous skills and trades associated with the Hebrides, for example fishing, or Harris Tweed weaving, are still active sources of income to the economy. Tweed weaving is flourishing, in 2019, but it is a very fashion-led business, tending towards periods of boom and bust, and has a history of sharp decline as well as growth. Crofting – the cultivation of small, tenant landholdings – is common in the islands, but most crofters are also self-employed or employed doing something else as well. Typically, crofts are now largely used for livestock grazing rather than arable cultivation.

The history of the islands

The factors that make the Outer Hebrides seem isolated today – its distance from the coast of Scotland and the surrounding sea – were those which made it a desirable place to live in the past. As the ice melted away from the islands at the end of the last Ice Age, *c.* 10,000 years ago, the land was separate from the mainland and, as a result, there were no large predators on the archipelago. No bears, boar, wolves or wild cattle, or other large animals survived on the islands, which could nonetheless be easily accessed by sea by people travelling along the western coasts of the British Isles by boat. These early settlers, arriving about 9,000 years ago, were the first of many immigrants to the islands over thousands of years, who were to shape the landscape by removing trees and importing grazing animals. The environment of the islands was attractive and welcoming – safe from predators, rich with plants, trees and birds, and with all the resources of the sea and freshwater lochs easily available.

Over time, the islanders and their environment interacted. Deforestation in an area of such high rainfall encouraged peat growth, and the introduction of farming and increase of grazing animals inhibited woodland regeneration. The sea level rose, inundating and eroding the shallow western coasts, driving sand and machair up ahead of it. These two factors pushed year-round settlement into the coastal areas and encouraged use of the interior and hills of the islands for summer grazing. The climate changed, sometimes rapidly, sometimes more slowly, and animal and human epidemics lowered the population sharply at various times. New people arrived, with new ideas and technologies, and were absorbed into the local populations, particularly at the beginning of the Bronze Age, and again in the Viking Age.

Links to the other islands, the mainland, and other peoples and ideas were always mediated by the sea, and the history of the islands is therefore dominated by the sea, with settlement largely orientated towards the sea. The good cultivable land seems to have ensured that most farming settlement was on the western coasts, but as boats got larger in the Middle Ages, the most important ports moved from the western side of the islands to the eastern, where there were deep water harbours.

It is only in the last 150 years that travel in northern Scotland has become primarily focused on the road network. This means that throughout most of the human history of Scotland, the northern and western islands were the opposite of isolated – they were well connected by water. The Outer Hebrides are on the main shipping routes from northern Europe to Ireland and control the northern entrance to, and much of, the length of the Minch, the sound between the islands and the mainland and Inner Hebrides. This gave islanders good connections and wealth in the past, encouraging the development of a largely maritime economy, based on trade, fishing and, in the past, toll-taking (or piracy, depending on your point of view).

The islands' fragile ecology, and low ecological carrying capacity, means that another characteristic of its culture over the years has been the export of people. From the earliest documented times, islanders have moved throughout the world. Blood groupings mapped in Iceland and the Faeroes demonstrate links with the Hebrides dating back at least 1,000 years, and Hebrideans could be found throughout the British Isles and in every area with which the British had contact from the Middle Ages onwards. Once again, this emphasises the wide cultural links which the islands had in the past and have at present.

Visiting the islands

You will enjoy your visit to the islands most if you take a little time to prepare. I hope that this book will give you an idea of some of the places you might like to see, and how they fit into the islands' past and present day. You will find a lot of further information about getting around the islands published online and in books and pamphlets. Don't be afraid to ask for information or help if you need it; you are very welcome to the Western Isles.

1. A Mobile People:
Mesolithic Hunters and Gatherers
7000–4500 BC

About 1,000 years after the end of the last glaciation, the first people arrived in the Outer Hebrides. The islands are far enough off the coast of Scotland that it would have been necessary for these early ancestors of ours to travel by skin boat or dug-out canoe to reach the archipelago, and we can guess that they probably came across from the Inner Hebrides to *Uibhist a' Tuath* (North Uist), where the sea crossing is narrowest. The process of sea-level rise means that the islands were larger at this time, and many islands would have been part of larger land masses. It might even have been possible to walk from the southern end of the islands, from *Ceann Barraigh* (Barra Head), to the northern end, *Nis* (Ness). There would have been more land on the western coastline, where the slope of the land is very shallow, and many of the small islands off the western coast, such as *Tarasaigh* (Taransay) in *Na Hearadh* (Harris), would not yet have been separate.

Environmental evidence from archaeological excavations, and from pollen sampling of peat and lake sediments, indicates that the landscape was very different then. After 1,000 years with no human occupation, there were extensive mixed woodlands, with lots of birch, alder and hazel, and with stands of oak and pine in sheltered areas. The remains of tree stumps and wood can sometimes be seen under later peat deposits, particularly at the coast where erosion has removed the peat, for example at *Lionacleit* (Liniclate) in *Beinn na Fhaoghla* (Benbecula), or where peat has been cut.

Because the Outer Hebrides' landscape had been covered with ice and separated from the rest of the country from the end of the Ice Age, no large animals had survived, and the islands were a paradise for birds, with few land predators. The lochs were full of fish. The wealth of resources and the lack of the dangerous animals found else-where, such as wolves, bears and boar, would have made offshore islands very desirable places to live.

The first evidence that we have for the arrival of people in the islands is found in the environmental samples. About 7000 BC, there was a sudden decrease in the amount of tree pollen and an increase in the quantity of tiny particles of air-borne charcoal, suggesting that areas of woodland were being cleared by burning. This is a pattern that is seen elsewhere in Scotland, and it has been suggested that people were trying to create and keep open woodland clearings, where grass would grow and attract grazing animals, particularly deer. This would have been very important as these early people were hunter-gatherers, not farmers. They moved round the landscape seasonally on a regular route, going to places where they knew that they could find food and other resources, for example particular types of stone for making tools.

It is interesting that we see this pattern of woodland clearance in the Outer Hebrides, because this is the only evidence that there might have been deer present on the islands then. We know that there were red deer in the Inner Hebrides and on the Scottish mainland, from excavations at Mesolithic settlements such as Kinloch on the Isle of Rum. Finds of headdresses made from red deer skulls and antlers, from Star Carr in Yorkshire, suggest that the deer may have had symbolic or religious importance, as well as being a source of food, skins, sinew, antler, and other useful materials. It isn't possible to say with certainty, but it is unlikely that deer could have swum across even the shortest gap between the Inner Hebrides and the Isle of North Uist, so it is possible that deer were deliberately introduced to the islands by these first settlers, or that woodland clearance was taking place for other reasons that we don't yet understand.

Woodlands, and particularly woodland margins, were important sources of food during this period. Hazelnut shells are a very common find on Mesolithic sites; nuts are high in protein, fat and calories, easy to harvest and preserve, and very tasty. The nuts ripen just before the winter sets in, and people would have gathered at known areas of hazel trees in the autumn to gather them.

There are few Mesolithic sites to visit in the islands. As these were mobile people, they lived in skin tents, caves and rock shelters and didn't construct large, permanent buildings or religious sites. Their tools were made of stone, particularly very small stone blades set into wooden, bone or antler handles, and the stone tools are commonly all that survives as evidence for human presence. The changes in the landscape since that time, particularly the rise of the sea level, and the spread of peat, have also removed or hidden the slight remains of their settlements. Many sites would have been beside the sea, focused on fishing and gathering marine resources, and have therefore been eroded or submerged by the rising waters or covered by the moving sand which forms the machair. Other settlements were probably by inland lochs and rivers and are now concealed beneath the peat. It is only in the last decade that conclusive archaeological evidence of Mesolithic human presence in the Outer Hebrides has been found, and there is certainly much more to discover about this period.

GAZETTEER

The known sites are associated with later archaeological sites, which are cross-referenced below.

Na Hearadh (Harris)

1. *Baile Deas* (South Town),   NF 9753 9125
   Taobh Tuath (Northton)

Walk 2km from *Taobh Tuath* along an unpaved path.

A multi-period settlement site, with Mesolithic, Neolithic, Bronze Age, Iron Age, mediaeval and Early Modern settlement (Sites 24, 46) is located on the southern coast of *Gob an Tobha* (Toe Head), a peninsula just to the north of *Taobh Tuath* on the west coast of Harris. The Mesolithic evidence, which was first uncovered in the mid 1960s and re-excavated in 2001, is a thin layer of soil immediately on top of the glacial till sub-soil. It is covered by the machair sand, and by later settlement from the Neolithic onwards. Only a very small area of the site has been excavated, but stone settings, possibly the remains of tents, chipped stone tools, and burnt hazelnuts were found. The hazelnuts provided radiocarbon dates, the earliest of which was 7050 BC, providing the first, and still the earliest, definite confirmation of Mesolithic settlement in the Outer Hebrides.

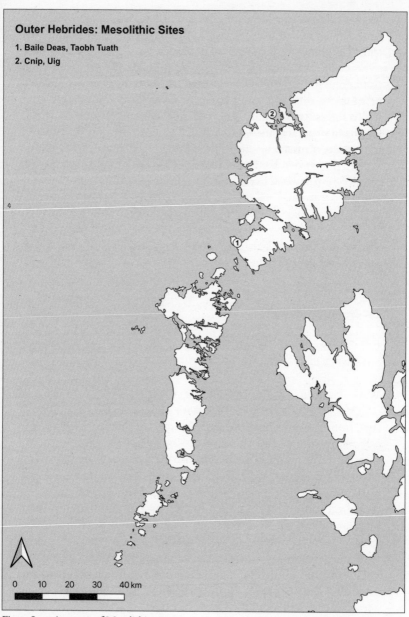

Outer Hebrides: Mesolithic Sites

1. Baile Deas, Taobh Tuath
2. Cnip, Uig

0   10   20   30   40 km

Fig. 2. Location map of Mesolithic sites

Leodhas (Lewis)

2. *Cnip* (Kneep), Uig

NB 1003 3634

From the campsite car park, walk 400m along the shore, or 200m across the beach if the tide is out.

At the bottom of the *Cnip* headland, at the northern end of *Rif* beach, is a small, rocky outcrop which provides shelter for the remains of a Viking or mediaeval naust, or boathouse (Site 95). On the top of the outcrop are the slight remains of a Mesolithic midden, or rubbish heap, consisting largely of limpet, razor clam, clam and oyster shells, which was excavated before it was finally destroyed by erosion. Further to the north, following the eroding edge of the headland, further middens of fish bone were excavated. This site was visited and revisited over many seasons, particularly for fishing young saithe, which still swim in the channel between the headland and the island of *Pabaigh* (Pabbay), about 300m offshore.

2. Shaping the Landscape:
Neolithic Farmers 4500–2000 BC

The greatest social and ecological change in the history of human life in the islands was the introduction of farming around 6,500 years ago, at the beginning of the Neolithic Period (the New Stone Age). Initially, this may have seemed to be a relatively minor adjustment; food crops, particularly wheat and barley, and new animals – sheep and cattle – were introduced, perhaps by incomers from the south of the British Isles. The first certain evidence for the presence of red deer on the Outer Hebrides also comes from this period; bone and antler are found on settlement sites. As people were already used to managing the landscape, following and hunting animals, clearing woodland and encouraging the growth of plants such as hazel trees, these new introductions might have been quite easy to adopt. There is recent evidence that suggests that early attempts to cultivate wheat may have failed, and the local people in the Northern and Western Isles of Scotland could have started farming as herders, managing cattle and sheep, then later cultivating barley as a staple crop.

The type of sheep which were first introduced to the islands still survive on the offshore archipelago of *Hiort* (St Kilda). Soay sheep are similar in size and shape to the Neolithic sheep and retain many characteristics lost by more modern breeds, including the ability to shed their wool.

Despite the introduction of agriculture, gathered and hunted wild food continued to be a very important part of the islanders' diet. Animal bones from excavations show that there was some shoreline fishing, birds, small mammals and red deer were hunted, and leaves, nuts and wild fruits were gathered.

In the landscape, this period was marked by further clearance of woodland, as grazing land was needed for animals and fields were cleared for crops. Samples from peat and from loch sediments show us that tree pollen in the atmosphere declined and, for the first time, cereal pollen from wheat and barley appears. The reduction in trees would have started to have a wider effect on the landscape, as trees draw up a lot of water through their roots and transpire it out of their leaves, so woodland clearance and the grazing of the open areas, preventing regeneration of trees, would have made the soil drainage worse in places and caused the gradual spread of peat.

Sea levels also continued to rise, as the wider landscape of Scotland settled after the removal of the ice sheet. Shell sand was pushed ahead of the rising sea, forming the sandy coastal plain of the machair, particularly on the shallower west coast of the islands. This soil was light and easy to cultivate, so it became one of the areas where farming was concentrated. The sea also started to separate the islands, creating the channels and straits that we are familiar with today.

Permanent settlement

After the introduction of farming, people became increasingly sedentary. They travelled less through the landscape and built longer-term settlements, of small, one-roomed, oval houses. Frequently, and perhaps surprisingly, these new settlements seem to have been founded on islands in freshwater lochs, such as *Eilean Domhnuill* on *Loch Olabhat* in *Uibhist a' Tuath* (North Uist) (Fig. 3). Here, two small oval buildings of stone, turf and timber were built on an island partly enclosed by a wattle fence and linked to the shore of the loch by a wooden causeway. It's not clear why the practice of living in lochs was adopted, but recent research has shown that it was widespread at this time throughout the Outer Hebrides. Divers surveying loch islands in the Isle of *Leodhas* (Lewis) have found evidence for Neolithic settlement at *Loch Langabhat* and *Loch Borghasdail* in *Carlabhagh* (Carloway) on Lewis, amongst others. These islands, called crannogs, were partly or wholly artificial, with large timber piles and stone used to create a building platform, and they represent a huge investment of time, effort and materials. Suggested reasons for the creation of crannogs include a need for defence, or the possibility that people found that the space on the island felt controlled and domestic, as opposed to the dangers of the wider landscape. Some archaeologists have even suggested that they were built to escape the clouds of midges that swarm over the islands in the summer! Why they were constructed is a question that we really can't answer yet, but there is little other

Fig. 3. Reconstruction of the Neolithic settlement on *Eilean Domhnuill* (Site 19), *Uibhist a' Tuath* (North Uist) (© Alan Braby)

evidence from this period in the islands for fighting or conflict, so it seems probable that these small islands had a symbolic or cultural significance. The Neolithic crannogs in the Outer Hebrides are the earliest known from Scotland, though there is evidence from Ireland of Mesolithic occupation of crannogs, so it wouldn't be surprising to find earlier occupation here in the future.

Another pair of houses was found, this time near the modern coastline, at *Taobh Tuath* (Northton) in *Na Hearadh* (Harris) (Site 24), a site which had previously been a Mesolithic camp. The reuse of this earlier site suggests the possibility that the same family group might have adopted the new practice of farming, continuing to occupy the land they knew before. The two houses were placed tightly side by side. They were oval, with walls of stone and turf, and were entered at the southern end. Their architecture was like that of the houses at *Eilean Domhnuill*, and like Neolithic houses from the Knap of Howar in Orkney, suggesting that there may have been cultural links between the islands.

Initially, people seem to have used wood for their houses, perhaps making wattle frames, and building turf walls around them. Such buildings would have been very similar to the temporary structures built in the Mesolithic Period, when people were more mobile. A Neolithic settlement at the coastal valley of *Allt Chrisal/Easdail* on *Barraigh* (Barra) provides an example of this. Excavations by the University of Sheffield revealed the remains of a timber-framed building, constructed on a stone platform, which may have been round or oval. Later renovations of the building were constructed in stone, and stone and turf soon emerged as the most commonly used building materials throughout the islands. This shift in building materials probably reflected a decrease in woodland on the islands, as it was cleared for farming. Stone buildings are easier for archaeologists to recognise, so it may also be that we are missing settlements constructed largely of turf and wood. We also need to remember that the Neolithic peat cover of the Outer Hebrides was less extensive; later peat certainly covers archaeological sites which are inland, away from the shore.

Although most houses of this period in the islands were relatively small and lightly built, there is one possible exception, which was found during peat cutting in the 1920s, at Steinacleit in *Siadar* (Shader) (Site 39), on the west coast of the Isle of Lewis. This is a much larger structure, built of huge stones, which may be the remains of a very large building. It has not been archaeologically excavated, so this interpretation has been hotly debated; some archaeologists believe that it is the remains of a chambered burial cairn. A better-preserved large building in Shetland, at Stanydale, which mimics the shape of a burial cairn, but has a large open room within it, gives some suggestion of what the Steinacleit site might have looked like (Fig. 4). Steinacleit is so unlike the other Neolithic buildings in the Outer Hebrides that we wonder whether it might have been a special building, perhaps with a religious function.

In addition, recent excavation and surveys have shown that sea cliffs and sea stacks were used, possibly for settlement. These sites are now difficult and dangerous to access because of erosion and rising sea levels, but were probably easier to reach in prehistory. However, they are likely to have been sites on or near the edge of the land even then, and most are not in the middle of land that can be easily cultivated, so they were probably not ordinary farms. Excavations on the sea stack of Dunasbroc in *Nis* (Ness) in Lewis have shown that the site was used for about 500 years and fires were built on it. It's not clear whether there was a building or not, as the site was reoccupied

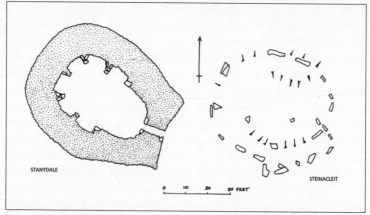

Fig. 4. Stanydale Temple in Shetland and Steinacleit in *Leodhas* (Lewis)

during the Iron Age (Chapter 4), and the top of the stack was reshaped then. Other coastal stacks, for example *Eilean nan Luchruban* (Site 41) and *Stac Dhomhnuill Chaim*, both in Lewis, and Biruaslum on *Bhatarsaigh* (Vatersay), show the same pattern of Neolithic use, followed by later prehistoric reuse.

Changes in technology

There were important technological changes in the more settled Neolithic Period. In addition to the flaked stone tools which had been used for many thousands of years, people polished and ground stone. Polished axes and broad, flat knives of stone were produced, some of stone types which were too soft to be functional, for example the limestone axe found during building work on 20th-century vernacular houses at *Gearrannan* (Garenin) in Lewis (Plate 1). Some of these may have had a symbolic value both for their original maker and, in the case of the *Gearrannan* axe, also for the person who put it into the wall of a house thousands of years later. An unused porcellanite axe, probably imported from Antrim in Ireland, was found still in its handle in a bog in *Sulaisiader* (Shulishader) in Lewis (Fig. 5); it may have been placed in the bog as an offering of value and beauty. Other ground stone tools, however, were entirely functional, and are chipped and re-polished.

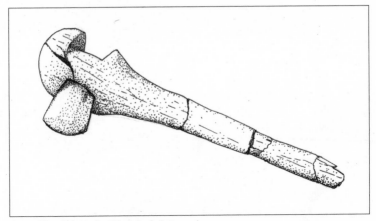

Fig. 5. The *Sulaisiader* (Shulishader) Axe

Another significant change was the introduction of pottery-making. Using the local clay, large amounts of highly decorated hand-made pottery was produced (Fig. 6). Pots were probably made at home and fired in the domestic hearth, and broken pieces are found on all settlement sites from the Neolithic Period onwards. The styles and shapes changed over time, sometimes following styles in neighbouring areas and sometimes showing local developments, helping to date archaeological sites in the islands. This was the start of a tradition of handmade pottery which continued unbroken in the islands for more than 6,000 years, until the beginning of the 20th century.

Imported stone tools and the changing styles of the pottery show that people were travelling by sea between the Outer Hebrides, Ireland, and the west coast of mainland Scotland. The islands were not isolated from developments elsewhere in the British Isles, and cultural and stylistic influences from outside the islands had an impact upon how the local community developed.

Communal burial

Although Neolithic farmers in the Outer Hebrides built small houses, they could build much larger structures. Community efforts were needed to erect the enormous communal burial cairns which are the earliest easily visible monuments in the Hebridean landscape. Most

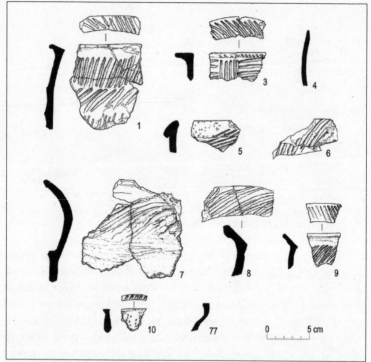

Fig. 6. Neolithic pottery from Dunasbroc, *Leodhas* (Lewis)

of these cairns were built on slopes of hills, sometimes in places which were visible from a long distance away, like *Barpa Langais* in North Uist (Site 22; Fig. 7), but in other cases in areas which had very limited visibility, for example *Dun a' Bharpa* (Site 5; Fig. 11) in Barra. They were rarely built on the highest point of a hill, and they may have acted as territorial markers for the areas that they overlooked.

Neolithic burial cairns had internal chambers, and the form of the chamber is used by archaeologists to distinguish different types of cairn. There are two types in the Outer Hebrides: passage graves, such as *Bagh Chornaig* on Vatersay, which were entered by a long, narrow passage leading into the body of the cairn; and Clyde cairns, which have a short passage and long, rectangular chamber. Excavations show that cairns were visited repeatedly to inter the dead and possibly to perform ceremonies. At *Cairinis* (Carinish) in North Uist, small,

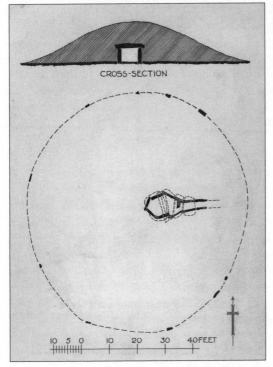

CROSS-SECTION

10 5 0   10   20   30   40FEET

Fig. 7. *Barpa Langais* (Site 22), *Uibhist a' Tuath* (North Uist) (© Crown copyright: HES)

ephemeral buildings, probably tents or benders, were repeatedly set up near the long cairn (Site 13) during the Neolithic Period, probably to house people attending activities at the cairn.

Similar burial cairns are found all over north-western Europe, but in each area the cairns seem to have been used slightly differently. Some contained the remains of cremated bodies, while others contained whole bodies. Bones were sometimes sorted into different types, with skulls in some areas and long bones in others, suggesting that bodies were either exposed to the elements outside the tomb before being moved in, or moved around inside the tomb after they had decayed. In Orkney, one cairn on South Ronaldsay contained the bones of sea eagles, and others contained those of red deer, or dogs, in addition to human bones. Perhaps these animals were totems for a community, symbolising the group who used the cairn for their dead.

Most of the excavated Outer Hebridean cairns were dug in the earlier part of the 20th century, for example *Uneabhal* (Unival) in North Uist, dug by Sir Lindsay Scott in the 1930s. As archaeological techniques were less sophisticated then, such excavations could only produce relatively limited amounts of information. However, in the 1990s, a team from the University of Edinburgh excavated at Geiriscleit chambered cairn in North Uist, an unusual, coastal cairn which was being destroyed by erosion, and their work has given us a more detailed understanding of the structure. Although the cairn had been damaged and had also been excavated in the early 20th century, enough survived to show that it had been used for the burial of both cremations and inhumations. Sometime later in prehistory it was reused, possibly for a building constructed into the chamber. This long, complex history is typical of excavated cairns in other areas, which were often closed at the beginning of the Bronze Age, and then sometimes had buildings constructed on top of them in the Iron Age (see Chapter 4). No tomb on the Outer Hebrides has survived intact to be excavated using modern techniques, so we cannot be sure whether these tombs were used for everyone in the Neolithic community, or only some individuals.

The distribution of chambered cairns is very uneven in the Outer Hebrides. They are heavily clustered in North Uist, where there are over 30, while on the larger island of Lewis and Harris, only 16 are known, most of them very poorly preserved. The explanation for the difference is not clear: North Uist may have been a landscape of particular importance in prehistory, but it is also possible that later cultural differences between the islands may have meant that more cairns were dismantled in Lewis and Harris, and their stones reused for building other structures.

Raising the stones

The other great monuments that survive from the Neolithic Period are the standing stones. For most people, the English site of Stonehenge is the iconic stone circle, but many of the standing stones in the Outer Hebrides and northern Scotland are earlier than Stonehenge. They are part of a wider movement that saw people all over the coastal areas of north-western Europe creating megalithic (big

Fig. 8. *Calanais* (Callanish) 1 Stone Circle, *Leodhas* (Lewis) (Site 37) in the 19th century (Proceedings of the Society of Antiquaries of Scotland)

stone) monuments, and, in each area, the patterns and uses of the monuments were slightly different.

There are standing stones and stone circles throughout the Outer Hebrides, and many of them are distant from modern roads and not now particularly accessible. However, research suggests that most were set up in areas that were farmed in the Neolithic and Bronze Ages, overlooking fields and settlements. They are often on slightly raised ground, ridges or slopes, though, like chambered cairns, they are rarely on peaks or summits. The best example of this is the group of standing stones, a flattened circle with radiating stone rows and an avenue, at *Calanais* (Callanish) in Lewis (Site 37) (Fig. 8 and Plate 2). This impressive stone setting is on a ridge overlooking the sea inlet of *Loch Rog* (Loch Roag), which would have been a largely dry valley, occupied by small farms surrounded by walled fields, when the stones were raised, but has since been inundated by the sea. The stone circle is near, but not at, the end of the ridge, just below the highest point, a pattern which is followed by other circles and stone settings around *Calanais*. Over 20 such sites are known around *Loch Rog* (see Sites 33–37), and there probably would have been many more in the past, as some have been accidentally or deliberately toppled and then covered by the growth of peat over the years, for example at *Achadh Mor* (Achmore) (Site 32).

Recently, it has also become evident that we have limited our understanding of monuments by focusing on those which are largest, most complex and obvious in our modern landscape. In Barra, at the southern end of the islands, in contrast to Lewis, there are no large stone circles; instead, individual stones or pairs of stones mark coastal valleys and important inland routes, for example on the coast at *Borgh* (Borve) (Site 6) and at *Beul a' Bhealaich* (Site 4). In addition, circles of smaller stones or boulders, such as that at *Aird Mhidhinis*, may date to the Neolithic Period, suggesting that how stones were used to mark the landscape and what they meant to the communities who set them up was different in different areas of the archipelago.

There is, of course, speculation about the function of stone circles and standing stones. Early visitors to the islands suggested that they were people who had been turned to stone, or that *Calanais* was a 'druidical temple'. More recently, some archaeologists have argued that such sites were observatories, marking the progression of the sun or moon. Significant alignments between the stones at the main site at *Calanais* and the rising and setting of the moon over the ridge of hilly landscape to the south, known as *Cailleach na Mointeach* ('the Old Woman of the Moor'), suggest some truth in this argument. In recent years, emphasis has also been put on the communal effort necessary to quarry, move and raise the stones, and how doing this would have affected early society, creating and strengthening bonds and relationships between people. Each site as we see it today is the end result of decades, if not centuries, of development and change.

Truly, such sites probably had multiple functions, marking seasonal changes and events with ceremonies, like places of worship today. The effort of raising the stones must have been important but, equally, the care that is shown in the placing of each stone in relation to each other and the wider landscape indicates that planning and location were a priority, and the underlying concepts behind the planning of each site were sufficiently important to be taught and passed on over generations. They give us a picture of people who had sufficient time to spare from subsistence that they could teach and transmit knowledge over time and work together to create communal monuments reflecting their views and beliefs of the wider world.

GAZETTEER

Barraigh (Barra)

3. *Allt Chrisal/Easdail* settlement   NL 6425 9773

Signposted. Park in the layby on the northern side of the road and walk 70m upslope and across a small stream.

The south-facing valley created by the stream, *Allt Chrisal*, also called *Allt Easdail*, on the southern coast of Barra, is a multi-period focus of settlement, much of which was excavated by archaeologists from the University of Sheffield in the 1990s. The earliest site here is the fragmentary remains of a Neolithic settlement, on a terrace on the eastern side of the stream. It lies behind the footings of an 18th-century house, which was probably built using stone from the Neolithic houses.

The Neolithic occupants cut out and constructed the terrace as a foundation for their house, which was initially a building of timber and turf, replaced over time by structures built of stone and turf. Finds from the site suggest that the occupants grew a little barley and were dependent on fishing. They burned peat in their fires, and the remains of a small, temporary, clamp kiln show that they made pottery in the house for their own use.

4. *Beul a' Bhealaich* standing stone (fallen),   NF 6834 0086
    Baile na Creige (Craigston)

Walk 2km east from the end of the paved road at *Baile na Creige*, initially following a peat track, to the high point of the valley crossing the island.

The walk to this fallen standing stone is worth it to see the very large, now fallen, standing stone which once stood close to the highest point of the pass.

The stone, which was probably visible from both sides of the island when standing, is nearly 5m in length and 1.5m wide. It has not been excavated so its precise date is uncertain, though it probably

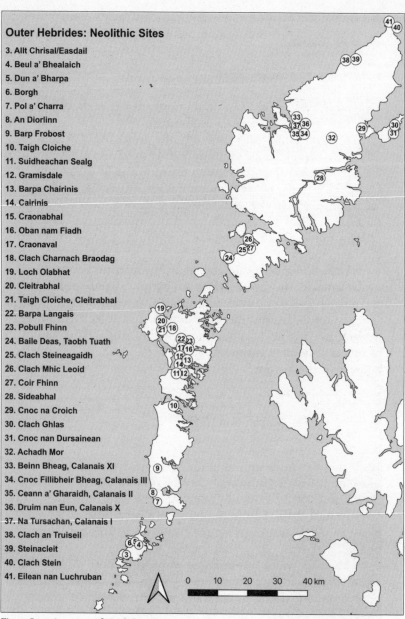

Outer Hebrides: Neolithic Sites

3. Allt Chrisal/Easdail
4. Beul a' Bhealaich
5. Dun a' Bharpa
6. Borgh
7. Pol a' Charra
8. An Diorlinn
9. Barp Frobost
10. Taigh Cloiche
11. Suidheachan Sealg
12. Gramisdale
13. Barpa Chairinis
14. Cairinis
15. Craonabhal
16. Oban nam Fiadh
17. Craonaval
18. Clach Charnach Braodag
19. Loch Olabhat
20. Cleitrabhal
21. Taigh Cloiche, Cleitrabhal
22. Barpa Langais
23. Pobull Fhinn
24. Baile Deas, Taobh Tuath
25. Clach Steineagaidh
26. Clach Mhic Leoid
27. Coir Fhinn
28. Sideabhal
29. Cnoc na Croich
30. Clach Ghlas
31. Cnoc nan Dursainean
32. Achadh Mor
33. Beinn Bheag, Calanais XI
34. Cnoc Fillibheir Bheag, Calanais III
35. Ceann a' Gharaidh, Calanais II
36. Druim nan Eun, Calanais X
37. Na Tursachan, Calanais I
38. Clach an Truiseil
39. Steinacleit
40. Clach Stein
41. Eilean nan Luchruban

0   10   20   30   40 km

Fig. 9. Location map of Neolithic sites

dates to the later part of the Neolithic Period. Its huge size and dominant position in the landscape suggest that it had great significance to the local population.

5. *Dun a' Bharpa* chambered cairn,   NF 6718 0190
Baile na Creige (Craigston)

Walk 1.2km from the end of the paved road at *Baile na Creige*, following the edge of the croft land to the north of the road.

    Dun a' Bharpa is a large, round, chambered cairn, edged with upright stones on the western side, in a raised valley on the northern side of the *Borgh* (Borve) Valley in Barra. Despite its size, about 30m in diameter and 5m high, it is visible from a very limited area of the valley, emphasising the care with which Neolithic ritual monuments were placed in the landscape. This cairn is probably the earliest visible

Fig. 10. *Beul a' Bhealaich* standing stone, *Baile na Creige* (Craigston), *Barraigh* (Barra)

Fig. 11. *Dun a' Bharpa* chambered cairn, *Barraigh* (Barra)

archaeological monument in the valley.

The tops of the upright megaliths (large stones) which formed the chamber and passage inside the cairn can be seen sticking up through the stones of the cairn, and they show that the entrance was to the east, facing the rising sun. The cairn stones have been rearranged on top to form numerous small, circular or oval hollow shapes, which are probably the remains of later sheiling huts.

In the landscape to the south of the cairn, spreading down the slope into the *Borgh* Valley, is a network of small, irregular, stone-walled fields which pre-date the modern crofting landscape. The walls of these fields may have been built using stones from the cairn. Within, and earlier than these fields, are three smaller cairns with kerbs around them, probably Bronze Age in date, and to the west of them are the remains of prehistoric building. This is a landscape in which we can see evidence of continuous use and occupation since the Neolithic Period.

6. *Borgh* (Borve) standing stones and possible cairn

NF 6527 0144

Situated 100m west of the A888 circular road around Barra, on the machair at *Borgh*.

Two standing stones, 12m apart, stood on the machair at *Borgh* until the early 20th century. One is now fallen but the other is still visible, though shifting sand has partially buried it. It is not entirely clear whether these were Neolithic stones, or whether they marked the location of a Viking Age burial which is said to have been found here (Site 85). Elsewhere in the islands, incoming Scandinavians sometimes reused prehistoric ritual sites for burials, and that may have been the case here.

Just to the north of the stones is a grassy mound which is the remains of another archaeological site. This is known locally as a cairn, but it has become entirely overgrown and we cannot be certain whether the story is true.

Uibhist a' Deas (South Uist)

7. *Pol a' Charra* (Polochar) standing stone   NF 7459 1439

Park at the car park for the Polochar Inn, and the stone is immediately visible on the grass between the parking area and the shore.

The place name *Pol a' Charra* means 'the inlet of the large stone', and it was probably named after the standing stone which is adjacent to the parking place for the Polochar Inn. A local tradition suggests that the stone may have been moved from its original location, but no archaeological excavation has been carried out to confirm or deny the story.

8. *An Diorlinn*   NF 7300 1733

Park at the end of the machair road, on the shore, and walk 200m out along the headland.

This site, which was fully excavated in 2013, is the eroded remains of a Neolithic–Early Bronze Age settlement located halfway along a ridge joining the small island of *Orasaigh* (Orasay) to the shore. In the Neolithic Period, it was probably either on an island in a freshwater loch, or on a natural knoll on the loch shore. Sea-level rise has eroded away the softer ground, leaving this and Orasay as tidal islands.

Although there is not much to see at the site now, the excavations revealed a site which had been occupied for around 1,500 years, with the remains of timber and stone houses and the archaeological deposits that had built up during their use. Decorated Neolithic and Early Bronze Age pottery were found, along with stone tools made of flint and quartz. Most of the site had been destroyed by erosion, and a visit here provides a clear illustration of just how much the coastline and landscape of the islands has changed over the last 6,000 years.

9. *Barp Frobost* chambered cairn   NF 7547 2496

Turn east off the main road towards *Minngearraidh* (Mingarry) and park at the end of the unsurfaced road at NF 7478 2640. Walk along the road for 800m, then turn south across the moor towards the cairn, which should be visible throughout.

This is a rather damaged, round, chambered cairn, which was probably originally about 23m in diameter, but has spread out over time. It had a ring of upright stones around the outside, some of which are still present, indicating where the original edge was. The large flat stones which form the wall of the internal chamber can be seen sticking up from the body of the cairn. If you look around the edges of the cairn, you can see the circular footings of later small huts, which were probably used during summer grazing on the moor.

10. *Taigh Cloiche* chambered cairn   NF 7919 4471

Just south of the turnoff to *Loch a' Charnain*, park on the side of the road at NF 790 448 and enter the grazings through the gate. Walk south-east for less than 200m to reach the cairn, which is visible from the road.

This is another damaged round cairn, in a similar landscape setting to the cairn at *Barp Frobost*, on what is now moorland, quite far away from the coast. It seems to have been a little smaller, at about 12m in diameter, and there are several large stones around the south-western edge that suggest it might have had a peristalith, or surrounding kerb, of upright stones. It has also been reused as a site for shielings.

Beinn na Fhaoghla (Benbecula)

11. *Suidheachan Sealg* stone circle   NF 8247 5522

A walk of 250m from the road, using gates into the grazings. Stop near the thatched cottage, to avoid having to cross deep drains in the peat.

At the northern end of Benbecula, as the road approaches the causeway leading to North Uist, are two stone circles, of which this is the one to the south. It is located on a hillock on a ridge extending northwards and down from the hill to the south and looks over the low-lying tidal flats towards North Uist, which would have been Neolithic farmland.

The stone setting is oval, measuring about 33m x 27m, and is missing several stones. The largest remaining stone shows signs of having been broken off and is now only about 1.5m high. As the geology of the islands is metamorphic and the stone thus tends to break into irregular blocks, large flat stones have been valued as lintels for doors and windows in the past, so that stone circles were sometimes dismantled for building stone. There may also have been times when such monuments were deliberately thrown down for religious reasons.

At the centre of the circle is a grass-covered mound, the remains of a burial cairn. This pattern of a burial cairn inside a stone circle appears elsewhere in the Outer Hebrides and can also be seen at the *Calanais* stones. The large stones of the chamber in the cairn are clearly visible.

12. Gramisdale standing stones   NF 8250 5614

Situated about 30m south of the Gramisdale road, which turns east off the main A865 spinal route immediately after it reaches Benbecula.

Just south of the causeway linking North Uist and Benbecula is a second possible stone circle. This is to the south of the Gramisdale road, in an area which has been cultivated in the past, and the stones are badly damaged and thrown down. One upright stone remains, and at least 5 further stones and additional stone settings are visible, forming a circle around 25m diameter, extending west of the survivor.

The position of this circle, to the north of *Suidheachean Sealg* and overlooking the same tidal area, which was probably low-lying cultivated ground in the Neolithic and Bronze Age, suggests that the two circles are located in relation to each other as well as their surrounding landscape.

Uibhist a' Tuath (North Uist)

13. *Barpa Chairinis* (*Caravat Barp*)   NF 8367 6031
   chambered cairn

Park by the main road in the disused quarry and use the forestry gate to get into the woodland area. Follow the rough path for about 200m north, to the cairn.

This long cairn is one of the largest burial cairns in the Outer Hebrides. It is orientated east to west and is over 50m long, a triangle with the wider eastern end tapering to a point at the west. The entrance was from the east, orientated towards the rising sun, and the remains of an open area in front of the entrance, a forecourt, can be seen by tracing the line of an enclosing wall extending from the southeastern corner of the cairn. This would have been matched by a similar wall on the north-eastern corner, but the north-eastern wall has been lost, probably from the reuse of the cairn for later shielings and animal enclosures.

The location of the chamber is clear from the six large slabs that can be seen towards the eastern end, but there is no sign of the passage which would have entered it from the forecourt and, again, this was probably removed when this end of the cairn was adapted for a later animal enclosure.

In the late 1980s, archaeological excavations in the peat banks to the north of the cairn found the remains of hearths, enclosures and tent sites left by Neolithic people visiting and revisiting the cairn. This gives an unusual glimpse of how such a communal burial monument might have been used, perhaps forming the focus of seasonal celebrations or ceremonies.

14. *Cairinis* (Carinish) stone circle NF 8321 6021

This monument is directly beneath the main road. Park on the hard standing beside the road and take care crossing from one side of the circle to the other.

When this stone circle was first recorded by Erskine Beveridge in 1911, at least 16 stones were identifiable, forming an oval about 36m x 37m, orientated north to south. Five of the stones were still upright. By 1928, only one stone was upright, and the reorientation of the main road in 1960, when the North Ford Causeway was constructed, caused further damage to the site.

One fallen stone and three broken stumps are visible on the northern side of the road, and one small standing stone is still present on the southern side. Elsewhere, there are fragments of stones and stumps, covered with heather, but large amounts of aggregate have been added to the surface to level and support the road, and these deposits may contain much of the remains of the stones.

15. *Craonabhal* (Craonaval)

Park at NF 8332 6341, and follow the moorland track south about 600m, to the following group of monuments, which form an important Neolithic landscape. Wander around the wider area and you will see other possible fallen standing stones or cairn remnants, but remember that it can be difficult to distinguish between what is artificial and what is natural, particularly in a heather-covered landscape.

Craonabhal (Craonaval) chambered cairn NF 8331 6276

A chambered cairn, about 16m diameter, is located on the west-facing slope of the hill after which it is named. It has been robbed of stone, but remains about 1m high, and the square chamber in the centre of the cairn has been uncovered and is empty.

Craonabhal (Craonaval) North chambered cairn (A)   NF 8332 629

Around 200m north of the previous site, this cairn is a turf-covered oval mound about 22m x 19m and less than 0.5m high. As is usual, it has been robbed to supply stone for shieling buildings on and around it.

Craonabhal (Craonaval) North chambered   NF 8321 6298
cairn (B)

This possible cairn is an oval 20m x 15m turfed mound, about 50m north-east of the previous cairn. There are several large stones sticking out from the body of the mound, including one long slab, which might be part of the chamber of a chambered cairn. It has later shieling huts on and around it.

Sornach Coir' Fhinn (*Sornach a' Phobuill*)   NF 8289 6303
stone circle

About 200m west of the above monument is a large oval stone setting, about 39m in diameter. There are 14 visible standing stones, the largest of which is just over 1m high, but the peat has built up around the stones, reducing their apparent height.

If you continue around *Craonabhal* (Craonaval) to the north, over the moorland, a walk of a further 2km will pass by two further chambered cairns (Sites 16 & 17).

16. *Oban nam Fiadh* chambered cairn   NF 8417 6247

A chambered cairn about 19m in diameter, which has been robbed of stone to build later sheilings and enclosures around its edges. There are two upright stones on the southern and eastern edges which indicate that it probably originally had a surrounding kerb of standing stones, known as a peristalith. The central chamber had a passage to the south, which is marked by two parallel stones protruding through the turf. The chamber itself is roughly circular and still partly roofed by two large slabs of stone.

17. *Craonabhal* (Craonaval) chambered cairn   NF 8384 6290

This cairn is on open land above the tidal loch of *Oban nam Fiadh*, at the foot of *Craonabhal* (Craonaval). It has, as usual, been robbed for the construction of shieling huts, and the diameter is not wholly certain as peat is encroaching around the sides. It is worth a visit, though, as the passage and chamber are very clear. The passage opens to the east, and the chamber is 4.5m x 3.5m internally. The roofing slabs have been removed and lie next to the chamber.

18. *Clach Charnach Braodag* standing stone,   NF 7864 6909
    Beinn a' Charra

Park on the Committee Road in a passing place and use the gate at the bend in the road to access the grazings. Walk 300m north-east across the rough grassland, up the shoulder of the hill, to the stone.

This large standing stone is on the shoulder of the hill, located with wide views over most of the surrounding landscape. It is 2.7m high and has been progressively leaning further and further over during the last 100 years. It has quartz veins on the northern face, a feature which is now recognised as characteristic of standing stones, and which was clearly an important element choosing a stone.

19. *Eilean Domhnuill* crannog, *Loch Olabhat*   NF 7470 7533

Park at the layby on the A865, walk down the Griminish road for 85m and turn west onto an old track across fields to the loch side, for 600m.

This site is an island, accessed by a causeway linking to the southern shore of *Loch Olabhat*. Excavation on and around the island during the 1980s revealed that it was occupied for hundreds of years during the Neolithic Period. During the occupation of the site, the water level of the loch fluctuated; initially the island was perhaps twice the size that it now is.

The excavations exposed the fragmentary remains of two parallel buildings of turf, timber and stone, with central hearths, surrounded by a yard, enclosed by a stone and timber palisade along the shore of the island (see Fig. 3). The underwater excavations suggest that earlier buildings were probably made mostly of timber, and that the island may have been largely artificial. As the water level rose, the occupants of the island built up the surface by dumping rubbish, and the water-logged debris that accumulated provided a wealth of archaeological information. Baskets, rope, pottery, structural timbers and wattle hurdles were all recovered from the site, along with organic debris which has the potential to provide much information about diet and environmental conditions at the site.

To the east, along the shore of the loch, is a later Iron Age and mediaeval site (Site 66), occupying a headland.

20. *Cleitrabhal* (Clettreval) chambered cairn   NF 7499 7135

Accessible either from the road to the top of *Cleitrabhal a' Deas* (South Clettreval), which leads up to the mast, or by climbing up the hill from the peat road to the south of the hill.

This chambered long cairn is orientated east to west and has a later Iron Age wheelhouse – a complex roundhouse – over the western end (Site 65). It was originally wedge-shaped and around 29m long with a fine façade of upright stones at the eastern end, from which the passage to the chamber opened. Many of the façade stones are now fallen, and the large stones which seem to have formed a kerb around the cairn have been displaced. The cairn stones have been used for the construction of the Iron Age roundhouse.

The form and chamber of this cairn are of the Clyde type, which is widespread on the west coast of Scotland, but unusual in the Outer Hebrides. We cannot know whether this might have been built by people from elsewhere in Scotland, but it does show that there was contact between communities in different areas, and ideas and archi-tectural forms were copied across the west coast and islands during prehistory.

This site was excavated in the 1930s and 1940s by Lindsay Scott, and the pottery from it included sherds of Beaker pottery, perhaps suggesting that it was last used at the end of the Neolithic and begin-ning of the Bronze Age.

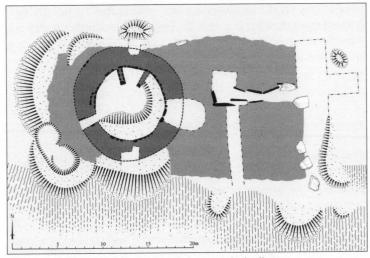

Fig. 12. *Cleitrabhal* (Clettreval) chambered cairn and wheelhouse
(© Crown copyright: HES)

Near the southern edge of the cairn is a cup-marked stone, with one cup-mark. Such stones have often been found in Bronze Age contexts, but the practice of carving stones in this way, with cups, rings and other decorative motifs, may have started in the Neolithic Period.

21. *Taigh Cloiche* chambered cairn,   NF 7516 7101
    Cleitrabhal (Clettreval)

Situated about 400m downslope of the above cairn, and across a fence, this site is most easily accessed from the peat road to the south.

    Taigh Cloiche, or the 'stone house', is a further chambered cairn with a southern outlook on the lower slopes of *Cleitrabhal*. The name of the hill, which means 'the hill of large rocks (or rock outcrops)' in Old Norse, may have referred to these cairns.

    Once again, the monument has been used for the construction of at least two later buildings, and its original shape and structure are therefore damaged. The chamber survives in part, represented by four large stones on the southwestern side, and it appears to have been entered from the east, as is typical. Some of the chamber stones may have been reused to roof one of the later buildings, but the size of these lintel stones and sheer volume of stone strengthen the interpretation of the site as a chambered cairn, despite the damage.

22. *Barpa Langais* chambered cairn   NF 8381 6573

Park in the parking place above the main road and walk 160m uphill on a surfaced path to the cairn.

This is the best-preserved chambered cairn in the Outer Hebrides (see Fig. 7) and is clearly visible from the main road. Its location dominates the surrounding landscape, with open views particularly to the north and west. It is around 25m in diameter and survives to a height of 4m, with a peristalith of upright stones around the edge. The intact oval chamber is entered by a passage from the eastern side and has been, until recently, accessible through the roof of the entrance passage. Cracked stones now mean that entering the chamber is unsafe and inadvisable.

The cairn has been broken into in the past, presumably in the 19th century, when a second chamber was reputedly also accessible from the north. Finds from the monument include pottery of the Beaker Period (transitional Neolithic–Bronze Age), and flint and burnt bone of the Iron Age. It may be that this Neolithic tomb was last used in the Beaker Period, a pattern seen elsewhere.

23. *Pobull Fhinn* (*Sornach Coir'Fhinn*)   NF 8427 6502
  stone circle

Follow an unsurfaced path for 1km or directly east from *Barpa Langais* over *Beinn Langais* and down the south-facing slope to find this stone circle. Alternatively, park at Langass Lodge and follow the signposted path.

The well-preserved oval stone circle consists of 31 stones, most still upright. It sits on a terrace on the south-facing slope of *Beinn Langais*, and the land around and within the stone setting appears to have been levelled. A bank of earth and stone forms a partial enclosure around the southern part of the monument, but it is not clear whether it is contemporary with the stones or later. Two of the stones lie fallen outside the south-western part of the circle.

Na Hearadh (Harris)

24. *Baile Deas* (South Town), *Taobh Tuath* (Northton)   NF 9753 9125

Walk 2km from *Taobh Tuath* along an unpaved path over the machair, following the coastline.

A multi-period settlement site, with Mesolithic, Neolithic, Bronze Age, Iron Age, mediaeval and Early Modern settlement (see the relevant chapters) is located on the southern coast of *Gob an Tobha* (Toe Head), a peninsula just to the north of *Taobh Tuath* on the west coast of Harris, close to an Iron Age broch and mediaeval chapel.

There were excavations here in the 1960s, and the site was revisited in 2001 and 2010–11. These showed that a cross-section of the whole development of the settlement was being exposed by coastal erosion. Before the development of the machair in this area, the landscape was intermittently used by Mesolithic hunter-gatherers, and the use of the site continued following the introduction of agriculture. Neolithic structures, dated to about 3200–2900 BC, were built on the site. They were similar to the fragmentary remains from *Loch Olabhat* – oval buildings about 5m wide – with stone walls revetted into the surrounding sand, but once again the remains of the two houses found were very partial and insubstantial (see earlier in the chapter for further discussion). This may have been because the stone from the buildings was reused for later buildings on the site, but it is more likely that Neolithic houses were generally insubstantial and probably frequently rebuilt.

The Neolithic settlement at this site may be larger; the site was only partially excavated and much of it remains. Given that this was also the location of an Early Mesolithic seasonal settlement, more evidence for the use of the area in the centuries between the Early Mesolithic and the Neolithic may still be here, but it may have been eroded by the sea. The Neolithic settlement would probably have been the first permanent, year-round occupation of the site, and settlement continued here, through the Bronze and Iron Ages, until the 19th century. The remains of 19th-century houses can be seen on top of the accumulated mound of archaeological deposits on the site.

25. *Clach Steineagaidh* stone circle, *Borgh* (Borve) NG 0209 9388

Park in the parking area further west along the road and follow the footpath to the field gate. There is an interpretation board on the wall.

This field was the location of a larg, Neolithic stone circle, of which the 1.9m-high standing stone is the last remaining upright element (Plate 3). Geophysical survey of the site by the University of Birmingham showed the remains of a stone circle around 40m in diameter, with 12 or 13 stones to the south of the existing stone. Around it was a large ditch, which has since been filled in. You can still see several fallen stones in the area of the circle, or the heaps of smaller packing stones that mark the places where they stood.

From this site, you have clear views of the standing stone on *Tarasaigh* (Taransay) (Site 75), and the very large stone, called the *Clach Mhic Leoid* (MacLeod Stone) (Site 26), on the headland to the north. These landscape-wide views were important to the location of the circle here, and all the stones in the landscape would have been located in relation to each other, as well as to their landscape setting.

To the north of the standing stone, between it and the sea, is a large artificial mound, which may be the remains of a Neolithic chambered burial cairn, or possibly of a later circular monument, such as a broch, which was built next to the stone circle.

26. *Clach Mhic Leoid* (MacLeod Stone), Nisabost NG 0408 9727

Park in the layby above *Traigh Iar*, Horgabost, and walk 600m along the beach or the edge of the dunes to the stone.

Clach Mhic Leoid is a very large standing stone, possibly the sole remnant of a circle, in a dominant position on the headland of Nisabost. The area has been a focus of archaeological finds of all periods, indicating its importance over thousands of years, and survey suggests that there are the remains of an Iron Age building under the sandy mound between the stone and the end of the headland. The stone itself is visible from both the *Clach Steineagaidh* (Site 25) and Taransay (Site 75) standing stones, across the very shallow strait between Taransay and the mainland of Harris.

The stone is about 3m high, with veins of quartz and feldspar, and is surrounded at the base with an area of packing stones. Two slabs of stone set on edge were visible at right angles to the stone early in the 20th century, although these are less obvious now, and it has been suggested that perhaps there might have been a burial cairn here as well. Only excavation of the area would answer this question.

27. *Coir Fhinn* chambered cairn, Horgabost   NG 0471 9664

This cairn (Fig. 13) can be seen from the main road, in the front garden of a house to the south of the road.

The chamber of this cairn survives as an oval setting of six large stones, with a single roofing slab lying inside. The capstone has two carved cup-marks on its upper surface. All the covering material was removed before the cairn was first mapped in the 19th century by the Ordnance Survey.

The National Museum of Scotland holds a skull of a man which was reputedly found in this cairn in the mid 19th century. When the

Fig. 13. *Coir Fhinn* chambered cairn, Horgabost, *Na Hearadh* (Harris)

skull was recently scientifically dated, it proved to date from the 18th century and it must therefore have come from a body which was buried outwith a Christian cemetery for some reason. It may have been the remains of a drowned man, or someone who was outside the bounds of society at the time, but it is also interesting that there may then have been a tradition associating the cairn with burial.

Leodhas (Lewis)

28. *Sideabhal* (Sideval) stone circle   NB 2781 1662

Park at the fank on the main road and walk down the croft track, or walk east along the shore from *Aird Sithaig*.

The remains of a stone circle have been built into the walls of a 19th-century house, later used as a sheep fank. The site is sometimes locally known as the Fangs, after the two free-standing stones to the north-west of the fank. Seven stones of the circle are still visible, ranging in height from 0.91m to 1.52m, around the circumference of a circle 16.5m in diameter. Other than the two free-standing stones, the remainder are incorporated into the buildings on the site, and it is an interesting exercise to see if you can locate them, and then try to work out where the missing stones might have been.

The area around and the slopes above the stone circle also contain less easily dateable and smaller sites. A circular stone setting, 4m in diameter, is in the intertidal zone to the south of the circle, and there are two possible Bronze Age kerb cairns at NB 28025 16709 and NB 27948 17032, which may have been reused to build later shielings. Erosion and sea-level rise have changed the position of the shoreline, but it is still possible to see how the basic form of the surrounding landscape, the south-facing slope and valleys, have ensured that this was a focus of settlement and ritual use over thousands of years. Work by local archaeologists has suggested that the *Sideabhal* circle may be part of the wider landscape of standing stones and other ritual monuments, including those at *Calanais* (see page 45), that are orientated in relation to the moon rising and setting over the hills of Lochs, the *Cailleach na Mointeach* ('the Old Woman of the Moor'), also known as the 'Sleeping Beauty' range.

29. *Cnoc na Croich* (Gallows Hill)   NB 4170 3229
chambered cairn, *Steornabhagh* (Stornoway)

Park your car at Lews Castle or Woodlands Centre and follow the surfaced paths about 2m southwards through the designed gardens to the monument and viewpoint.

This high point above the town of Stornoway was the execution place for the Isle of Lewis. The location of the gallows is marked by a modern cairn, built in 1902 to commemorate the visit of King Edward VII to the island. Below this, and spreading out westwards from it, are the remains of a large Neolithic chambered cairn, probably around 30m in diameter. The edge of the cairn is marked by three upright stones and one fallen one, which are all that survives of the edge stones that would have circled the perimeter of the monument. The stone from the body of the cairn has been taken away, perhaps to build the settlement of *Gearraidh Cruiadh*, which was cleared from this area in the 19th century to lay out the planned landscape in the castle grounds. Stone field walls and boundaries in the area probably also used the stone from the cairn.

The chamber of the Neolithic cairn is still visible, though, aligned north-east to south-west, just to the south of the modern cairn. It consists of seven large stones set on edge to form the walls of a room at least 5m long and a maximum of 1.25m wide inside.

30. *Clach Ghlas* standing stone   NB 5281 3340

Park by the church and walk down the side road leading south-east, past Hebridean Seafoods, to where a waymarked stile crosses the fence at the grazings gate. Follow the waymarked path, which will take you past the standing stone and onto the chambered cairn at *Cnoc nan Dursainean* (overleaf).

Until recently, this triangular standing stone was difficult to see under overgrown heather, but it has been cleared and is now much more obvious. It is 1.7m high and set on a long mound, which is partly artificial. There is a stone-lined rectangular hollow in the surface of the mound behind the standing stone, and the whole structure may have been a burial cairn, which has been robbed of much of its stone.

Dating a monument like this is not straightforward, and it is possible that it is Bronze Age rather than Neolithic in date. One of the features that suggests this is that the shape of the mound is formed by an enhanced and augmented natural feature, an economy of effort which is characteristic of some Bronze Age burial mounds.

31. *Cnoc nan Dursainean* chambered cairn   NB 5238 3307

Follow the signposted path described in Site 30.

This monument is the very heavily robbed remains of a chambered cairn which was probably originally square or nearly rectangular in plan. So much of the stone from the cairn has been taken away, presumably to build houses in nearby Garrabost, that when it was first described in the 19th century, it was initially identified as being a stone circle around the remains of a cairn. Since that time it has been realised that the standing stones are the remains of the kerb, the peristalith, around the outside of the cairn, and a small façade of upright stones on the south-eastern edge of the cairn marks the opening of the entrance passage; the chamber is oval. The large, upright stones that can be seen poking through the surface of the cairn beyond the visible chamber may be the remains of a further, additional chamber.

32. *Achadh Mor* (Achmore) stone circle   NB 3174 2926

Park on the main road in *Achadh Mor* and take the signposted path for 220m, uphill.

Peat cutting from the 1980s onwards has progressively revealed the remains of a stone circle about 40m in diameter. Eighteen or more stones, some of them still set upright, form a true circle. Some of the fallen stones have been re-erected by local people, but none are very stable, and weathering repeatedly dislodges them. At least one of the stones is as much as 2m high, and the circle must have been an impressive monument when it was first constructed.

This monument is visible from the main stone circle at *Calanais*, and it also has very clear views to the south, towards the hills of Lochs and Harris, which are believed to have been significant for the location of the stone settings in the *Calanais* landscape (see below). There is, therefore, a strong argument for considering this circle part of a wider landscape of stone settings in the *Calanais* area, scattered through landscape around the inundated valley which forms the eastern half of what is now *Loch Rog* (Loch Roag).

Calanais (Callanish)

The *Calanais* district on the western coastline of Lewis has one of the finest groups of Neolithic standing stone settings anywhere in the British Isles. There are also numerous small and large cairns in the district, and this landscape may link more widely with the location of other monuments further south and east in Lewis, the locations of which can be related to movements of the moon over the ridge of hills known as *Cailleach na Mointeach* ('the Old Woman of the Moor'). The following are just a selection of the monuments in the area; other, more detailed references can be found in the Further Reading section.

33. *Beinn Bheag, Calanais* XI, Breascleit   NB 2223 3569

Park on the Pentland Road to the east of Breascleit, just outside the croft fence, and walk north uphill for 140m to a natural terrace on the southern slope of the hill.

Two burial cairns and the deliberately broken and displaced remains of a stone circle are located at this site. The larger of the cairns is 11.5m x 9.3m, and up to 2.25m high, with a kerb visible around part of its edge, and what may be part of a central chamber visible under a flat slab. As is usual, the stones of the cairn have been robbed to build a more recent shelter on top, which could have been used as a shooting hide.

The smaller cairn, which is around 7m x 5m, is also kerbed, and has also been robbed to construct a shelter.

The single visible standing stone is one of at least seven and possibly originally ten or more stones which formed a large circle of around 50m diameter here. The remainder of the stones have been robbed from their settings, or displaced and broken, and local tradition states that the monument was quarried in the 19th century to provide lintel stones for local houses – always a temptation in an area where flat slabs of stone are scarce and difficult to find. It is also possible that this monument was never completed but was abandoned in a state of partial construction. Evidence for this may survive under the surrounding peat.

The monuments are on a natural terrace of land, with open outlooks towards the west, south and east. The cairns may well be more recent than the stone circle and could easily date to the Bronze Age, as there is evidence elsewhere for the continuation of use of this landscape from the Neolithic on into the later period.

34. *Cnoc Fillibheir Bheag, Calanais* III   NB 2250 3269

Park in the signposted layby on the main road and follow the unsurfaced path through the gate in the fence along the ridge for 270m to the stones.

This unusual stone circle is located on a ridge to the south of the main *Calanais* circle. It consists of a double ring of stones, with the outer ring of about 13 stones, 7 or 8 of which are upright, and an inner ring of 4. The uncertainty about the count of stones in the outer ring is not for some mysterious reason, but just because one of the stones, on the north-western side, is between the two rings, rather than perfectly on the outer ring, and could therefore be interpreted as part of an oval, rather than circular, inner ring. This is unlikely to be accidental, but what the meaning of the anomaly is, we may never know.

North of the circle, about 60m away, is a setting of upright stones which has been disturbed or dismantled, and to the south of the circle is a small cairn, with a large, fallen standing stone nearby. If you continue south, to the top of an adjacent knoll, you will also find a roughly rectangular setting of stones. Walking 148m north-north-east of the circle will also take you to the broken stump of another standing stone, while next to the access path from the road, 60m north-north-west of the circle, are the wall footings of a small circular hut, which appears to have had a door opening directly towards the stone circle. Some people have called this the Watcher's House, thinking that it would provide shelter for someone watching the stones on a cold night!

What appears at first sight to be a (relatively) simple megalithic monument proves, on closer examination, to be the focus of a complex landscape with a wide variety and chronological range of remains, all located in relation to each other, within it.

35. *Ceann a' Gharaidh* stone circle, *Calanais* II   NB 2220 3260

Either follow the waymarked footpath for 300m from *Calanais* III, above, or turn off the main road, and park at the end of the side road nearest the stones.

This well-preserved stone circle is oval and about 20m in diameter, made of tall, flat stones, surrounding the remains of a cairn about 8.5m in diameter. As with the main stone circle at *Calanais* (see Site 37, *Calanais* I), the cairn is not in the centre, but off-set. There are seven surviving stones, five of which are still upright, but it is likely that there were more in the past.

The location of this monument in the landscape is very similar to that of *Cnoc Fillibheir Bheag* (Site 34) and Calanais I. They are on parallel ridges, which extend out towards the tidal sea loch to the south. This shallow loch would have been a valley during the Neolithic Period, and it was probably valuable agricultural land. All the monuments are set back from the ends and highest points of the ridges, and such a consistent pattern must have meant something to the people who set up the stones. In two cases, at *Calanais* I and *Cnoc Fillibeir Bheag*, there is good evidence for the use of the knolls at the ends of the ridges for activities relating to the stones, but no excavation or geophysical survey has yet been carried out at *Ceann a' Gharaidh*.

36. *Druim nan Eun, Na Dromanan,*   NB 2297 3362 and
Calanais X   2293 3360

Park by the fank, enter the grazings through the gate on the right-hand side, and walk north-north-west for 1km across rough, and sometimes wet, grazing land and peat, to the ridge of *Druim nan Eun*.

This monument has been known locally for a long time as a place where flat stones could be quarried, and the remains of a quarry can be seen at NB 2293 3360, which was thought likely to be the source of stone for the circles at *Calanais*. Close to the quarry, a rough circle of fallen flat stone slabs can be seen sticking through thin peat cover on the top of the ridge.

Excavations between 2003 and 2006 examined both the quarry and the stone circle site. Many of the stones at the other circles around *Calanais* have black blobs of hornblende in them and the stone at this quarry does not seem to contain these, so it is possible that we have yet to find the quarry for the main stone circle.

When the peat was removed from the stone circle, a double ring about 22m in diameter was revealed, with 17 stones in the outer circle and 5 in the inner. None of these had had proper excavated sockets but had been set up on the rock outcrops from which they had been quarried, propped with piles of stones. They had therefore fallen over the years.

The form of the circle was flattened on one side, directly comparable to the form at *Calanais* I. A short avenue of stones led to the circle from the south, suggesting the direction from which it might have been approached in antiquity. Druim nan Eun would have been very clearly visible on the skyline from *Calanais* I, II and III, and it would seem likely that the stones were set up with this in mind, though during the course of the excavation the excavator came to feel that the location of individual stones was less important.

37. *Na Tursachan, Cnoc an Tursa, Calanais* I   NB 2130 3302

Park at the visitor centre and follow a surfaced path 220m uphill to the stones, or park adjacent to the stones and enter through the gate at the northern end.

When people speak of the *Calanais* standing stones, this is the monument they are referring to. Many writers who visited the island over the centuries have mentioned it, so we know, for example, that one of the early stories about it was that these stones were the remains of people who were turned to stone for dancing on a holy day! In the 19th century, it was assumed to be a druidical temple, and is recorded as such on the early editions of the Ordnance Survey maps.

As interest in the monument grew in the 19th century, the owner of the island, Sir James Matheson, had the peat, which had built up around the stones to a depth of nearly 1.5m, removed (Fig. 8). This revealed the circle virtually as it can be seen now and exposed the cairn between the central monolith and the eastern side of the circle. Further excavations within and around the monument over the years have expanded our understanding of the history of the stones, and a sequence of the monument's development can now be put together.

This ridge was being cultivated when the first of the standing stones were set up, and the development of the monument took place within an agricultural landscape. The small, 5m diameter, central circle, which is not a perfect circle but is flattened on the eastern side like the circle at *Druim nan Eun*, was erected between about 2900 and 2600 BC. The equally small chambered cairn, which incorporates the central upright stone into its kerb and uses two of the eastern stones of the circle as its façade, was built shortly thereafter. The central stone, which is over 4.5m tall, was put up when the circle was constructed.

The height and close setting of the 13 stones of the central circle give a feeling of enclosure from the inside and a feeling of exclusion from the outside. This is emphasised by the fact that the later long avenue of two parallel rows of stones, which extends to the north of the circle, was constructed so that the approach to the circle is blocked by one of the circle stones. This is a monument that is very clear about inside and outside.

The furthest stone of the eastern row of the avenue fell in the past and has been re-erected in its original socket. The stone which stands to the east of the southern 'arm' extending from the circle is also re-erected; this was done in the 19th century, and it is not clear whether it was originally in this position or not.

Secondary 'arms' extend from the circle to the south, east and west. The southern of these seems to align with a natural rock hollow on the northern side of the knoll at the furthest and highest point of the ridge on which the monument is erected. Excavations on the top of this knoll revealed that a kerbed burial cairn had been located here.

The motives surrounding the location of individual stones in this complex and impressive setting are strongly debated. Local archaeologists believe that many of them are placed to mark different parts of the cycle of the moon through the heavens, particularly in relation to its rising and setting over the ridge of hills to the south of the island, known as *Cailleach na Mointeach* ('the Old Woman of the Moor'), which is sometimes known in English as 'the Sleeping Beauty'. Other archaeologists are less convinced of this, but visitors frequently gather at the site at the equinoxes and solstices, and the last lunar standstill, which occurs every 18.6 years, saw huge numbers of visitors to the monument.

Finds from the 19th-century excavation indicate that the latest use of the central chambered cairn was at the end of the Neolithic or beginning of the Bronze Age, as fragments of Beaker pottery were found in the cairn when the peat was removed. The roof of the cairn chamber may have been removed later in the Bronze Age. However, the main circle probably continued in use throughout most of the Bronze Age, and a Bronze Age cairn in nearby *Calanais* Park (Site 48) was built in the same flattened-circle shape as the central circle. Outside the north-eastern sector of the circle, the footings of a small house built against the stones can still be seen on the ground. This may date to this period of continuing, secondary use.

The mid 19th-century uncovering of the stones was contemporary with the Clearance of the local township of *Calanais*, and its replacement with the present planned crofting township which stretches north along the ridge from the site. The footings of 19th-century, pre-Clearance houses and a corn-drying kiln can be seen to the south-west of the stone circle, and over the field wall.

38. *Clach an Truiseil* standing stone,   NB 3755 5377
    Baile an Truiseil (Ballantrushal)

Park at the layby and walk 50m up a grassy track between walls to the stone.

This single standing stone is the most massive standing stone in Scotland and reputedly the tallest, at over 5.5m high and nearly as much in girth at the base. Local traditions have always stated that it was originally part of a stone circle, and recent survey and excavation by the University of Manchester has proved that there was indeed a circle on the artificial terrace of land next to the stone. The sockets of four further stones have been located, one of which had originally had a wooden post in it, later replaced by a stone. This sequence of wooden posts replaced by stone pillars is one that has been seen at other monuments in Scotland.

The field walls adjacent to the remaining stone, which may have been too large to break up easily, contain pieces of stone which probably derived from the circle. They can be distinguished as being roughly cylindrical and more regular in their shape than the field stones which were used for the rest of the walls. One large slab still lies on the ground just to the north of the stone.

39. Steinacleit, *Siadar* (Shader)   NB 3962 5407

Turn off the main road following the signs, and park at the parking area adjacent to the loch. Walk uphill 280m on an unsurfaced path.

This mysterious site has been variously described as a stone circle, a chambered cairn and a monumental building. Of these three possibilities, the latter seems most likely, but it is still a site which is poorly understood and dated. Until 1920, the site was just an amorphous heap of stones, but the removal of over a metre of peat revealed a very large oval enclosure over 82m in length around a megalithic structure, measuring about 16m in diameter. The outside of the structure is edged by upright stones, like the peristalith of a chambered cairn, but the interior of the structure is much more open than is likely for a cairn. Archaeologists have argued that the open interior is the result of reuse of an original cairn to provide the base and building material for a later house, or homestead, which is surrounded by the remains of its fields. Surveyors in 2003 concluded that the site had been used and restructured at least twice, but the arguments continue, and only excavation of the site would provide the evidence needed to answer some of the questions.

40. *Clach Stein* standing stones,   NB 5348 6418
Cnoc Aird (Knockaird), *Nis* (Ness)

Park at the bottom of the track signposted for *Dun Eistean* and walk 80m up the track. The stones are visible immediately to the north of the track in an adjacent field. Continuing along the track will take you to the late mediaeval fort of *Dun Eistean* (Site 120).

When this stone setting was first described in the mid 19th century, it consisted of four stones, each around 1m high, set in a rectangle. By the early 20th century only three were present, one of which had fallen over, and the fallen slab, which had been the flattest and straightest of the three, disappeared in the 1930s, so only two stones remain now.

The remaining two stones are relatively short, stout and boulder-like. One is around 1m tall and nearly 3m in girth, and the other is a little taller. Geophysical survey carried out by the University of Glasgow as part of a wider archaeological survey of Ness revealed that the two remaining stones may originally have stood within a wider circle of stones, which has been robbed.

41. *Eilean nan Luchruban, Nis* (Ness)   NB 5078 6601

Park by the lighthouse and walk west along the coastline for 1.4km to a point overlooking the island. The surface is relatively level, but the grass can be slippery when wet, so keep back from the cliff edges.

This sea stack or small island, whose name means 'island of the little people', is the site of a complex archaeological monument, which was partly excavated during the 19th century. Originally, this was interpreted as a monastic site. The early descriptions mention small, underground rooms linked by staircases. However, recent reinterpretation suggests that it may have had an Iron Age roundhouse on it.

This settlement is one of a series of coastal sea-stack sites, including *Stac Domhnuill Chaim* in Uig and Biruaslum in *Barraigh* (Barra), which have revealed evidence for Neolithic settlement, and which were later reoccupied in the Iron Age. It isn't clear whether these coastal sites were islands or promontories in the Neolithic Period, but they would have been on high land close to the coast, and were likely to have been in unusual, exposed and marginal situations even then. Little is known about these sites, and why they were reoccupied thousands of years afterwards, but *Eilean nan Luchrubain* is the most easily viewed of these intriguing monuments.

3. Working with Metal:
The Bronze Age 2500–800 BC

In the second half of the third millennium BC, between 2500 and 2000 BC, the first understanding of metalworking arrived in the British Isles. It seems to have arrived from continental Europe, and recent analyses suggest that it was probably brought by groups of migrants travelling by sea, who also brought with them new fashions in pottery, and a preoccupation with archery and the artefacts associated with it. These styles and fashions rapidly spread to the indigenous population, who adapted them to suit their own interests and culture, but in some areas there may also have been a significant amount of replacement of the local population. In the past, archaeologists have argued at different times both for the idea that the incomers wiped out local populations, committing genocide, and for the idea that the new fashions spread solely by trading contact with no migrants, but recent advances in DNA analysis make it clear that there were immigrants from mainland Europe into Britain at this time, and also that local populations mixed with the immigrants, adopting and absorbing the new fashions.

The Bronze Age was a period of change throughout the British Isles. Initially, settlement, subsistence and ritual practices had strong links to the culture of the preceding Neolithic Period but, by the end of the period, material culture and the social values and practices that produced it had changed dramatically. Neolithic and Early Bronze Age concerns with remembering the dead, marked by the building of monumental burial cairns and standing stones, were replaced by a culture that emphasised domestic life and constructed monumental and long-lived stone houses. How and why these changes happened is one of the most fascinating questions about the Bronze Age.

Environmental changes

The environment of northern Scotland changed between the beginning and end of the Bronze Age, and this was probably one of the factors triggering the wider social changes of the period. At the end of the Neolithic Period, the islands still had extensive areas of woodland, as shown by pollen samples taken from peat cores throughout the archipelago. The central area of *Uibhist a' Deas* (South Uist), for example, around *Cille Donnain*, seems to have been covered with deciduous woodland, and sheltered areas of *Barraigh* (Barra) had stands of trees. Peat was much less extensive than it is now; landscapes around *Calanais* (Callanish) in *Leodhas* (Lewis) were not covered by peat. The landscape would therefore have looked very different to the modern landscape, with patchy woodland, open ground, and settlements in areas which are now under blanket bog. Settlements would probably have been scattered relatively widely across the landscape, rather than being focused on the coastline as they are at present. On the coast, the shoreline was still some distance out from the modern shore. Many areas of land which are now machair were not yet covered by sand in the Early Bronze Age, and in other coastal areas the machair had only just begun to accumulate.

In the years after 1159 BC, however, there is evidence for a change in the climate. One of the ways to date archaeological material is by counting tree rings, called dendrochronology. Each year, a tree makes more or less growth, depending upon the conditions that year. Trees growing in the same climatic area will show the same pattern of thick rings for good years of growth and thin rings for poor ones. For nearly two decades after this date, Irish tree rings show very poor growth indeed, and given that the Western Isles are part of the same climate area as Ireland, it seems likely that this was a long period of poor weather in the islands as well. This bad weather in the 12th century BC was the start of a period of marked climatic decline, which continued through the later part of the Bronze Age and into the Early Iron Age, between around 1000 and 500 BC. This had a significant effect on the ecology of the Outer Hebrides and the ease with which crops could be cultivated.

The pollen record also shows that people had continued to clear woodland in the islands throughout the Bronze Age, probably to create more grassland for grazing and to provide wood for building. In a fragile, wet ecology like the Outer Hebrides, removal of woodland tends to lead to poor drainage, and poor drainage encourages the development of peat. Peat development would also be encouraged by a shift towards cooler weather, as it became more and more difficult for surface vegetation on the wet ground to rot down completely.

By the end of the Bronze Age, peat had covered extensive areas of what had been earlier farmland, as shown by excavations in the landscape around *Calanais* in Lewis. Here, field walls and the ruins of houses lie beneath up to two metres of peat in the areas around the standing stones. By this time, the islands' landscape would have looked familiar to the modern eye, with wide open areas of blanket bog, machair developing along the coastlines, and only limited areas of trees left.

Drinking and shooting: the Beaker Period

In the Outer Hebrides, prehistoric changes are particularly clearly seen in changing fashions in pottery. The transitional period between the Neolithic and the Bronze Age is known as the Beaker Period, named after the highly decorated new style of pottery (Fig. 14) that appeared with the new metalworking in Britain sometime before 2200 BC. This name is given to the pottery because, although the size of

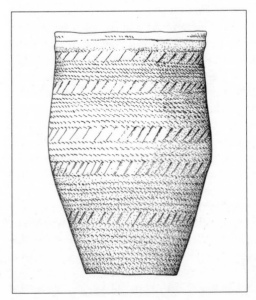

Fig. 14. Beaker pottery from *Allt Chrisal/Easdail, Barraigh* (Barra)

the pots varies from small cups to large jars, all of these new and fashionable pots were made in the deep, upright, relatively straight-sided form of drinking beakers with open mouths rather than narrow necks. The pots are decorated with horizontal or vertical bands of patterning, made by impressing string, comb-teeth, or other small, delicate tools into the surface of the wet clay, and Hebridean Beaker pottery is particularly finely made and highly decorated.

Elsewhere in the British Isles, Beaker pottery is normally found in burials, and there is very good evidence from Ashgrove in Fife, amongst other sites, that these burial Beakers often contained alcoholic drinks. This is the earliest certain evidence of alcohol from Britain, though there is much earlier evidence from Europe and the Near East. Maybe the technique of fermenting drink was also introduced by the new arrivals, or maybe not, but we can say that from this time onwards, alcoholic drinks were part of the culture of Scotland. In the Hebrides, though, Beaker pottery is found in settlements as well as burials, and does not appear to have been reserved for special occasions.

Along with the change in pottery came technological developments in hunting. Chipped and flaked stone arrowheads continued to be used, but their shape changed from the leaf-like form of the Neolithic Period to more specialised shapes, which were typically barbed and tanged (Fig. 15). The tang allowed the arrowhead to be attached more securely to the shaft of the arrow, while the barbs ensured that it did not fall out as easily once it hit its target. Beaker burials from the south of England, such as that of the Amesbury Archer, from near Stonehenge, often include multiple arrowheads, and stone wrist guards to protect the archer from the slap of the bowstring as it was released.

Metalworking in gold and copper was also introduced to the British Isles at this time. The first metal objects of the period are tools, weapons and jewellery, and recycling of metal means that most metal artefacts are found in graves, where they were left undisturbed. The burial of the Amesbury Archer included three small copper knives, which is probably a reflection of the high value of metal when it was first used. As yet, no Beaker Period metalwork has been found in the Outer Hebrides, and stone would still have been the main material for tools.

There are more known buildings of the Beaker Period in the

Fig. 15. Barbed and tanged arrowheads from *Barabhas* (Barvas), *Leodhas* (Lewis) (© B. Ballin Smith)

islands than anywhere else in Europe (Fig. 16). In Barra, the valley of *Allt Chrisal/Easdail* has a small settlement (Site 43). In South Uist, there was a settlement, now destroyed by erosion, at Gortain on the south coast, with three, relatively evenly spaced clusters of settlement at *Cladh Hallan, Cille Donnain* and *Machair Mheadhanach*. On *Beinn na Fhaoghla* (Benbecula), a settlement was excavated at *Roisinis* (Roshinish) on the eastern coast and, on *Uibhist a' Tuath* (North Uist), there was a Beaker Period settlement at *Coileagan an Udail* (the Udal). In Harris, there was a Beaker Period building at *Taobh Tuath* (Northton), and buildings have been excavated at *Cnip* (Kneep), *Dail Mor*, and *Barabhas* (Barvas) on the western coast of Lewis.

At most of these sites, the houses are like those of the Neolithic Period: small, U-shaped or oval buildings, with low walls of stone and turf, and roughly central hearths. There is no pattern of where the door is orientated. At *Cladh Hallan, Taobh Tuath* (Northton) and *Dail Mor*, the buildings took advantage of the sandy soil, and were

Fig. 16. Beaker Period
settlements in the islands

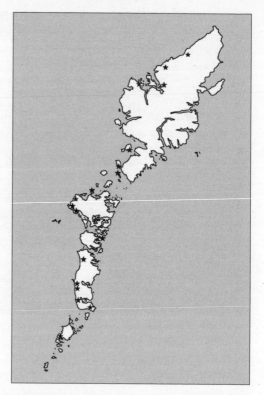

semi-sunken, with stone-lined and soil or turf walls. Unfortunately, most of these buildings were excavated before the sophisticated sampling techniques of modern archaeology became available, which allow us to investigate how the interior of a building was used and organised. Their small size – at most about 10m long and 4m wide – and ephemeral construction may be one of the reasons that settlement sites of this period are so rarely discovered elsewhere, particularly in regions where timber would have been the main building material.

Most of the excavated sites are located on the machair, but we cannot assume that all settlement of this period was coastal; there were probably settlements further inland as well, as the peat grew rapidly during the middle and later part of the Bronze Age and would have covered Beaker Period settlement. The remains of field systems adjacent to the standing stones at *Calanais*, which were covered by later peat growth, and the settlement at the higher end of the *Allt Easdail* valley in Barra both suggest that settlement was still widely spread across the landscape of the islands. Interestingly, however, excavations on several of the Neolithic islet and crannog settlements mentioned in the last chapter show that they were not occupied in the Bronze Age.

Allt Chrisal (also known as *Allt Easdail*, Site 43) is an important site for our understanding of the Beaker Period, as it contrasts with the other settlements in many ways. A substantial stone and turf roundhouse, rather than a slight, U-shaped building, was constructed on the remains of the earlier Neolithic buildings (Chapter 3) at the southern end of this steep, south-facing valley. It reused the flooring of an earlier house, and the site appears to have been continuously occupied from the Neolithic Period. A second roundhouse and two smaller structures were built further north up the valley during the same period, all of which contained the distinctive Beaker pottery. One of the smaller roundhouses contained a complete beaker in a small annex (see Fig. 14). This cluster of houses formed a settlement, while the other sites are of only one or two buildings, and the site at *Allt Easdail* therefore emphasises how much there still is to learn about settlement in this period. Perhaps a variety of buildings and settlement types served different functions across the wider landscape.

Fields have been excavated at two Beaker sites in South Uist – *Sligeanach* at *Cille Donnain*, and *Cladh Hallan* – and at *Roisinis* in Benbecula, all of these settlements on machair. The soil surface was worked with a simple plough and by spades. On these sites, small bits of worn pottery, tiny fragments of bone and charcoal show that the people cultivating the land were spreading household rubbish, known as midden, onto the fields to maintain their fertility, suggesting intensive cultivation. Barley and emmer wheat came from the associated houses.

In contrast to these, the site at *Taobh Tuath* revealed little evidence for grain production or processing, and the excavator suggested that the occupants may have had a largely animal-based, pastoral economy, including hunting as well as managing herds of sheep and cattle. The finds from the house at *Dail Mor* in Lewis, on the other hand, suggest that the occupants may have been specialising in producing fine quartz arrowheads. This has led some authors to suggest that people may have moved from one resource to another at different times of the year, and that settlement may have been flexible, with a variety of houses belonging to one group.

Beaker beliefs – closing the tombs

As mentioned earlier, there are no excavated Beaker Period burials yet from the Outer Hebrides. However, several earlier Neolithic chambered tombs seem to have been finally closed during the Beaker Period, a pattern also seen in Orkney. When the chambered tomb inside the stone circle at *Calanais* (Site 37) was emptied in the mid 19th century, sherds of Beaker pottery were found in it, but no later artefacts. Similarly, sherds of Beaker pottery were found within the chambered tomb at Geiriscleit in North Uist, when it was excavated, and have also been found in *Barpa Langais* (Site 22) in North Uist. The survival of these, apparently deliberately broken, sherds emphasises the likelihood that the great chambered tombs went out of use with the arrival of metal-working in the islands. However, they were not slighted, but apparently carefully closed, suggesting reverence and respect from the local population.

Recent excavations on the Neolithic crannogs and islets mentioned in the previous chapter have led to the suggestion that, rather than being settlements, they were religious or ritual sites. Many are similar in size to chambered burial cairns, and the evidence suggests that they also ceased to be used at the end of the Neolithic Period and were not reused in the Bronze Age. Whether they were religious or domestic sites, it is interesting that they follow the wider pattern of abandonment at the end of the Neolithic Period, when new cultural and technological ideas arrived in the islands.

Elsewhere in the British Isles, individual inhumations with Beaker pots have been found under circular mounds, or barrows – a burial practice which continued throughout the Bronze Age – but none have yet been discovered in the Outer Hebrides. Clearly there was something different about how the dead were treated in the islands, reflecting once again a distinctive local culture which adapted the new ideas to suit itself.

The shift towards an emphasis on individual burial happened at a time when stone circles and standing stones were still being erected, adapted and used. In the south of England, the stone circle at Stonehenge continued to be reconstructed and remodelled until around 1600 BC. In northern Scotland, and particularly in the islands, we know less about the life history of the great stone circles, but we are confident that they continued to be used and developed during the earliest part of the Bronze Age, in contrast to the chambered tombs.

Archaeologists have pointed out that the greatest concentration of standing stones in the islands is on the Isle of Lewis, while the focus of Neolithic chambered tombs is in North Uist. A certain amount of this pattern can be attributed to later cultural attitudes to archaeological remains, as there are several large chambered tombs in the Isle of Lewis, for example at *Cnoc na Croich* (Gallows Hill) in *Steornabhagh* (Stornoway), which were later dismantled to provide building stone. Nonetheless, the pattern does seem to be real enough that we can say that the ritual or religious focus of the archipelago may have shifted in the later part of the Neolithic Period and earlier part of the Bronze Age.

Moving on

By about 1800 BC the Beaker pottery was gradually replaced by plainer styles of pot, including large vessels decorated with applied strips of clay, called cordoned urns. As this was happening, many Beaker Period settlements were abandoned, often with local people moving only a short distance away, for example at *Barabhas* (Barvas) in Lewis (Site 49), at *Cladh Hallan* in South Uist (Site 45), and probably also at *Roisinis* in Benbecula. At *Barabhas* and *Roisinis*, the population who moved away reused the earlier settlements as burial sites for their dead; at *Cladh Hallan* a cemetery was created on the site after the earlier settlement had been covered with sand and was presumably invisible. Was this a coincidence, or does it reflect memory of the earlier settlement?

What can these changes tell us about the Early Bronze Age society of the islands? Importantly, it was still a society where buildings and houses were relatively short-lived, and people quite mobile. However, land may have been more important than houses, as the distance people moved was short – at *Barabhas* less than 500m – and memory and links to earlier settlements would seem to have been important as well. Perhaps reusing an earlier settlement for the burial of the dead was a way to emphasise links to the land, and the right to use it.

In this context, it is particularly interesting that survey in South Uist has found clusters of Beaker Period and Early Bronze Age settlement sites at three areas of the machair – *Iochdar* in the north, *Cille Donnain* in the middle, and *Cladh Hallan* in *Dalabrog* (Daliburgh) in the south – all areas where sea lochs from the east coast stretch almost to the machair, meaning that people had good arable land, but also good routes for travel from one side of the island to the other. These continued to be important areas for settlement for many generations after the Bronze Age, so it makes sense that settlement clustered here in prehistoric times, and that the occupants would want to reinforce their right to use this land.

We cannot know why pottery styles changed from the beautiful beakers to plainer and less well-made wares, except perhaps that the population put less value on pottery and started to invest status and value into other materials, maybe metal. Increasingly, cordoned urns and the plain wares that succeeded them later in the Bronze Age are found in burials, typically of single individuals, though occasionally of two or three people, as at *Roisinis* in Benbecula. This shift in burial, more than anything else, reinforces the social change from a communal Neolithic burial practice to more emphasis on individuality in the Bronze Age. After the closure of the chambered tombs, throughout the rest of the Bronze Age, individuals were given separate burials, sometimes in stone-lined graves (cists) (Fig. 20), with or without smaller cairns raised over them, sometimes cremated and sometimes inhumed (buried whole). There is no evidence that there was any practice of re-entering the grave, as had been the case earlier, though it is clear from the clustering of burials, for example at *Cladh Hallan*, *Cnip* in Lewis, and *Treseabhaig* (Tresivick) in *Bhatarsaigh* (Vatersay), that it was important to be buried near to others, probably from the same extended family. This suggests that kinship and ancestry continued to be very important to the local population.

The importance of ancestry to Bronze Age islanders is reinforced by one extraordinary find from *Cladh Hallan* in South Uist. Excavation of later Bronze Age and Early Iron Age houses (Site 45 and discussed below) uncovered human burials under the floors of the houses. One skeleton, of a mature man who had been tightly wrapped into a bundle before burial, was stained dark brown – an unusual colour for bone that has been buried in machair shell-sand. When the bones of the body were analysed, it became evident that the intact body had been buried in peat for long enough to preserve it, and then removed from the peat and probably dried. The skull and lower jaw which were found with the body belonged to different people; it was a composite body. Dating of the bones indicated that the man might have died as much as 500 years before the house was built and had been kept out of the ground until just before the house was constructed. This means that although the house dated to the later part of the Bronze Age, the man himself had died in the Early Bronze Age, and he had been kept as part of the family to which he belonged for generations after that, before being interred under their new house.

Investing in the living – the Late Bronze Age

The poor weather in the 12th century BC and the following climatic decline between around 1000 and 500 BC may be key to understanding some of the social changes that occurred in the later part of the Bronze Age. As the climate worsened, crop yields would have decreased; wheat would have grown poorly, if at all in the islands. Areas of hill and moor, which could have been cultivated in the Early Bronze Age, became wetter, and peat spread across poorly drained land. Increasingly, the machair became the only land that could be cultivated.

For many years, the only archaeological information about the later part of the Bronze Age in the Outer Hebrides came from chance finds made by people who were cutting peat for fuel. In the 19th century, two bronze swords were found at Aird, *Dail bho Dheas* (South Dell), in Lewis, and two more at *Iochdar* in South Uist. In the early 20th century, a spectacular hoard of spears, axes, chisels, razors, beads and whetstones were found within the remains of a large bronze cauldron at *Adabroc* in the Eoradail Grazings, in *Nis* (Ness) in Lewis, and, in 1975, a hoard of four bronze spearheads were found at *Cairinis* (Carinish) in North Uist. All of these had been carefully placed in the peat, some of them far below the modern surface, and although archaeologists initially assumed that these had been buried in order to keep them safe, more recently we have reconsidered. Hoards of valuable metal objects are only found in wet or boggy places, and it is now assumed that these are sacrifices, buried in the peat because they were valuable to their owners. Perhaps it might be that they were an attempt to slow or stop the spread of peat over valuable land? Or might they have been aimed to improve the weather, guarantee a good harvest, or provide protection against raiders? We cannot know, but their presence hints at a context where life might have been precarious, and it was necessary to appease greater powers. As peat cutting has decreased, no more recent finds have been made, but there may be more objects buried on the moorland.

The burial of weapons and other luxurious metal items highlights that the Bronze Age was a time when value and wealth were invested in portable objects, which were widely traded. The two swords from *Nis* in Lewis were of a style and quality found elsewhere in Europe, emphasising the international networks of which the islands were part. We also know that these weapons were used. A burial of this period from *Cnip* in Lewis (Site 47) was of a middle-aged man who had suffered severe injuries to his face and jaw as a result of a sword or axe blow. He survived these, but his jaw was dislocated, and he had to eat a soft diet, evidence of which showed in the build-up of tartar on his teeth.

Until recently, there was little excavated information about settlement of this period in the islands, but we now have information from one key and very important site – *Cladh Hallan* in South Uist (Site 45) – excavated by the University of Sheffield in the 1990s. This settlement has already been mentioned as the location of a Beaker Period house, an Early Bronze Age cemetery, and a composite mummy. In keeping with the themes mentioned above, of settlement mobility in a limited area, and remembering earlier places in the landscape, when the local community here built new houses in the later part of the Bronze Age, they built on top of the earlier cemetery.

The new houses were very different to the Beaker Period buildings. A terrace of six or seven very large, round houses, with east-facing doors, was constructed, of which three have been fully excavated (Fig. 17). These houses were built and rebuilt on the same site over hundreds of years; the longest-lived of the three was occupied for over 700 years and rebuilt 14 times. Each was constructed into a hollow cut in the ground, carefully walled with stone, and with a massive bank of turfy soil built up around to form the bulk of the wall. Each of the buildings

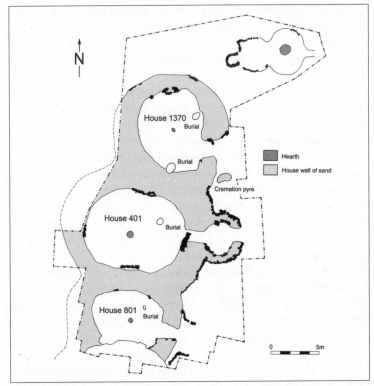

Fig. 17. Plan of settlement at *Cladh Hallan, Uibhist a' Deas* (South Uist)
(Irene De Luis, © M. Parker Pearson)

was much larger than earlier houses, with about 50–60m² of floor space, but the size varied, and the finds from the houses varied as well. The smallest of the buildings contained less metal and rougher stone tools than the others, which suggests that belongings and house size had become a way of measuring relative status between different families.

The houses had central hearths, and careful analysis of the deposits on the sand floors of the buildings revealed that they were organised in a clockwise direction around the hearth. To the left of the door was an area in which food was prepared. On the far side of the hearth from the door was an area with evidence for craftworking of antler, metal and stone, and to the right of the door was an area where beds had been made. These activity areas mirror the movement of the sun through the skies during the day, and the fact that human remains and animal sacrifices were found under the sleeping area suggests that this cycle also reflected life, from birth to death. Interestingly, the concern with a clockwise, sunwise movement in the house is one that persisted in European culture; the Gaelic language has a word *deiseil* which means 'sunwise', and moving around something anti-clockwise, or widdershins, is seen as unlucky in many cultures.

The burial under the northernmost of the houses was that of a middle-aged man – the composite mummy discussed above – who had died hundreds of years earlier, and this practice reinforces the fact that the people who constructed these buildings were actively thinking of previous family members and earlier times. Although there was a major change in architecture, continuity with the ancestors remained to be a reference point for belief and practice.

The middle house contained a lot of evidence for metalworking – moulds for casting, scraps of metal, and metal artefacts (Plate 4). When the house was rebuilt, and a new sacrifice was needed, a pair of bronze chisels was placed under the floor of the new house. This was the largest of the three buildings, suggesting that the metalworkers were important people. Metal ores are not found in the Outer Hebrides, so gold, and the copper and tin needed for bronze-working, had to be imported. Gold and copper probably came from Wales, Ireland or mainland Scotland, but tin was imported from Cornwall in the south of England. Clearly, there were trade routes linking the islands to other areas in the western British Isles, and the people who lived at *Cladh Hallan* had access to imported metal.

Food and warmth

The environmental finds from this village give us some idea of the impacts of the changing climate. Wheat was no longer grown, and barley was the staple food crop. Household rubbish and midden were apparently no longer being spread on the fields, but instead allowed to build up around the houses, and crops were being cultivated right up to and over the soil walls of the houses.

The pottery that was used for food preparation absorbed traces of liquid from its contents, so analysis of the chemical traces within the pot tells about its original use. Many pots held milk, often cooked with either meat or barley to make staple meals of stew and porridge. The bones of young calves indicate that cattle were being managed primarily for milk production; removing a calf from its mother at birth means that people can take all the milk the cow produces, and that the size of the cattle herd can be kept at a manageable level.

We know that sheep were kept, from bones found in the middens that piled up around the houses. Weights from spindles, for spinning wool, were also found and, for the first time in Scotland, the marks left by the posts of a loom and a loom weight show us that weaving was taking place. Lots of stone scrapers and other tools from leather-working also indicate the importance of leather, probably for clothing and shoes as well as making things like bags, straps and containers.

Many of these glimpses into Late Bronze Age life are only available to us because *Cladh Hallan* was excavated to modern standards. As more modern excavations take place on other sites in the islands, we can expect to find out much more about the detail of everyday lives in prehistory.

Saunas or smoke houses?

One of the most distinctive site types of the Bronze Age are burnt mounds. These are crescent-shaped mounds of broken, fire-damaged stone, found by freshwater sources. On excavation, some mounds are shown to have formed around small buildings, while others just have the remains of a pit in the centre. The mounds built up over time, as stones were heated in a fire and dropped into water to warm it. The broken stone was thrown away on the mound.

Stones were used like this to heat water throughout prehistory, but in the Bronze Age and Early Iron Age people seem to have used these sites specifically for water heating. Their location by water suggests that a lot of water was used. Some archaeologists believe these to have been places where large amounts of meat could have been cooked by boiling. Others think that they may have been saunas or smoke houses. *Ceann nan Clachan* in North Uist (Site 65, Fig. 18) is a good, if late, example of a burnt mound, dating from the Early Iron Age.

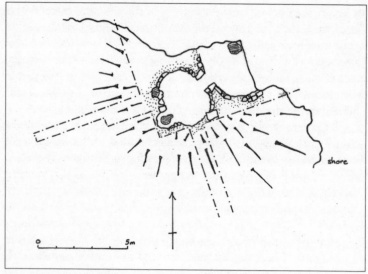

Fig. 18. *Ceann nan Clachan* burnt mound, *Uibhist a' Tuath* (North Uist)

The vanishing dead

As these monumental houses were being built, the tradition of marking burials with cairns came, gradually, to an end. The kerbed burial cairns which had been built in the islands from the Early Bronze Age onwards disappeared, and fewer burials are found from this period. At *Cladh Hallan*, immediately before the construction of the houses, there was a small cemetery of cremations on the site. These were marked only with very small rings of stones, and it is unlikely that they would have been discovered if not for the excavation of the overlying buildings. During the Bronze Age, the community had changed from one focused on memorialising the dead to the extent of preserving their remains above ground in some cases, to a culture that emphasised the permanence of the living. This may reflect the difficult environmental times, when more effort had to be put into staying alive.

This change in attitudes to the dead has an unfortunate side effect for archaeologists. We can learn much about the lives of individuals in the past by studying their physical remains. Chemical analyses of skeletons, for example, can tell us about food habits; prehistoric people in northern Scotland, after the Mesolithic Period, ate almost no seafood, despite the amounts of shellfish sometimes found on excavated sites. Analyses of tooth enamel can suggest whether a person was born in a different area from where they are buried, because adult tooth enamel forms in the gums in the first decade of a person's life and reflects the chemical makeup of the food and water from the local area. These are things that we cannot find out without studying the actual remains of human beings and we have little or no evidence from the later part of the Bronze Age for much of the next millennium.

New priorities

The islands' culture, as the end of the Bronze Age grew near, had changed radically. The relatively mild climate of the earlier part of the period, during the 2nd millennium BC, had shifted to a cooler and wetter, and probably stormier, one, in an environment that had grown progressively more limited. Trees were fewer, areas of peat wider, and arable land increasingly confined to the coastal machair. Settlement had taken on the coastal pattern which was to characterise it from this time forward, and within that coastal area massive, long-lived houses were being built and rebuilt on the same site, accumulating great settlement mounds that would have been visible from long distances. Instead of the earlier, large-scale, communal, ritual or religious monuments, these monuments to the living now dominated the landscape.

GAZETTEER

It is very noticeable that there are far fewer known Bronze Age sites than sites of other periods. There are several reasons for this: the landscape and settlement patterns in the islands changed significantly during this period; housing was small-scale and unobtrusive for a very long time; and ritual monuments first built in the Late Neolithic Period continued in use. But, most of all, it is probably because insufficient research has yet been carried out on this most interesting period.

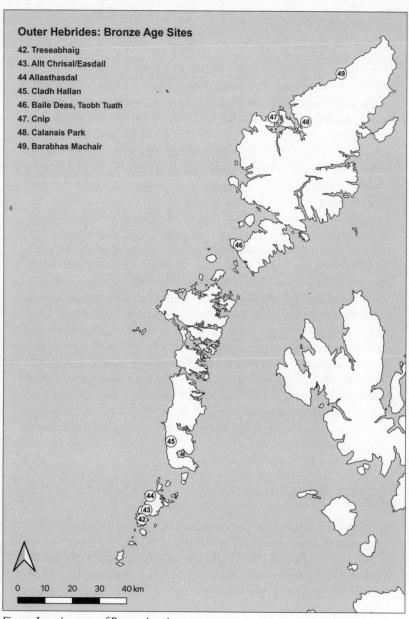

Outer Hebrides: Bronze Age Sites

42. Treseabhaig
43. Allt Chrisal/Easdail
44. Allasthasdal
45. Cladh Hallan
46. Baile Deas, Taobh Tuath
47. Cnip
48. Calanais Park
49. Barabhas Machair

Fig. 19. Location map of Bronze Age sites

Bhatarsaigh (Vatersay)

42. *Treseabhaig* (Tresivick)   NL 6244 9596

Park at the Vatersay hall and walk west across the machair. Follow the coast of the bay, continuing westwards, and walk up the second stream valley, staying on the eastern side of the stream. Total walk of just over 1km, with no path.

This site is in a rich archaeological landscape that is worth taking time to explore. There are 9 kerbed cairns at this site, and a further 9 nearby, giving a total of 18 cairns in one small valley. All are on the eastern side of the stream.

The cairns vary in size from 9m in diameter to less than 3m, and are recognisably Bronze Age rather than earlier because of their location on higher ground and their small size, circularity and kerbs. Each was the burial place of only one person, or at most two people. Excavations of such cairns elsewhere have shown that they have one main burial or cremation in the centre of the cairn, and perhaps a second, presumably of a closely related person, buried later into the body of the cairn material. If this is the case, we must assume that this is probably the burying place for a local community.

Across the stream, on the western bank, are four or five roundhouses. When these were first found, it was assumed that they were too large to date to the Bronze Age. However, excavations at *Cladh Hallan* in South Uist (Site 45) have demonstrated that very large roundhouses were built in the Bronze Age, so the houses in this valley may have been where the people buried in the cairn cemetery lived.

Barraigh (Barra)

43. *Allt Chrisal / Easdail*   NL 6417 9785

Signposted. Park in layby on northern side of road and walk 100m upslope.

The Neolithic and Early Bronze Age settlement in *Allt Chrisal* is upstream from the Neolithic and Early Modern buildings (Site 3), and is a roundhouse located on a hillock adjacent to the point where the stream emerges from the narrow defile higher up the hill, and the land starts to open out. Excavations here in the 1980s showed that the hillock had been built out and extended using boulders and soil, with a stone retaining wall, to increase the area around the house.

The house was first built in the Neolithic Period and appears to have been in use during the same time range as the building lower downstream, but it continued in use into the Beaker Period. The entrance opened to the south, and the building was around 4m in diameter internally. There were small, external structures associated with this site, including a square box or cist that had been built onto the northern wall at the time that the building was constructed. This contained an entire, though broken, Beaker vessel (see Fig. 14). A further small hut immediately to the south, with an internal diameter of only 1.8m, was a store house or shelter. It had not been occupied, and there were no obvious floors or hearth, but a lot of damage had been done by burrowing rabbits, which had certainly destroyed evidence. Flint flakes were found within it, so it is assumed to be of the same period as the adjacent roundhouse.

44. *Allathasdal* (Allasdale) settlement and burials   NF 655 028

Park on the edge of the road next to the turn-off onto the machair and walk 250m south, parallel with the road towards the shore, to the erosion hollows.

Stormy weather in 2005 exposed the remains of four Bronze Age burials in an eroding hollow of the machair at *Allathasdal*. These were excavated as a matter of urgency, and a year later *Time Team* visited the still-eroding site. Their rapid excavations uncovered a further Bronze Age burial and the remains of at least one Bronze Age house, as well as the remains of a large Iron Age roundhouse. Depending on the winter weather, the remains of the buildings can sometimes still be seen.

The people who were interred at *Allathasdal* were buried near to each other and were probably related. Their graves were lined with upright stones, and they were lying on their sites, crouched.

Fig. 20. *Allathasdal* (Allasdale) burial, *Barraigh* (Barra)

Uibhist a' Deas (South Uist)

45. *Cladh Hallan*   NF 7305 2203

Park adjacent to the modern cemetery, and walk 600m north and west, following the machair track. The site is in a grassed-over hollow immediately south of the track.

Settlement on the machair near *Cladh Hallan* in South Uist began in the Early Bronze Age with a small Beaker Period settlement and cemetery. However, these had been abandoned and covered with wind-blown sand before the Late Bronze Age settlement started. The creation of the new Late Bronze Age settlement began with a small cemetery of cremations, and a house was built over one of these crema- tion burials, with the hearth of the house carefully placed on top of the burial, reinforcing a strong association between the living and the dead on this site.

The initial house on the site was only 6m long and 3m wide, and was built using wooden posts, probably with wattle panels between them. The proportions and shape of the house are very similar to those from the Neolithic and Beaker Period houses at *Taobh Tuath*

(Northton) (Sites 24 & 46), despite being nearly 600 years later. On abandonment, this building was replaced by a line of pits, in which pieces of unburnt and cremated bone, some at least from the earlier cemetery, were deliberately placed. The pits were filled in, and a tiny, semi-sunken stone building was constructed, perhaps as a test run for the techniques which were then used to build a substantial row of roundhouses, joined together in a terrace. Three of these were excavated; the remainder remain under the adjoining sand dune.

These new houses (see Fig. 17) were much bigger; the largest had a floor area of 60m², which is the same as a two-bedroom flat. They were also very substantial, semi-sunken into the sand, with stone walls, and carefully laid floors with central hearths that formed the focus of the building. The door in each house faced east, towards the rising sun. The roof rested on the wall head and on posts inside the building. This circular, massive, permanent form of architecture was a new thing, and was the beginning of the trend in massive building that was to continue into the Iron Age.

Inside the buildings, craftworking debris shows that people were spinning fibres, weaving, working leather and antler, and metal. They cooked at the hearth, and for the first time in Scotland we have evidence that their diet included dairy products. The evidence for an upright loom here is also the earliest in Scotland; previously people probably wove textiles on wooden frames. These activities took place in specific parts of the house, and it seems that daily activities, and people, may have moved around the building in a clockwise, or sunwise, route, with sleeping areas to the right of the door, in the north-eastern quarter.

And they lived with the dead. Burials of the dead were made under the houses as they were constructed – a child in the southern-most house, a teenager in the middle one, and the famous *Cladh Hallan* mummy discussed earlier in the chapter in the northern house. In addition, there was a second mummified body of a woman buried under the northern house. The people who were buried here were already dead; the child's body had been kept for some time before it was buried. Most of the burials, apart from the woman in the northern house, were buried in the north-eastern quarter of the house, emphasising the pattern of different areas for various activities.

These buildings were reused and rebuilt over a long period of time. Each time the houses were rebuilt, new burials of people or animals, including dogs, were made under the floor. The southern house fell out of use relatively early, but there were still people living in a renewed but recognisable middle house 500 years later, in the Iron Age. This was a real change in priorities, marking a shift from investing effort in the huge communal monuments of the Neolithic Period and very early Bronze Age, towards showing the status of a specific kin group or extended family in their home.

Na Hearadh (Harris)

46. *Baile Deas* (South Town), *Taobh Tuath*   NF 9753 9125
    (Northton)

Walk 2km from *Taobh Tuath* along an unpaved machair path, following the track along the southern coast of the headland.

This site is most easily visible from the shoreline but can be identified from up on the coastal path by the grassy rectangular footings of 18th- and 19th-century houses, with enclosure walls around them. If you walk on the shore, you will see deep layers of dark coloured soil, with shells, stones, pottery and bone eroding out from the exposed edge of the land.

Partial excavation of this site during the 1960s revealed the remains of a settlement first occupied seasonally in the Mesolithic Period, and then permanently occupied from the Neolithic onwards (Sites 1 & 25). Beaker Period occupation here included an oval house cut into the sand with stone-revetted walls and a roof supported on central posts. The entrance to the house was at the narrow end. This pattern of relatively small, oval or sub-rectangular architecture is very similar to the building found at the bottom of the sequence of Bronze Age houses at *Cladh Hallan*, suggesting that houses were small and relatively ephemeral, possibly frequently replaced or moved, in much of the first half of the Bronze Age.

As this site is being destroyed by erosion, it is likely that the Bronze Age settlement was larger than the excavated area. There could still be more evidence for the use of the settlement in the centuries between the Early Mesolithic and the Bronze Age, yet to be uncovered.

Leodhas (Lewis)

47. *Cnip* (Kneep) cemetery   NB 0996 3639

Park at the campsite parking area on the beach, and then walk 500m north to the headland above the beach. The site is enclosed in a fence to prevent damage from grazing animals and to encourage grass to regrow over the eroding surface. Please close the gate behind you.

This area was first identified as an archaeological site in the early 20th century, and when a Bronze Age cairn eroded out of the ground in the late 1970s, it was excavated. This large and complex cairn had been reused and rebuilt three times. First, a D-shaped cairn had been built over a burial in a stone box, or cist. Another cist was then dug through the cairn, to contain a pot with a cremation in it, and both of these were then covered by a later, round cairn, built to contain a cremation. The remains of these three cairns are the heap of stones in the middle of the eroded hollow.

Further excavations have taken place here since then. Another Bronze Age cist, containing the body of a man, was found adjacent to the cairns. This man had been badly injured by a blow to the face, possibly from a weapon. He had survived, but the damage had left him eating a soft diet, shown by tartar on his teeth.

Then, in 2009 and 2010, excavations to the south of the cairns found three further burials (Fig. 21), containing parts of at least nine people. The bodies had been put on a ring-shaped mound to decompose and fall apart, or buried in shallow graves, over about 150 years from the time of the first reconstruction of the main cairn, between about 1770 and 1620 BC.

Clearly, this place was used by a group of people as their cemetery over a very long time. Probably the big cairn formed the central focus of the other burials, which were less clearly marked out on the surface. The variety of different ways of disposing of the dead also shows us why we find relatively few prehistoric burials. If the cremations and the burial sites of the disarticulated bodies had been exposed by marine erosion, they would probably have been lost without record.

Interestingly, the main cairn was probably still visible in the landscape in the Viking Age, when this site was reused as a Viking burial ground (Site 95).

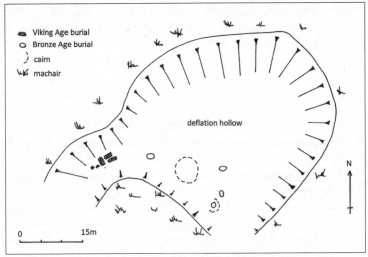

Fig. 21. Plan of *Cnip* (Kneep) Bronze Age and Viking Age cemetery, *Leodhas* (Lewis)

48. *Calanais* (Callanish) Park cairn   NB 2179 3473

Park in the small parking area to the east of the road and cross to the cairn.

This cairn was discovered during road widening in the 1990s. Excavation revealed a large Bronze Age cairn about 8.5m in diameter, which had two kerbs. The outer kerb was circular, but the inner kerb formed a flattened circle the same shape as the plan of the main stone circle at *Calanais* (Site 37). In the centre of the cairn was a cist containing a cremation in a plain pot, and a paved path led up to the central cist from the north-east. The body of the cairn had been remodelled in prehistory, and it appears that an earlier path led to the centre of the cairn from the south, possibly aligned with the northern avenue of the stones at *Calanais*, reinforcing the impression that this cairn was part of the wider related landscape.

There were later hollows and disturbances in the deposits of peat and burnt peat which had been laid over the stones of the cairn. In these were the broken remains of another pot, which may have contained a cremation. The whole of the cairn was covered by quartz pebbles. Under the cairn itself, further post-holes, pottery, stone tools and plough marks indicated that the site had been intensively used before the cairn was built.

49. *Barabhas* (Barvas) Machair
NB 348 518

Park at the modern cemetery and walk south and west around the fence towards the sea, through the eroding remains of the prehistoric landscapes.

Walking around the machair to the south and west of the modern cemetery at *Barabhas*, you enter an area where a vast, multi-period prehistoric landscape has been exposed by erosion and is now progressively stabilising and being re-covered with grass. Small-scale excavations, field walking and survey have taken place here since the 1970s.

Two Bronze Age buildings were excavated here. In the 1970s, a small excavation took place on a very fragmentary roundhouse, which had been extremely badly damaged by rabbit burrowing. The house was built with turf walls, faced in stone, and was about 5m in diameter internally, but it was difficult to say anything about the internal arrangements of the building due to the damage. It was on top of a settlement mound of earlier archaeological remains, showing that this

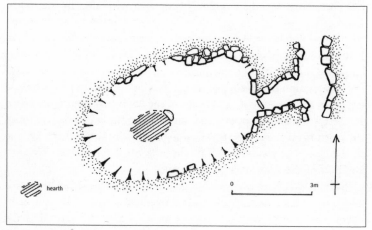

Fig. 22. *Barabhas* (Barvas) Beaker Period house

location had been used and reused over time. The pottery from the site was very plain, and the radiocarbon dates confirmed that this building was used in the middle of the Bronze Age.

In 1986, about 300m away, a tightly crouched skeleton was discovered in eroding archaeological deposits. The following year, three further crouched burials, inserted into the remains of an earlier house, were discovered. This was particularly exciting, as the pottery from the site showed that the building remains dated from the Beaker Period. The house (Fig. 22), which was about 5.5m x 4m internally, was similar in size and shape to other Beaker and earlier Bronze Age houses in the islands, but had had a porch added to the entrance, perhaps to stop sand blowing in. At a later stage, but before the burials, a smaller building had been constructed at the entrance end. Then, when that building went out of use, the burials were put into the heap of building remains. Dates from the buildings and burials suggest that the Middle Bronze Age house is only a little later than the burials in the Beaker house, so that there is a sequence of Bronze Age activities in this landscape.

4. Monumental Buildings:
The Iron Age 800 BC – AD 800

The Iron Age is, perhaps, the most visible prehistoric period in the Outer Hebrides. It covers a long duration; ironworking first arrived in the islands around 800 BC, and the period continued until the arrival of Scandinavian incomers 1,600 years later, around AD 800. By the beginning of the Iron Age, the coastal settlement pattern which characterises the islands today was established, and the remains of Iron Age settlements are found close to later settlements. They are, therefore, often found during croft work or house building. In addition, Iron Age culture in Scotland was preoccupied with building monumental houses to demonstrate status, and the islands are littered with the massive remains of these buildings.

This period also saw significant social change; the population gradually converted to Christianity and, for the first time in the years after 0 BC/AD, historical documents refer to the area, complementing the results of archaeological survey and excavation. None of the surviving documents were written in the Outer Hebrides and, therefore, the few sources that talk about the islands refer to places that the authors may not have seen, and record events that were indirectly reported. This period, though, marks the end of prehistory and the emergence of the historical periods during which we have increasing written sources of information.

Importantly, this period in the Outer Hebrides was non-Roman. In southern Britain, the Iron Age ended with the arrival of the Romans in the 1st century AD, and the four hundred years of Roman occupation had important impacts on the structure of the landscape and culture. However, although there are occasional Roman finds from the Outer Hebrides, perhaps reflecting indirect trade links, there is no evidence that Romans ever set foot on the islands, and there was therefore uninterrupted local cultural development.

The surviving documents suggest that, from the 4th or 5th century AD, Scotland was divided amongst three or four ethnic groups, two of which – the Scots and the Picts – were resident in the north of the country. The Picts are associated by archaeologists with a material culture that is mostly found in eastern Scotland, while the Scots, who were Gaelic speakers with close links to Ireland, were resident in western Scotland, particularly where the west coast is closest to Ireland. Some documents suggest that the Scots came from Ireland originally, but the sources are so few that this is impossible to be certain about. Given the proximity of the Hebrides and Northern Ireland, the Scots probably had long-standing links across the water.

Archaeology remains our richest source of information about this period, given the scarcity of documentary evidence, but also given that it focuses on the physical lives and circumstances of the population. This is particularly true for the Outer Hebrides, for which there are no local surviving documents, though this is something that will be discussed later in this chapter.

Settlements and subsistence

Archaeologists use the emergence of ironworking as a convenient marker for the beginning of this new period, but the technological change did not produce an immediate cultural change. Many of the characteristic elements of Iron Age culture, particularly monumental house building and a concern with personal adornment, had their roots in the Bronze Age, and continued and developed in the earlier part of the Iron Age.

Cladh Hallan (see Fig. 17), the village of roundhouses excavated in *Uibhist a' Deas* (South Uist) by the University of Sheffield, was occupied from the Bronze Age into the Iron Age, until around 400 BC. During this time, the buildings were built and rebuilt, the remains accumulating into a great mound – 'an ancestral pile' as the director of the excavation described it. Clearly it was very important for the occupants to continue to live in the exact location their ancestors had lived, the structure of the houses somehow embodying their identity and their claim to the land from which they took their subsistence.

Internally, these round buildings were centred on a hearth, with activities arranged radially around the hearth, so that the rising sun entered the south-east-facing doorway and daily life moved around the house sunwise, following the progression of the light. This pattern, established in the Bronze Age, persisted as a basic domestic principle of domestic organisation throughout most of the Iron Age, and elements of this concern with sunwise, or clockwise, activity and organisation lasted until the 20th century in the islands. As late as the 1950s, for example, it was considered ill luck to turn a boat anti-clockwise after it was launched into the water, or to wrap the securing rope around a haystack in an anti-clockwise direction.

The size variations between the houses in the settlement at *Cladh Hallan* suggest that buildings were increasingly important as a way of demonstrating status in the earlier part of the Iron Age. The objects that were found inside the buildings also varied; the biggest house – the middle house of the excavated part of the site – contained lots of metalworking debris, including fragments of moulds for making ornate and valuable weapons, pins and razors. The Outer Hebrides do not have metal ores, so the metal was imported from elsewhere in the British Isles. The association of a big house, occupied over hundreds of years, with the skills and trade links to work metal, suggests that metalworking was a high-status trade, and that this was demonstrated both in the beautiful and valuable portable objects that were created, and in the size and quality of the house that the metalworkers lived in.

Brochs and fortifications – the Middle Iron Age

This concern with large houses underpinned the development of the most dramatic of Iron Age building types – the broch. There have been endless archaeological arguments over the definition of a broch, few of which have progressed our understanding of the buildings and the culture that produced them. However, one of the key elements of Early and Middle Iron Age culture in northern Scotland was showing status by investing effort, materials and technical skill in constructing the largest possible houses. Another is that they defined domestic buildings – houses – as rounded or perhaps ideally circular. The roundhouses of the Iron Age, therefore, became ever larger and taller, with the most prestigious houses developing into enormous circular towers, up to 13m in height, with two or three storeys of accommodation inside (Fig. 23). These towers are called 'brochs', a Gaelic word borrowed from the Scandinavian Old Norse language,

Fig. 23. Reconstruction of a broch (© Alan Braby)

which arrived in the islands at the end of the Iron Age. The incoming Scandinavians saw towers and massive houses throughout the islands, and called them '*borg*', meaning fort, and this was borrowed into Gaelic as the word '*broch*'.

Although the original meaning of 'broch' was simply 'fort', in the last 200 years it has come to be used specifically to describe Middle Iron Age towers. These were constructed of unmortared 'dry' stone, with concentric double walls, linked and tied together by broad, flat stones, forming corridors and a stairway between the walls. The bottom of the wall is normally built as a solid block, with two or three small rooms inside it. This is typically 6–8m thick and is heavy and solid enough to support the weight of the walls above. From the first-floor level, there are two concentric walls, and these grow narrower and closer together the higher up they go. The tallest surviving brochs in Scotland are around 13m high, probably their full wall-head height.

Inside the broch, ledges were built into the wall to support wooden floors. In some brochs, most of the living space was at first-floor level when they were first constructed, with the ground floor being reserved for storage or animal housing. In an increasingly treeless environment, brochs used large amounts of timber for wooden floors and their great, conical wooden roofs.

Dun Charlabhaigh (Dun Carloway) (Plate 5) on *Leodhas* (Lewis) is an excellent example of a broch, and is particularly useful for understanding the construction of this type of building, as half of the wall has collapsed, providing a cut-away view of the structure. There has only been a little excavation there, so we do not have a good date for its construction, but the earliest construction dates thus far for any broch come from the site of Old Scatness in Shetland, built in the 3rd or 4th century BC. In the Outer Hebrides, the only modern dating evidence for a broch comes from *Dun Mhulan* (Dun Vulan) at *Bornais* (Bornish) in South Uist, constructed around 100 BC. It seems likely that the peak of broch construction was in the 1st and 2nd centuries BC, but this is an area of archaeological studies where there is a lot of ongoing excavation, and our understanding of these dates may easily change.

Dun Mhulan (Fig. 24) is typical of many brochs in the islands. Prior to its excavation, it survived as a heap of rubble, with short lengths of curving wall visible in some areas. Excavation by the University of Sheffield took place in the 1990s and showed that the broch was originally built on the shore of, or an island in, a freshwater loch. Rising sea level has pushed the coast closer to the broch, burying the loch and the southern edge of its island in shingle. Removal of the shingle revealed rectangular buildings constructed against the southern

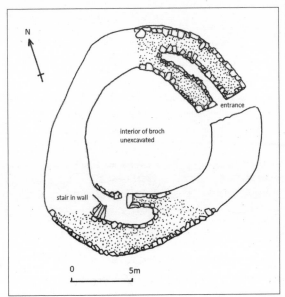

Fig. 24. *Dun Mhulan* (Dun Vulan), *Uibhist a' Deas* (South Uist)

edge of the broch in the 1st and 2nd centuries AD, suggesting that there may have been a small village clustered around the central point of the broch tower, a pattern of settlement unusual in the Hebrides, but commonly found in both Orkney and Shetland.

Typically, there are two brochs or other fortified sites in any one of the west coast townships in the islands. Remembering that the basic outlines of the settlement pattern, including the lines of boundaries between the major townships, were set by the end of the Bronze Age, then this helps to explain the social function of brochs in the Iron Age. Often one broch or other fortified site is near the coast and another is on higher ground set back from the coastline. A good example of this pattern can be found on the *Bhaltos* (Valtos) Peninsula in Uig (Fig. 25), on the west coast of Lewis. Here a circular broch, *Beirgh* (Berie), in a coastal machair loch, is paired with a very small, but massive broch-like round house, *Dun Bharabhat* (Dun Baravat), on an island in an upland loch, *Loch Bharabhat*. Coastal brochs are often on the edge of an area of cultivated land, with views out towards the sea to the west, and may have been lookout points as well as houses, keeping watch over the coastal shipping routes and the shallow

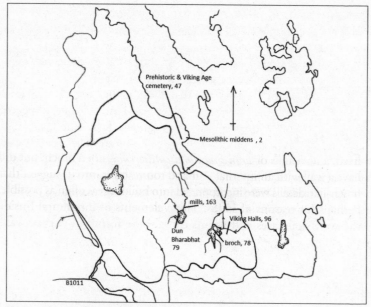

Prehistoric & Viking Age
cemetery, 47

Mesolithic middens , 2

mills, 163

Viking Halls, 96

Dun
Bharabhat
79

broch, 78

B1011

Fig. 25. Map of *Bhaltos* (Valtos) Peninsula, Uig, *Leodhas* (Lewis)

beaches where boats could be drawn up. Their position is frequently obvious as you approach the shoreline from the water. Upland brochs or fortified sites are frequently set at the edge of a pass through hills, or a valley in the hills, perhaps to keep an eye on the movement of people up into the summer grazings, or to monitor land routes between one area and another.

Dun Mhulan and *Dun Bharabhat* also demonstrate another important thing about brochs. The upstanding brochs, like *Dun Charlabhaigh*, or Mousa in Shetland, are the minority. These are the structures that were best-built and most functional. Most brochs are now heaps of stone, and many buildings, amongst them *Dun Mhulan* and *Dun Bharabhat*, collapsed either as they were being built or during their use. Many were built onto the remains of earlier Iron Age and Bronze Age settlement, frequently on islands or promontories where part of the ground may have been bedrock, and part softer soil. The unevenness and variable strength of the underlying surfaces clearly made construction difficult; *Dun Bharabhat* was built on an island that was partly artificial, which progressively compacted and sank under the enormous weight of the round house, causing it to collapse. Given these difficulties, and the trial and error which were involved in the construction of any broch or monumental round house, most probably never reached anything like 13m in height.

Although brochs dominate our understanding of the Middle Iron Age, most people did not live in brochs. There are many unexcavated sites where simple, if substantial, round house foundations or walls survive, and these are probably the type of house where most people lived. The details of *Dun Bharabhat*, which was not a broch, but did have a wall with an internal stair and rooms built into it, suggest that broch-like details were incorporated into buildings as often as possible, perhaps for reasons of status. These elements of intramural (inside the wall) staircases and rooms can also be found in curved walls protecting fortified promontories, a type of building often called a 'block house', for example at *Stac a' Chaisteal* in *Gearrannan* (Garenin) (Plate 6 & Fig. 26).

Changing society

In the first two centuries AD there was a decline and end to the building of brochs. No broch has, thus far, produced a construction date later than AD 200. However, brochs were still the focus of high-status settle-

Fig. 26. *Stac a' Chaisteal, Gearrannan* (Garenin), *Leodhas* (Lewis)

ment. Sometimes, as at *Dun Mhulan*, buildings were constructed outside and immediately adjacent to the broch, and the interior of the broch itself was remodelled, dividing the large, open, central space into smaller rooms. A similar pattern of internal building can be seen at *Beirgh* (Berie) in Lewis, where the broch wall stood to at least two storeys in height during the use of the later house. Why, then, was a secondary house built inside the intact wall? There may have been cultural reasons for this change, for example people may have felt that the separate functions of life – cooking, sleeping, storage – required separate rooms. However, there may also have been practical ones. Brochs and monumental round houses used extravagant amounts of timber for flooring and roofing. In contrast, from the 1st century AD onwards, buildings were constructed in ways which minimised the use of large pieces of wood for roofing; perhaps these smaller, sub-divided houses were easier to roof.

Outside the brochs the population of the islands was probably rising, and new settlements were being founded in many areas of the machair. While in Shetland and Orkney this new settlement appears to have clustered immediately around the broch buildings, in the Hebrides, in contrast, this expansion infilled previously unoccupied areas of the machair, as shown by extensive survey of the South Uist machair. Small clusters of settlement mounds, containing one or two houses each, were founded during the first centuries AD. Perhaps this indicates that the Hebrides were safer and more politically stable than the Northern Isles, allowing the growth of undefended settlements.

The houses constructed in these small farms were roundhouses called wheelhouses. This name comes from the fact that, in plan, these buildings look like a wheel, with the central hearth forming the hub and radially arranged walls subdividing the circular interior. Effectively, these are a continuation of the roundhouse building tradition. Where earlier stone-walled roundhouses would have needed internal wooden posts to support their roofs, wheelhouses used radial stone walls instead. Well-preserved wheelhouses have been found, for example at *Cille Pheadair* (Kilpheder) in South Uist, and *Cnip* in Lewis, and they show that the small, radially arranged rooms formed by this construction method were roofed with stone slabs. At Jarlshof in Shetland, where wheelhouses associated with a broch village survive intact, you can see that this construction method formed a series of dramatic arches around the central hearth (Fig. 27), leaving only a small central area to be covered by a wooden roof. Building like this allowed Iron Age people to build big houses using the minimum amount of timber, suggesting that timber was either rare or tightly controlled in the islands.

Wheelhouses varied in size; the smallest excavated example is from *Cille Donnain* (Kildonan) in South Uist, and was only 5m in diameter internally, whilst larger examples could be over 10m internally. This suggests that this was the preferred architectural form for houses, whether large or small. The central hearth and circular structure allowed for the continuation of the sunwise organisation of internal spaces, as previously. Most wheelhouses still had entrances that faced towards the east or south-east, in the direction of the rising sun. However, a significant proportion of both brochs and wheelhouses had entrances that faced west, towards the setting sun, and their internal space seems to have been either rotated by 180° or reversed (mirrored). Clearly the sun and its movement through the heavens

Fig. 27. Jarlshof wheelhouse interior, Shetland

remained crucially important to Iron Age people's understanding of the universe and their place in it, so what could this reversal imply? We can only wonder whether there might have been a group or class of people in society for whom the rules and practices of everyday life were reversed for some reason, whether religious or social or both.

We used to believe that the wheelhouse, as an architectural form, died out in the first two or three centuries AD, but the recent excavations at *Cille Donnain* show that they continued to be built and occupied until after AD 400, continuing the tradition of monumental circular building for over 1,000 years, before the architecture of the islands started to change in the 5th and 6th centuries.

Food and agriculture

The Iron Age environment was like that of the present day. Progressive deforestation had removed much of the woodland on the islands, though pollen samples suggest that there were stands of trees in some inland, sheltered areas. Peat bog had spread widely across the centres of the islands, and much of the settlement was coastal, focused on the machair. We do not know whether seasonal transhumance to shielings had started by this time, but it would seem likely, as moving livestock onto the moorland for grazing during the summer would maximise the productivity of the landscape and protect the growing crops on the shore. Wheelhouses are also found on the moor and these may have been summer houses, rather than permanent settlements, though more research is needed to confirm this.

New crops, particularly oats, were introduced during the Iron Age. There is some evidence of oats from pollen and from soil samples on earlier prehistoric settlements, but the amounts are so tiny that these earlier examples were probably weeds in barley crops. However, in the Iron Age, oats became one of the staple food crops; they grow well on acid soils and tolerate lower temperatures and higher rainfall better than barley. Oatmeal porridge would have been a commonplace dish in the islands from the Iron Age onwards.

Milk, butter and cheese were important sources of calories and protein, and keeping sheep and cattle was a way of changing grass into food that people could eat and that could be kept over the long winter season. Meat, from animals slaughtered at the end of the summer, would have been an important supplement to a diet that would probably have been largely vegetarian. Curiously, however, chemical analyses of Iron Age skeletons and food remains suggest that not much seafood was eaten. Although fish bones and shells are found on many sites, they do not seem to have been an important part of people's diets, and there may have been social or cultural prohibitions or restrictions on eating seafood. The remains that are found suggest that small, coastal fish were being caught, probably from the shore, and seafood may have been a supplementary food that was only eaten when other, preferable, food was unavailable.

Pork would also have been in limited supply in the Iron Age, but it is found most frequently on broch sites and was probably a high-status food. Pigs were never much kept in the islands, and this may in part be because their habits of rooting and digging can be damaging to the fragile soil, and because they eat food which is also edible for humans. Wild boar were never present on the islands.

An additional advantage to keeping sheep was wool for making clothing, and Iron Age sites throughout northern Europe, including the islands, have huge amounts of evidence for sophisticated spinning and weaving of wool. Wool would have been plucked from the sheep towards the end of the summer, and then washed, combed and spun, using a weighted stick called a spindle. Different threads would have been used to weave the various types of textiles – smooth, thick, textured, fine or coarse – required for different purposes. Scraps of fabric found preserved in waterlogged conditions show that decorative patterns, particularly checks and stripes, were commonly made using the natural and dyed wool.

Red deer were also an important source of food during the Iron Age, and the amount of venison that was eaten varies significantly from site to site. Deer may have been in short supply on some of the islands, but at *Beirgh* in Lewis they were the commonest type of meat eaten. Here, the proportions of bones from young and older animals suggest that the deer herd was carefully managed, and that animals for eating were selected and slaughtered in a controlled way, keeping a core group for breeding. Remembering that deer were probably introduced to the islands by people in early prehistory, this suggests that in some places the deer herd may have been managed as if they were domesticated animals.

Living amongst the dead – religion and ritual

As archaeologists, we cannot understand people's thoughts, merely the practical outworkings of them. During the first part of the Iron Age, these practical effects of religious belief were very alien and remarkable and, initially, nearly invisible. There is little evidence of how most of the dead were disposed of during the period between about 800 BC and AD 400. Cremation may have been usual, with the ashes of the dead scattered or washed away. There have also been Late Bronze Age and Iron Age pots found buried in peat around the area of the *Calanais* (Callanish) Stones. Peat would dissolve the remains of cremations, and it could be that some of the cremated dead were buried in these pots, around the important, earlier ritual site that still would have been visible. However, only one cremation burial from the earliest part of the Iron Age, before 300 BC, has been discovered in the Western Isles, so this is speculation.

The long-lived roundhouses at *Cladh Hallan* in South Uist had the dead buried beneath their floors, and this pattern of incorporating human remains into housing continued in the building of brochs and wheelhouses. The outbuildings to the south of the broch at *Dun Mhulan* contained a piece of human jawbone built into a drain beneath the floor, and each had a piece of human skull laid on the floor when they went out of use. Although the buildings were added onto the broch in the first two centuries AD, the human bones that were used in their construction and closing dated to nearly 400 years earlier, around the time of the building of the broch itself.

A similar pattern was noted at *Cnip* in Lewis, where a piece of human skull was put into an unfinished wheelhouse, abandoned and gradually filling with sand, and where two other pieces of skull, shaped and worked, were found in midden deposits during the excavations.

At *Thornais* (Hornish) Point in South Uist, the construction of a new wheelhouse was marked by the burial of the remains of a young boy, whose partly decomposed body was cut into four pieces and buried under the floor of the new house. Animal remains buried with him, including cuts of lamb and young beef, showed signs of being butchered and eaten, but there were no signs of this on the remains of the child, who had clearly died some time before the burial. The burial was unusual in the Hebrides, but the pattern of animal remains being found under the floors of wheelhouses is much more common, sometimes intact, sometimes butchered, and sometimes cremated. All of these types of animal burial were found in the wheelhouse at *Solas* (Sollas), along with pits containing pottery, a crucible for melting bronze, and one pit covered by a rotary quernstone. Although some of these odd deposits clearly dated to the construction of the house, it would seem possible that these pits were dug in the floor of the house at intervals during its occupation, perhaps to mark special events, rituals or memories.

This concentration of human and animal remains in ritual deposits in houses emphasises the importance of the household and its domestic space not just in the everyday life of the islanders, but also in their belief system. For us, used to a separation of spiritual and domestic space, this may seem curious and uncomfortable, but the integration of the two realms was clearly essential to island society in the Iron Age.

This integration of domestic and ritual realms is emphasised after 300 BC, as inhumation, or burial, became a more common practice. There is a very wide variety of types of burial of all ages of people, some buried in a curled, foetal position, others stretched out, often in stone-lined graves, called cist burials. Commonly these burials are found in settlements. At *Gabhsann* (Galson) in Lewis, a cemetery built up over time, widely spread through and around a settlement site. Our Iron Age ancestors lived amongst their dead, in close community with their ancestors, and this was probably important to their religious beliefs.

This emphasis on the past and ancestors may also explain why excavation has revealed a pattern of Iron Age reoccupation of Neolithic sites. It has long been known that brochs were sometimes constructed on the remains of Neolithic chambered cairns. It could be argued that this was simply the convenient reuse of a source of stones, but the fact that the passage to the central chamber of the cairn was reopened in a number of these cases, for example at Howe in Orkney, allowing the occupants of the Iron Age building to crawl into the burial chamber of the Neolithic tomb, suggests an important symbolic meaning to the practice.

Underground chambers were also sometimes built close to houses, perhaps in imitation of the chambers of chambered cairns, for example on Hirte, *Hiort* (St Kilda) (Site 76). The purpose of these 'souterrains' has been widely debated; practical ideas have included refuges in case of attack, or storage rooms, but many are approached by long, narrow passages from the house which could only be passed through by crawling, which would certainly have been impractical for a storeroom. These small rooms probably had a ritual or religious function. An intact souterrain was recently discovered by accident at Newton House in *Uibhist a' Tuath* (North Uist), when a tractor bailing hay put a wheel through its roof, and there are many others in the islands, but they are rarely safe to visit.

Survey of coastal, sea-stack sites around Lewis has also indicated that many of these sites, which were perhaps narrow promontories in the Neolithic Period, were reused in the Iron Age after a period of abandonment. Only limited excavation has been possible, but at Dunasbroc in Lewis excavation showed that a series of walls were built around the stack, some possibly Neolithic in date, but others certainly Iron Age. On the enclosed top, little survived of Neolithic structures, but there were very large amounts of Neolithic pottery and worked stone tools, and a lot of wood charcoal, suggesting that fires had been lit here. In the Iron Age, the site was briefly reoccupied. Grain and pottery dating to this period were found on the site, mixed in layers of soil which contained Neolithic finds, and the whole surface levelled. A very hot fire, or possibly two fires in succession, were lit on this levelled surface. The small excavation, and the short periods of occupation, mean that it is difficult to understand these activities, but they fit with the wider pattern of Iron Age reuse of Neolithic sites.

Politics and architecture – shrinking houses

The second half of the Iron Age is the period during which the islands first feature in historical documents; most were written in either England or Ireland. However, the Outer Hebrides are only rarely mentioned, and there is no real indication as to the political history or society of the islands. Archaeologists and historians speculate as to whether the population and culture of the islands was Scottish or Pictish in character, and the archaeological evidence is not conclusive either way.

From around AD 400 the housing styles of the islands began to change. Most excavated wheelhouses were abandoned by this time, and smaller buildings began to be the norm, which must reflect a significant social change. For nearly 2,500 years buildings had been as large as people could manage, but now they began to shrink and change form. Typically, buildings of this later part of the Iron Age are shaped like a figure of eight in plan, with one large, oval room, normally with a central hearth, joined to a slightly smaller round room without a hearth. The main entrance is into the larger room, which appears to have been the living area of the house, and there is less evidence for the function of the smaller room, which may have been used for storage.

During this period, broch sites continued to be the focus of higher-status settlement, and both the broch at *Bornais* in South Uist and that at *Beirgh* on Lewis had houses built inside their circular walls that followed this pattern of one main and one subsidiary room, as far as was possible, within the circuit of the earlier wall. However, the clearest example of this type of house is at *Bostadh* (Bosta) on the island of *Bearnaraigh Mor* (Great Bernera) off Lewis (Plate 7 & Fig. 28). Here, a small village of these houses cluster together beside a beach; they were exposed by coastal erosion and excavated in the 1990s.

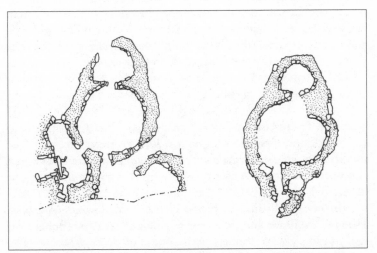

Fig. 28. Iron Age houses at *Bostadh* (Bosta), *Bearnaraigh Mor* (Great Bernera)

This architectural form also appears in Orkney, where it is associated with the northern Pictish kingdom, the political power in north-eastern Scotland in the Late Iron Age. The documentary evidence we have of the Picts comes from external sources; they were first referred to by the Romans, who encountered them during incursions into Scotland during the 1st century AD. It is not straightforward to bring together the scanty documentary sources and the archaeological evidence. The Romans recognised the Picts as a political unit and they provide us with the first use of the name 'Picts', which continued to be used to refer to the kingdoms of eastern Scotland up until AD 800. Otherwise, nearly all our evidence comes from the material remains that these people left behind in eastern Scotland, including some very distinctive carved stones, and evidence of literacy using a form of alphabet called 'ogham' to write a Celtic language with some similarities to Welsh.

English and Irish authors in the middle of the first millennium also refer to a kingdom in south-western Scotland called Dal Riata, occupied by people called 'Scots', who spoke Gaelic, also a Celtic language but one distinct from Pictish, and who had very close links to Ireland. Gradual political and cultural pressure over three or four hundred years led to the merging of the Pictish and Scottish kingdoms, and the disappearance of Pictish as a language.

By the 5th or 6th century, the Outer Hebrides were, therefore, in the middle ground between two kingdoms – Northern Pictland based in Orkney, and Dal Riata further to the south on the west coast. The islands were distant from both centres of power, and it is not clear which culture might have been dominant locally. The architecture of *Bostadh* hints at the possibility that there might have been Pictish influence in Lewis, and figure-of-eight houses were found during excavations at *Eilean Olabhat* and at *Coileagan an Udail* (the Udal), both in North Uist. However, excavations at *Bornais* machair in South Uist showed that an earlier wheelhouse was adapted and reused during this period, to form a smaller, oval building, less regular than those at *Bostadh*.

Two of the distinctive, carved Pictish symbol stones have been found in the Outer Hebrides, one in *Beinn na Fhaoghla* (Benbecula) and one in *Pabaigh* (Pabbay), to the south of *Barraigh* (Barra) (Fig. 29). However, both stones, which were probably used to mark boundaries or serve as a memorial for events or treaties, are relatively early and simple compared to some of the great carved stones of the east coast. Other evidence of Pictishness is elusive and ephemeral; a piece of bone found in North Uist in the early 20th century had an ogham inscription on it, possibly of a person's name, and another similar inscription on bone was found in 1996 by archaeologists from Sheffield University. In neither case can we be entirely certain what the inscription meant. Ogham is an alphabet, and in Ireland it was used to write Gaelic, so its occurrence in the islands isn't necessarily an indication of Pictish culture. There are no specifically Pictish language elements in the place names of the Outer Hebrides, and Pictish may never have been spoken there. It would seem likely, given the location of the islands in between these two power centres, that both the Scottish and Pictish kingdoms had influence in the area, but that the Outer Hebrides may have been largely independent of the growing political powers to the north and south of them.

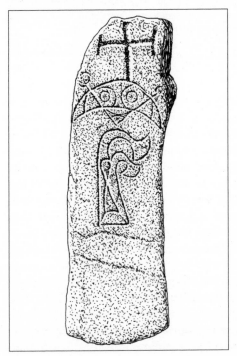

Fig. 29 Symbol stone from *Pabaigh* (Pabbay) (© Crown copyright: HES)

Personal display

Earlier Iron Age people focused their creative impulses on elaborate architecture and decorated pottery but, increasingly, in this time of political change, there is more and more evidence of a concern with personal adornment and decoration. Pottery styles changed, becoming very plain, and houses became smaller, but highly decorated pins of bronze, bone and antler were produced, used for pinning clothing or hair. Brooches of bronze and silver, decorated with gilding, glass or semi-precious stones, were produced. Evidence for decorative metalworking is found at many sites, including *Eilean Olabhat* in North Uist, where an earlier Iron Age building, rebuilt in the 6th to 7th centuries AD, was used as a metalworking workshop. Large amounts of metalworking waste, including broken moulds and crucibles for melting metal, were found here.

Another common find of this period, which supports the idea of an increasing preoccupation with personal presentation, is combs. Few personal combs were found before this, but during the Late Iron Age, decorated antler and bone combs were made, often with both coarse and fine teeth, both for hair styling and for lice removal. The styles of these changed quite rapidly, suggesting that they were fashionable display items as well as functional tools.

Converting a landscape

It is also during this period that the first evidence of local Christian belief is found in the islands. Although it has traditionally been believed that St Columba, settling on Iona in the mid 6th century, was the first missionary to Scotland, recent archaeological and historical research has emphasised that there was very early Christian religious practice at Whithorn in Galloway, which continued throughout the second half of the Iron Age. Galloway was linked to the rest of Scotland and the whole of the western part of Britain by maritime trade routes, so it is possible that there may have been pre-Columban Christianity in other parts of western Scotland. However, the surviving evidence for conversion in the Outer Hebrides is scanty. Old Norse place names, created by 9th-century incomers, sometimes include the names of Late Iron Age, early Christian, Celtic saints, for example Taran in *Tarasaigh* (Taransay) (meaning Taran's Island). There are also several place names including the word '*papa*', which meant a Christian priest or monk in Old Norse, for example *Pabaidh* (priests' island), *Paibeil* (priests' town) and *Pabanais* ('priests' headland').

Several holy or healing wells through the islands, including one at *Coileagan an Udail* in North Uist, have simple crosses carved next to them. Often these are wells with iron-rich water, which might have helped people suffering from anemia or other mineral deficiencies, and were probably used for healing purposes from earliest prehistory. In the process of conversion, some of these were given saints names and 'christened'.

On some of the offshore islands, including the Flannan Isles and *Ronaigh* (North Rona), where there has been little recent development, there are small chapels which may be very ancient. The chapel on the Flannan Isles is a small rectangular building, entered from the western end and roofed in corbelled stone. It was reputedly repaired and used by the 19th-century workmen who built the Flannan Isles lighthouse, and is very like some of the small, early stone chapels that can be found on the Irish West Coast and offshore islands, emphasising the links between Ireland and western Scotland.

On the larger islands, chapel sites and their surrounding burial grounds have been in use for many hundreds of years. The remains of the earliest chapels in some of the historic, coastal graveyards are buried deep under later churches. A strong suggestion of Late Iron Age origins, however, is given by the number of these coastal cemeteries which have eroding Iron Age settlements either immediately adjacent to or under them. The converting population probably built their first chapels where they lived.

In the southern Outer Hebrides, the Late Iron Age was also marked by the raising of stone crosses for outdoor worship, for memorials, and to mark boundaries of religious areas. Some of these, such as *Clach an Teampuill* on the island of Taransay (Site 75), may have been carved into Neolithic standing stones; others, for example that at *Cille Pheadair* in North Uist, are cross-shaped, and small, cross-incised slabs have been found as grave markers in ancient burial, for example on *Bhalaigh* (Vallay), off North Uist. Small crosses were also carved into bedrock and boulders, for example *Clach an t-Sagairt* in North Uist, where they may have marked the boundaries of sanctuaries or holy sites.

North of the Sound of Harris, the only crosses that survive in the landscape are found on offshore islands, such as Taransay or Rona. However, place names including the element 'crois', the Gaelic word for cross, do exist, suggesting that there may have been landscape crosses here as well. *Buaile na Croise* in *Carlabhagh* (Carloway) is a good example of this. Early Christian cross-marked grave markers were found built into and hidden in the 19th-century houses in *Hiort* (St Kilda), and excavations on the Shiant Islands, to the east of Lewis, uncovered an early cross-marked beach pebble, buried beneath the doorway of a later house. These concealed crosses suggest the possibility that later religious changes, discussed in later chapters, might be behind the lack of surviving crosses in Lewis and Harris.

This adoption of Christian practice would certainly not have been initially universal and, although burial became a more and more common way of disposing of the dead, burial practices were still very variable throughout the later Iron Age. People might be curled in foetal position or buried face down, and have their grave marked by a cairn or by a cross. In South Uist, at *Cille Pheadair*, a woman's burial of this period was excavated (Site 57; Fig. 32). Her burial was covered by a square cairn, in which she was orientated diagonally. Her burial had been initially covered only by stone slabs, and her body had been moved in the grave sometime after death, turned on its side and propped, at a point when it was decomposed enough that one of her hands fell off in the process. After this, the cairn had been filled in.

Changing times

Iron Age society, growing from prehistoric roots in the islands' culture, flowered and changed over 1,600 years. It moved over time from a culture which expressed status in great, monumental houses, rooted in the deep past and the life and death of the ancestors, towards a culture which was influenced by new religious beliefs and new political developments. Kin groups gave way to small kingdoms, and Christian beliefs, spreading along trade routes from the Mediterranean and the Roman world through the Irish Sea, strengthened and enhanced existing links to wider Europe and its ideas. By the end of the Iron Age, many of the cultural and material elements which would determine the development of the mediaeval history of the islands were in place.

Small coastal farming settlements were scattered across the landscape, some with churches and chapels, or near the remains of a broch in which the locally important family lived. In the summer, some people probably took the livestock to the moors and hills for grazing, while others may have stayed on the coast, repairing houses, cultivating the crops, or perhaps travelling for trade. This landscape, occupied, farmed and rich, must have looked very desirable to travelling raiders coming from the North, who began to appear in the years around AD 800, and who would have a dramatic impact on the islands, discussed in the next chapter.

GAZETTEER

Bhatarsaigh (Vatersay)

50. *Dun a' Chaolais*   NL 6285 9707

Park south of the cattle grid and walk 200m south-west over rough grazing to the top of a prominent knoll.

Dun a' Chaolais ('the fort of the Sound') is in a prominent, indeed dominant, position on a hilltop overlooking both the rich arable land of the northern part of the island of Vatersay and the sound between Vatersay and Barra.

The walls of the broch are largely fallen but stand over 1m high in places. It is 16m in diameter and both the external and internal wall faces can be seen. It seems to have had a north-eastern entrance, with small rooms to either side in the thickness of the wall. The gallery between the two concentric walls can be traced for much of the circumference of the building, and there is a small external enclosure or courtyard on the western side.

Outside the broch, to the south, are the remains of buildings, including later shielings. It is difficult to determine whether some of the buildings might have been contemporary with the broch or not, given the spreads of fallen stones masking the area around.

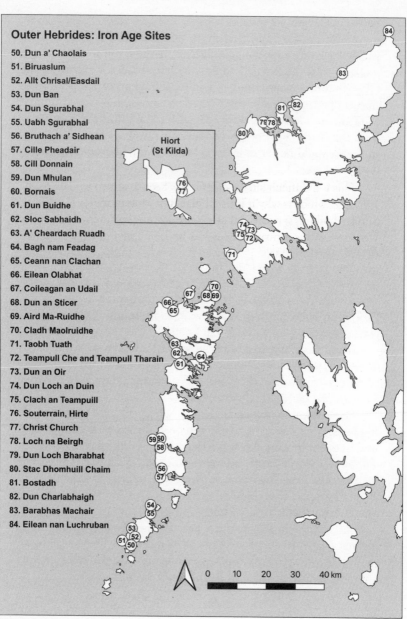

Outer Hebrides: Iron Age Sites

50. Dun a' Chaolais
51. Biruaslum
52. Allt Chrisal/Easdail
53. Dun Ban
54. Dun Sgurabhal
55. Uabh Sgurabhal
56. Bruthach a' Sidhean
57. Cille Pheadair
58. Cill Donnain
59. Dun Mhulan
60. Bornais
61. Dun Buidhe
62. Sloc Sabhaidh
63. A' Cheardach Ruadh
64. Bagh nam Feadag
65. Ceann nan Clachan
66. Eilean Olabhat
67. Coileagan an Udail
68. Dun an Sticer
69. Aird Ma-Ruidhe
70. Cladh Maolruidhe
71. Taobh Tuath
72. Teampull Che and Teampull Tharain
73. Dun an Oir
74. Dun Loch an Duin
75. Clach an Teampuill
76. Souterrain, Hirte
77. Christ Church
78. Loch na Beirgh
79. Dun Loch Bharabhat
80. Stac Dhomhuill Chaim
81. Bostadh
82. Dun Charlabhaigh
83. Barabhas Machair
84. Eilean nan Luchruban

Hiort
(St Kilda)

0   10   20   30   40 km

Fig. 30. Location map of Iron Age sites

51. Biruaslum promontory fort   NL 6103 9626

A walk of 1.4km west around the coast of Vatersay will bring you to
a viewpoint where you can see this island. Note that the island is
difficult and dangerous to access and making the attempt is not recom-
mended.

Biruaslum is a fortified island which was probably a promontory
in earlier prehistory. The fort occupies a flat shelf of ground, defended
by a curving wall. A dozen small buildings are clustered along the
walls.

This is a difficult site to date; it has been assumed to date to the
Iron Age, which is why it is listed here, but its appearance is unusual.
Similar buildings, excavated at *Dun Eistean* in northern Lewis (Site
120) were 16th century in date, and finds collected from an eroding
midden on Biruaslum in the 1990s included Neolithic pottery. While
it is fair to presume that the site will have been used and reused at
various points in prehistory, its true date and function are likely to
remain a mystery until further research is carried out on the monument.

Barraigh (Barra)

52. *Allt Chrisal/Easdail* wheelhouse   NF 6418 9776

Signposted. Park in layby on northern side of road and walk 70m
upslope, on the western side of the stream.

The south-facing valley of *Allt Chrisal/Easdail* was occupied during
the Iron Age as well as earlier and later. Excavations by the University
of Sheffield on a terrace above and to the west of the stream, about
halfway up the valley, revealed the remains of a circular stone structure
that had been built and rebuilt around 2,000 years ago.

The first house on the site was a large roundhouse, probably
dating to the middle of the Iron Age, when brochs were being built.
This type of house would have been where most people lived, while
brochs were the homes of the local aristocracy. Internally, the timber
roof of this house was probably supported on wooden posts, but the
remains of the building had been heavily robbed to build the small

wheelhouse which succeeded it and is still visible on site. This had an internal space of around 40m², and its largely stone roof was supported on stone piers. This architectural shift reflected decreasing access to timber, perhaps because of deforestation, or perhaps the increasing control of the timber trade.

This site was only partly excavated – the lower floor layers within the wheelhouse, and much of the underlying roundhouse, are unexcavated. The southern wall of the wheelhouse had to be rebuilt for presentation; if you look carefully, you can see a slightly different style of stonework in the rebuilding.

After the wheelhouse went out of use, the site was reused for building a small rectangular house and several circular huts, all of which may have been much later shielings.

53. *Dun Ban, Beinn Tangabhal* (Ben Tangaval) NF 6311 0037

A walk of around 2km from *Tangasdail* (Tangasdale), west along the coast of the northern side of *Beinn Tangabhal*, brings you to the exposed headland of *Dun Ban*.

Dun Ban ('the fair or pale fort') is a headland on the northern coast of the hill of *Beinn Tangabhal*. The headland is cut off by a thick wall of stone, making it a promontory fort. There was an entrance in the north-eastern end of the wall, and within the enclosed headland are the remains of a substantial broch, around 18m in diameter. The broch entrance appears to have been on the eastern side, with an intra-mural cell or small guard room immediately beside it, as is typical. The southern wall of the broch is badly collapsed, and a great tumble of stone spreads out from it towards the promontory enclosure wall. This probably obscures the remains of other buildings in this area.

54. *Dun Sgurabhal* NF 6954 0810

Park at the corner of the road, near the shore, north of the site, and walk 250m south, uphill, to the remains of the dun.

The remains of *Dun Sgurabhal* are visible as a roughly triangular, collapsed structure on the top of a small hill, overlooking the sea to the north and west of Barra. Some of the details of the building, including the double wall with a gallery between, strongly indicate that it dates to the Iron Age. As you walk up the hill, you will cross the remains of field systems and walls, some of which may date to the same period as the fort.

The building has not been excavated, and we do not know whether it was a broch tower or not, but it has a scarcement ledge for supporting a first-floor level, so it was more than one storey high. Early descriptions of the site say that there were buildings around the outside of the main structure and an enclosure wall around the whole, so this may have been the site of an Iron Age village.

The Iron Age date is confirmed by finds of Iron Age pottery from the site, but a piece of a ground stone axe dating to the Neolithic Period was also found here. This could have been brought to the site by someone as a curiosity or amulet, but it could also indicate that the dun was built on top of a Neolithic monument.

55. *Uabh Sgurabhal* (*Uabh an Duin*) cave   NF 6956 0798

Situated to the south of *Dun Sgurabhal*, 140m downslope. Take care accessing the cave, which is halfway down the cliff.

In front of this narrow cave is a platform surrounded by a rough wall of large blocks of stone. A human skull is said to have been found in the cave about 50 years ago, and a small trial excavation here revealed that the cave was used in the Middle Ages and Iron Age. Some stone tools may also indicate that it had earlier prehistoric occupation.

Little is known about how and when caves were used in the Outer Hebrides. They would have been convenient shelters for people working outside and might occasionally have been lived in by people who were moving from one area to another or were homeless. The use of caves probably goes back to the earliest occupation of the islands.

Uibhist a' Deas (South Uist)

56. *Bruthach a' Sidhean* (*Bruthach Sitheanach*),   NF 7337 2022
   Cille Pheadair (Kilpheder) wheelhouse

Park where the *Cille Pheadair* machair road divides to north and south and walk 150m west-south-west over the machair to the site of the wheelhouse.

This wheelhouse was excavated in the 1950s as it became exposed by erosion. It was remarkably large inside, with 11 radial piers supporting the roof. The main wall of the wheelhouse can still be seen today (Fig. 31), though its piers have long since fallen. The excavator believed it was one of a cluster of wheelhouses, but none of these is evident today, and much of the machair to the north of the house has been eroded or dug away.

At the time of its excavation, the wall of the house survived to its full height, which was 2.73m, emphasising the monumentality of the

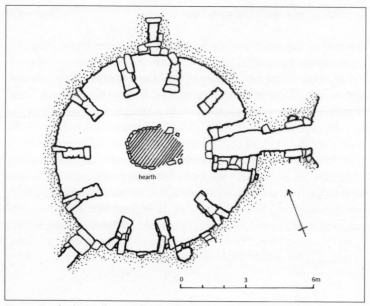

Fig. 31. *Bruthach a' Sidhean, Cille Pheadair* (Kilpheder), *Uibhist a' Deas* (South Uist)

building. It had started its life with free-standing piers supporting the roof, tied to the outer wall with flat lintel stones. This type of house is sometimes called an aisled roundhouse, where there is a small aisle between the circular wall and the piers. The lintels had cracked, and many of the gaps had been filled in with stone to strengthen the building – a pattern which is seen more widely in aisled roundhouses. Nothing remained of the stone roof which would have covered the small radial rooms formed by the piers, which must have been robbed for later building after this house went out of use.

The central hearth was made of a clay slab, with beach pebbles around three of its edges, and the clean floor and lack of finds in and around this central area indicates that it was swept regularly. Within the side rooms, small built-in shelves in the walls contained useful objects, including a late 2nd-century AD Roman bronze brooch, showing the status of the occupants and their access to valuable imported trade goods.

57. *Cille Pheadair* (Kilpheder) square cairn   NF 7292 1972

The site of this cairn has now been destroyed by erosion.

Coastal erosion on the shingle foreshore of *Cille Pheadair* exposed a square Late Iron Age (Pictish) burial cairn in 1998. This was excavated, and the cairn was reconstructed in the grounds of *Taigh Tasgaidh Cille Donnain* (Kildonan Museum), where it can be seen.

The skeleton in the cairn was of a woman about 40 years old, dubbed '*Cille Pheadair Ceit*' ('Kilpheder Kate') (Fig. 32). Her burial had been disturbed in the past, before the cairn was finally covered over, and her chest had been deliberately opened. The only object that accompanied her into the grave was a stone cobble.

This type of square cairn is more common in eastern Scotland, where it is associated with the culture of the Picts. Although a few further cairns like this have since been discovered in the Outer Hebrides, they remain unusual here, and indeed Iron Age burials are rare altogether.

Fig. 32. *Cille Pheadair Ceit* ('Kilpheder Kate') (© M. Parker Pearson)

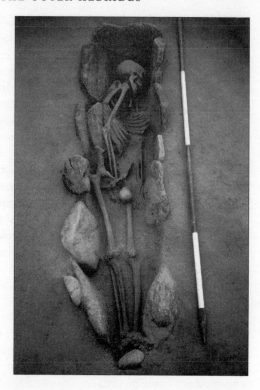

58. *Cill Donnain* wheelhouse

NF 7284 2857

The remains of this building have been reconstructed at *Taigh Tasgaidh Cille Donnain* (Kildonan Museum).

This small wheelhouse was located on the edge of a large settlement mound, surveys of which have shown that it was occupied from the Bronze Age onwards. It was excavated early in the 1990s and had already been very heavily robbed of its stone in prehistory, probably to build other structures in the settlement.

This small house was only 5m in diameter inside, a good example of the variability of size that wheelhouse architecture could be used for. Given that house size and monumentality reflected status in the Iron Age, this house was probably the house of a poorer or lower-status family in the community. Despite this, the house was used for at least 200 years, from about AD 200 onwards. There were probably only five or six internal piers, but the internal arrangements, with a central hearth, were the same as in much larger houses.

59. *Dun Mhulan* (Dun Vulan), *Bornais* (Bornish) NF 7140 2980

The machair road is suitable for vehicles, but you must stop at the parking place before the promontory begins, as the road thereafter has been badly damaged by storms and is only passable by foot.

The remains of the Iron Age broch of *Dun Mhulan* (see Fig. 24) lie on the southern edge of a promontory in the township of *Bornais*, which is named after the broch. It is increasingly damaged by sea-level rise and was unsuccessfully defended by a concrete sea wall to the south during the 1990s, which has now failed.

This broch was originally on an island in a machair loch, and the rising sea level has moved the shoreline progressively eastwards, leaving only small remains of the loch, with the broch standing half-buried on a shingle beach.

Excavations here in the 1990s examined the area of beach immediately south of the broch and the interior of the building itself. Within the building you can see a Late Iron Age figure-of-eight house, with one big room and smaller rooms leading off it. This was a secondary construction within the circular wall of the broch, and dates from the period after around AD 500. This form of building, whether within a broch or free-standing, is typical of the later Iron Age, and similar buildings have been found at *Bostadh* (Bosta) on *Bearnaraigh Mor* (Great Bernera) (Site 81) and elsewhere in the islands. This building is about the level of the first floor of the broch and excavation stopped at this level in the interior, which means that there is a whole storey of archaeological deposits below this before the original floor of the broch is reached. The entrance to this house reused the same line as the original broch entrance but at first-floor level; the flat slabs that pave the entrance are the ceiling of the original passage.

The archaeologists also dug within and between the two walls of the broch, and here they reached the bottom level of the building. Radiocarbon dates taken from beneath one of the walls of the broch indicate that it was constructed around 150 BC. Beneath this were soil layers dating from the earlier Iron Age.

Building expanded outside the broch over time, forming a small, clustered settlement extending into the area to the south which has now been eroded by the sea. During the 2nd century AD, two rectangular buildings were constructed outside the eastern side of the broch on top of layers of midden and rubbish deposits. These are the earliest known rectangular buildings in the Outer Hebrides. They were not houses, as they had no hearths. The later of these buildings contained a deliberately deposited part of a human jawbone in a drain under its threshold. After they went out of use they were replaced by a circular house with a hearth.

The broch was abandoned around AD 800, about the time the Scandinavians started arriving in Uist. The site remained unused until the Middle Ages, when it was reoccupied, with a rectangular building constructed on the north-eastern outer side of the broch. There is more discussion about this issue in the mediaeval chapter. In the 1940s, a fisherman's hut was built into the interior of the broch, using a German lifeboat as a roof.

60. *Bornais* (Bornish) Mound 1, settlement   NF 729 302

Follow the *Bornais* machair road until you get to the bend just north of *Loch Bornais*. Park here and walk north following the fenceline along a rough track for about 500m, before turning west for 100m. Make sure that you walk along the boundaries between the strips of cultivation and don't cross a crop.

There are three very large settlement mounds on *Bornais* machair, which have been subject to a long campaign of survey and excavation. This was the site of a large Viking Age and Norse settlement (Site 88) and of its predecessor, a Middle to Late Iron Age settlement, which was located on Mounds 1 and 2. This site would have been occupied at the same time as the later occupation in the broch at *Dun Mhulan* (Dun Vulan).

On Mound 1, a Middle Iron Age wheelhouse burnt down around the 4th or 5th century AD. Its burnt roof was left lying on the floor, and parts of the walls were reused to build a new sub-rectangular or oval house. This new house had a central hearth, edged at one end with cattle ankle bones; whether the bones were decorative or served

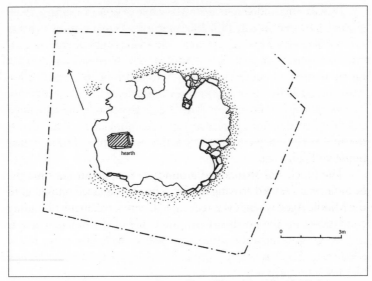

Fig. 33. Iron Age house at *Bornais* (Bornish), *Uibhist a' Deas* (South Uist)

as some sort of talisman, we will probably never know, but animal bones were often used in the structure of houses of this period.

Pictish finds from Mound 2 indicate that it was occupied in the Late Iron Age, probably right until the beginning of the Viking Age. What the relationship of the local people with the incoming Scandinavians was like is unknown, but when the Scandinavians arrived around AD 800, the broch at *Dun Mhulan* (Site 59) was abandoned, and this site became the focus of an important Scandinavian-style settlement, a pattern discussed more in the Viking and Norse chapter.

Beinn na Fhaoghla (Benbecula)

61. *Dun Buidhe*   NF 7942 5498

Park on the road that approaches nearest *Loch Dun Mhurchaidh*, at NF 7927 5491, and walk 360m south-east across a causeway, then an island, and carefully across a further causeway, to the dun on the second island.

Dun Buidhe is the most easily accessible of at least 14 island duns in Benbecula. Benbecula ('the hill on the ford') was until the recent past the wettest of the islands, interpenetrated by multiple brackish lochs and moved across by boats. All these strategic waterways, which gave sheltered access from the north to south of the island, were protected by settlements and fortifications.

The island is enclosed by a circular wall, inside which was a monumental, circular building. It is unclear whether this was a classic broch tower, as it has not been excavated, but it may well have been. Stone from the Iron Age structure has been taken and reused to construct rectangular post-mediaeval houses and a cattle fold or walled garden, and the causeways are likely to have been extended and reinforced in the Middle Ages as well.

This is a particularly good site on which to see clearly the process of use and reuse of Iron Age fortified sites in the mediaeval and later periods, and is very interesting to compare with *Dun an Sticer* in North Uist (Site 68).

Uibhist a' Tuath (North Uist)

62. *Sloc Sabhaidh, Baile Sear*   NF 7823 6085

Park at the parking area at the edge of the western coastal beach of *Baile Sear* (NF 7793 6131). Walk 560m south-east down the beach or coastal track to the settlement mound.

This settlement mound has been producing archaeological finds since the early 20th century, and sea-level rise and coastal erosion finally uncovered and damaged the western edge of the mound in a storm in 2005. Community excavation took place on the beach over a period of three years between 2017 and 2019, revealing the remains of a wheelhouse (Fig. 34).

The building had originally been constructed as a wheelhouse with free-standing piers (an 'aisled roundhouse'), with a foundation offering of a pot buried under the house wall when it was built. Further small pits containing pots and animal bones suggest that there might have been quite a lot of special activities and offerings in the area before the house was built. This building had later been modified to

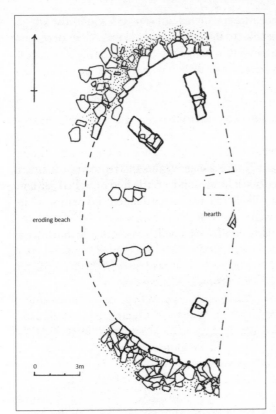

Fig. 34. *Sloc Sabhaidh, Baile Sear, Uibhist a' Tuath* (North Uist)

eroding beach

hearth

0   3m

reduce its internal floor area and remove two of the piers that supported the roof, one of which had been built over a pit and had collapsed during the use of the house. After the house had been abandoned and filled naturally with wind-blown sand, further pits that extended all the way down to the floor level of the house were dug into it, showing that the site was still being used and remembered.

Outwith the wheelhouse, on the beach, excavation revealed a complicated area of walls and small buildings, constructed and reconstructed over time, probably storerooms. Beneath these were further, complex archaeological remains, many filled in with later rubbish deposits. They included animal burials, pits, and post-holes, reflecting the use of the area around the building for a mixture of everyday and ritual activities.

Part of this wheelhouse remains unexcavated within the coastal dune, demonstrating one of the major practical difficulties of coastal, or indeed any, archaeology. Where do you stop digging? The wheelhouse is only part of a wider settlement site in this area.

63. *A' Cheardach Ruadh* ('the red smithy'),   NF 7763 6157
   Baile Sear

Park in the parking area at the edge of the western coastal beach of *Baile Sear* (NF 7793 6131). Walk 500m north along the beach to the settlement mound.

This site, one of a series along this beach front (see above and below), has been eroding for decades, producing Iron Age finds. Excavations of individual burials and a possible cremation indicate that this was one of many Iron Age settlement sites where some of the dead were buried scattered around or under houses.

The great storm of January 2005 caused huge erosion at this point along the coast, revealing the remains of a building. Small-scale excavations, carried out with the help of local school children in 2009, revealed deep archaeological deposits next to a piece of walling that was probably a pier of a wheelhouse.

64. *Bagh nam Feadag, Griomasaigh* wheelhouse   NF 8665 5736

Park beside the road just west of Loch Hornaraigh and walk around the northern end of the loch. The site is inside a field to the east of the loch.

There is a large wheelhouse overlooking *Bagh nam Feadag* on the northern coast of *Griomasaigh*. It is one of several sites in the area, including an island dun at the southern end of the loch.

The wheelhouse was excavated during the 1990s by an amateur archaeologist. It was one of a sequence of buildings that had been built on the same site, creating a settlement mound. If you look around the western edge of the wheelhouse, you can see the remains of an earlier curving wall underneath it, and there is a rectangular building built onto the southern side, with smaller huts constructed on the northern edge of the site. The buildings were adapted and modified over time, and the finds date the occupation from the Iron Age to the Middle Ages or later.

This site is a good example of a settlement that was sometimes permanently occupied, and sometimes seasonal.

65. *Ceann nan Clachan* burnt mound

Park beside the road by *Loch nan Clachan*, and the site is immediately to the east of the road, on the shore.

On the edge of the *Traigh Bhalaigh* (Vallay Strand), which would have been a low-lying fertile plain in the Early Iron Age, is the remains of a burnt mound that was excavated in the 1990s. The mound formed around a small, oval building, which had no fireplace. It was later replaced by a building with two circular rooms, the outer of which had a fireplace. Unusually, there was no pit or tank for holding water on the site, but it is close to a stream running out of *Loch nan Clachan*.

The lack of a fireplace in the earlier building, and the huge amounts of stone which built up around it and the building which replaced it, make it clear that these were not ordinary houses. The excavators suggested that it may have been a steam bath, or sauna, perhaps with additional functions, for example smoking food.

66. *Eilean Olabhat*   NF 7494 7529

Park at the layby on the A865, walk down the Griminish road for 85m and turn west onto an old track across fields to the loch side, for 600m.

On a promontory to the east of the Neolithic island settlement in *Loch Olabhat* is another former island settlement. The edge of the original island is surrounded by the remains of a wall, which has an entrance on the shoreline side.

Excavation produced evidence that the settlement had been used throughout the Iron Age, probably until around the beginning of the Viking Age. An early building was constructed around 0 BC/AD, and was replaced in the 2nd century by another, oval building, which continued in use, being adapted and repaired, for centuries afterwards. This second building was built with upright slabs at the bottom of the wall and coursed horizontal stonework above this, typical of later Iron Age building, and had a paved floor. The second building was used for fine metalworking, though it didn't have a formal hearth; moulds for pins and brooches were found. The lack of a hearth indicates that this was not an ordinary house, but the amounts of metalworking debris don't seem to be enough to suggest that it was used for full-time jewellery production.

Evidence of fine metalworking, mostly using bronze for jewellery, but also occasionally silver and gold, is often found on important sites of the Late Iron Age. There is never much debris, so each object was probably made individually and to order, perhaps so that they could be given as gifts. Giving this kind of gift may have been a way of making friendships and alliances between people and groups, so controlling this kind of metalworking would have been a way of gaining power. Metalworking might also have been seen as a bit magical, given the skill needed to produce delicate and beautiful objects. Perhaps there was an important, high-status Iron Age settlement in the area that we have not found yet, or perhaps this island on the loch, near the ancient Neolithic site, was a special place.

67. *Coileagan an Udail* (the Udal, Veilish)   NF 8249 7830

Park at the picnic area on the *Grenitobht* (Grenitote) road and follow the track north onto the machair headland for 3km, bearing west after 2.5km. Visit Outer Hebrides produces a walking leaflet for this route.

The ruinous remains of a large wheelhouse are visible at this site – all that remains of the longest-running and largest-scale excavations ever carried out in the Outer Hebrides. Excavation started in the early 1960s, finished in the late 1990s, and has yet to be completely published.

The site, which was scattered over three or four large settlement mounds on this strategically located peninsula extending north into the Sound of Harris, was occupied from the Neolithic Period through to the 17th century at least. The visible remains are Iron Age, but this wheelhouse was not the total of the Iron Age settlement here; the remains of other wheelhouses, and a village of smaller houses which succeeded them, have been fully excavated.

This was a pivotal site for a long-running discussion amongst archaeologists about the relationship between incoming Scandinavians and local people at the beginning of the Viking Age, because it produced evidence for the destruction of the Late Iron Age village. The excavator argued that the village had been burnt by incoming Vikings, and that this demonstrated that the Vikings took over the islands violently. However, this pattern of destruction hasn't been seen at other sites in Scotland, and it may be that the fate of the Iron Age village here was unusual.

68. *Dun an Sticer* NF 8972 7768

Situated on the road north to the Sound of Harris ferry. Stop in the parking area beside the road and walk along the road to the interpretation board. Take care crossing the causeway to the site.

Dun an Sticer is a broch, which was reoccupied and adapted in the Middle Ages as a small castle, on an island in a tidal loch at the northern end of North Uist. Considering the known sea-level rise, this may have been on a freshwater loch in the Iron Age, but the mediaeval reoccupation probably took place when the loch was open to the sea. The name means 'the fort of the skulker' and relates to its mediaeval reuse by the disreputable Hugh Macdonald of Sleat.

The broch has been partially dismantled and altered to provide the building stone needed for the later buildings, but it seems to have been around 12m in diameter originally, with double walls nearly 4m thick. It was entered from the south-west originally, but the door has been substantially altered. There is also a bad bulge in the western wall which has probably been caused by compression of the underlying island surface, resulting in subsidence of the wall. The eastern part of the wall tapers inwards, typical of broch towers. This is deliberate, as the walls became thinner higher up the building to reduce their weight.

To the right of the entrance, an original Iron Age room has partially collapsed, and it is easy to see the corbelled construction of the stone roof. This is the type of construction that was also used around the circumference of wheelhouses, where each course of stone

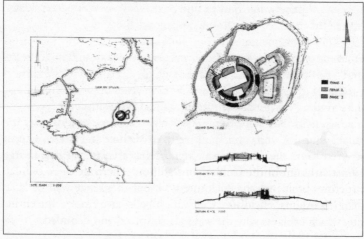

Fig. 35. *Dun an Sticer, Uibhist a' Tuath* (North Uist) (© Crown copyright: HES)

was set a little further inwards until the gap at the top could be bridged by one flat slab. You can also see the remains of the gallery between the walls at various points around the circle of the broch.

69. *Aird Ma-Ruidhe, Bearnaraigh* (Bernera)   NF 9145 7998
    ferry terminal, burial cairn

While you're waiting for the ferry to Harris, walk to the area of grass to the south of the ferry terminal and follow the rough path 70m west to the monument.

This is a square burial cairn, discovered during work to build the causeway between North Uist and Bernera. It has not been excavated, but the turf was removed to expose the stones and to confirm it was a cairn. The route of the road was then altered to allow the cairn to be preserved.

The square shape, which is formed by a kerb of stones filled in with quartz and gneiss cobbles, suggests that this is a burial of the Late Iron Age, contemporary with the burial of *Cille Pheadair Ceit* (Kilpheder Kate).

70. *Cladh Maolruidhe, Bearnaraigh*   NF 91215 80680
   (Bernera)

From the community centre, follow the waymarked path about 650m south-east to the top of the hill.

A turf wall encloses an area of ground at the top of this hill, above the sound that divides Bernera and North Uist. Within the enclosure is a Neolithic standing stone and the remains of a small, sub-rectangular building, which was built right up against the stone. This is reputed to be the chapel of St Maolrubha, a Late Iron Age (Early Christian) saint of the Columban tradition. There are three cellular structures built into the enclosure wall, but these may well be later than the original enclosure. Cultivation beds have crossed the entire site, which explains why the walls are so spread and denuded.

Na Hearadh (Harris)

71. *Taobh Tuath* (Northton) broch,   NF 9700 9134
   Gob an Tobha (Toe Head)

Park at the end of the township road and walk 2.5km along the track out onto the headland, bearing west to follow the south-western coast. The site has an interpretation board, and there are other sites to visit along the way (Sites 1, 24, 46).

The location of this broch is marked by the roofless late mediaeval chapel which is built on top of it. The chapel is visible for most of the length of the coastal walk, emphasising the prominent place that its predecessor, the broch, also had in the landscape.

The circle of the broch wall can be seen under the western end of the chapel, stripped down to its foundation, when stone was taken to build the chapel. It has a diameter of 16.6m. Excavation on the site in 2011 showed that it had been constructed onto the bedrock of the headland, and archaeologists uncovered part of a small ground-floor-level room, constructed within the wall, which was 4m thick at the base.

Tarasaigh (Taransay)

Taransay is a particularly lovely island, and a wonderful place to look at archaeology. If you get a chance to go over there, here are a few of the Iron Age sites that you can visit.

72. *Teampull Che* and *Teampull Tharain* NB 030 991
  (St Keith's and St Taran's Chapels)

The boat normally lands on the Paibeil beach. Walk south-west along the shoreline for about 290m until you reach the end of the village, where you will see the remains of the burial grounds.

These two related chapels both have Early Christian dedications, but continued to be used for hundreds of years. The name of St Taran is also embedded in the Old Norse place name for the island, *Tarasaidh*, which means 'Taran's Island', indicating that the dedication to the saint pre-dates the arrival of Scandinavians in about AD 800.

The remains of St Taran's Chapel, on the eastern side of the small stream, have been largely destroyed by coastal erosion. However, the foundations of St Keith's Chapel can be seen, a small rectangle of turf-covered walls approximately 6m x 4m, orientated east to west, on the western side of the stream, near a small rock outcrop.

Local tradition has it that women were buried in the burial ground around St Taran's Chapel, and men in that around St Keith's, and if either gender were wrongly buried, the body would appear on the surface of the ground the following morning, rejected from its rest. It has been a very long time since these burial grounds were used, and they are both now eroding, but please leave any bones that you see where you find them, and do not remove them from the site.

A cross-marked stone, reputedly from the area of St Taran's Chapel, was removed from where it had been built into the stone tacksman's house in Paibeil in the early 20th century, and it can now be seen in the National Museum of Scotland in Edinburgh.

73. *Dun an Oir (Dun Clach)* NG 0358 9961

If you follow the line of the old township road about 350m north-east along the coast from the landing place, you will come to the remains of this fort.

On the northern end of the head dyke of the township of Paibeil, set on rising ground slightly back from the shore, is the remains of what was probably a broch. Some sources describe it as D-shaped, but this is clearly the result of a later rebuilding on the remains of an earlier, massive, circular structure. The sheer size of the underlying building suggests that it was probably a broch and, as this type of monumental circular architecture is characteristic of the Iron Age, we can confidently date it to this period.

The location of the monument is typical for a broch, with good visibility over the sound separating Taransay from mainland Harris, overlooking the adjacent rich arable land. This advantageous location was clearly also important to the people who reoccupied it at a later stage, probably for similar strategic reasons.

74. *Dun Loch an Duin* NB 0216 0127

A 2.2km walk uphill from the landing beach, following *Allt a' Mhuillin* and the eastern side of the hill *Beinn na h-Uidhe*, will bring you to *Loch an Duin*.

Dun Loch an Duin is a circular stone structure on an islet in this upland loch. It is accessed by a causeway leading from the southern bank of the loch, which can be crossed with care when the loch levels are low. Once again, its non-circular superficial appearance seems to be a result of secondary reuse of the building at a later stage, though early drawings of the structure from the 19th century show it as positively rectangular (Fig. 36), in which case we should be discussing this in the mediaeval gazetteer.

In the light of recent results from underwater surveys of islet sites, we need to consider the possibility that this structure, whether Iron Age or not, is a reuse of a much earlier prehistoric crannog. There is, however, no evidence to decide the question one way or the other.

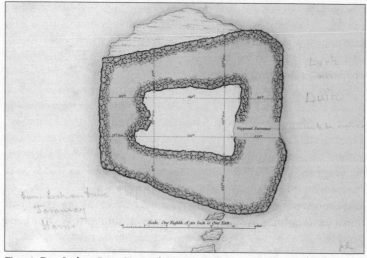

Fig. 36. *Dun Loch an Duin, Tarasaigh* (Taransay) (© Crown copyright: HES (Society of Antiquaries of Scotland Collection))

75. *Clach an Teampuill*   NB 0129 0077
    ('the stone of the chapel') standing stone

To reach this site, either walk 1.4km from *Dun Loch an Duin*, following first the south shore of the loch and then striking west over the shoulder of *Beinn na h-Uidhe* to descend to the sandy isthmus linking the two halves of the island, or follow the rocky south-western shore of the island around from the landing beach for 3km.

This small standing stone is visible from the *Clach Mhic Leoid* (MacLeod Stone) on the shore of Harris, and from the site of the *Sgarastadh* (Scarista) stone circle, suggesting that the Taransay stone may also have been Neolithic in its origins. It is also covered on one face with a sheet of natural white quartz, suggesting the same preoccupation with interesting stone formations that can be seen, for example, at some of the Calanais stones. However, it is included in this section because of the fine outline cross that is carved on one of the faces, and because of its name, which indicates that it was associated with a chapel.

The site has no surviving dedication to a saint, but a rectangular

122

platform, orientated east to west, immediately to the east of the stone, has the right shape, size and orientation to be the foundations of a small chapel. The arrangement of the site, with its association of a standing stone and possible chapel, is like that of *Cladh Maolruidhe* on Bernera, and they may both reflect a Late Iron Age process of Christening the landscape and its key features.

Hiort (St Kilda)

76. Souterrain, Hirte   NF 1001 9941

Walk 600m from the jetty through the village, past the graveyard and north up the slope to find the souterrain, about 30m north of the graveyard.

This souterrain was discovered in the mid 19th century. It consists of a long passage, roofed by flat stones, with a paved floor. It was investigated several times in the late 19th and early 20th centuries, and the finds from these digs included a Viking Age spearhead and brooches, net sinkers or loom weights, querns and stone lamps. Records suggest that there was a deep deposit of ash on the floor.

Further excavation took place later in the 20th century, and it became clear that the structure was associated with the remains of a large, circular or curved building above ground, which was part of more extensive settlement remains dating to the Iron Age. The presence of the Viking Age finds from the souterrain may show that it was also used for a later Scandinavian burial.

77. Christ Church, Hirte   NF 1000 9939

The circular graveyard in the Village Bay was the site of Christ Church, the main chapel for the island. It was one of three known chapels on Hirte and was used until the 17th or early 18th century. There are at least three small cross-marked stones built into structures in this area, including Cleit (storage house) 74, House 16, and the road. These stones are all dated to the 7th or 8th centuries, suggesting that at least one of the churches on the island dates to the Late Iron Age.

Leodhas (Lewis)

78. *Loch na Beirgh* (Berie) broch, Uig   NB 1035 3517

Park on the edge of the machair road and walk 260m south-west, crossing a large drain, to reach the site.

The remains of a large broch can be seen behind the beach at *Beirgh* on the *Bhaltos* (Valtos) Peninsula in Uig, on the western coast of Lewis. This building is dangerous, part-excavated, and flooded, and great care should be taken in visiting it.

The central open area of the broch is one of the largest known in Scotland, at around 10.5m in diameter, with an outer diameter of nearly 17m. Its construction date is not known, as the excavations which took place here during the 1980s and 1990s did not reach the base of the structure. However, it was clearly built on either an island or a peninsula in a freshwater loch, and as the adjacent sea level has risen, pushing the machair sand up ahead of it, the loch has gradually silted up and the water table has risen, flooding and burying the broch. The visible remains, like *Dun Mhulan* (Dun Vulan) (Site 59), are at first-floor level.

This broch formed the focus of local high-status settlement for a long time. There were at least three periods of rebuilding within the broch wall, the earliest dated to the 2nd century AD. The broch itself, therefore, might have been built around 0 BC/AD or a little later.

This earliest rebuild consisted of a roundhouse built with its wall resting against the broch wall. Following this, around the 3rd century AD, it was renovated and a cellular structure, with small round rooms opening off a central area, was constructed. This continued in use until the 4th century AD and was then replaced by a figure-of-eight building, with one large and one smaller room, again like that excavated at *Dun Mhulan* and dating to a similar period.

The site went out of use not later than the 9th century AD, around the time of the arrival of Scandinavian incomers bringing new patterns of settlement. This strengthens the pattern of the abandonment of brochs in favour of new, large Scandinavian-style halls built on nearby sites. Aerial photographs of the area around *Beirgh* have shown that there are the remains of at least three long, bow-sided buildings nearby (Site 96), probably the remains of a Viking Age and Norse settlement.

79. *Dun Loch Bharabhat* (Baravat), NB 0989 3532
Bearnaraigh Mor (Great Bernera)

Park at the campsite parking area, walk south, crossing the bridge on the road and then turning to walk 375m south across the machair to the southern end of the machair loch. Follow the small path around the southern end of the loch, turning south up a steep valley at the bottom of which is a watermill. At the top of the valley is an upland loch, and the dun is visible on an island in the loch.

Excavation here has shown that this small, broch-like building was constructed on an island that was at least partially artificial – a crannog. Access to the island was by the causeway that is still used. The structure had an intramural gallery with a staircase, a small room in the wall by the door, and a central hearth. There had also been buildings outside, covering the island, which underwater excavation showed to have been larger originally.

There has been a lot of debate about the dating of this site; the excavators were convinced that it dated to the 5th century BC or earlier, but this has been challenged by other archaeologists. The site continued in use intermittently until the 6th or 7th century AD.

80. *Stac Dhomhuill Chaim, Mangarstadh* NB 0022 3152
(Mangersta), Uig

Park where the peat road leaves the main *Mangarstadh* road, at NB 007 317, follow the peat road north to the edge of the grazings and then walk west following the edge of the grazings fence. When you reach the corner of the crofts, turn south along the coastline, taking care of the cliff edges, which can be very slippery. A total walk of around 900m to a point where you can look out over the site.

This site (Plate 8) is included in the Iron Age section, as it is typical of a class of promontory or sea-stack sites that have been traditionally dated to the Iron Age. However, recent survey on this and other sea-stack sites in Lewis shows that some were first occupied in the Neolithic Period and then reoccupied in the Iron Age, as seen at Biru-aslum in Vatersay (Site 51). The function of such sites is unclear – the long-standing assumption that they were defensive does not entirely stand up, as many are overlooked by higher areas of land. They may have been look-out points, as most prehistoric stack sites are on the western coasts, overlooking the sea lanes. They could also have had religious or ritual functions, as these would have been places on the edge – liminal places between land, sea and air – even in prehistory.

Stac Dhomhnuill Chaim is also known for its reoccupation in the 17th century. The visible remains of a rectangular house behind an enclosure wall on the top of the stack probably date to this period.

81. *Bostadh* (Bosta), *Bearnaraigh Mor* (Great Bernera)   NB 1373 4010

Park in the car park next to the cemetery. Follow the path for 70m around the north of the cemetery over the sandy machair to a gate next to an interpretation board.

The Iron Age settlement at *Bostadh* was excavated in the 1990s, following its exposure in a storm. The uppermost level of the settlement, which dated to the Viking Age, had been largely destroyed, but underlying this was a cluster of houses dating to the Late Iron Age – the 5th to 8th centuries AD. The site was only partially excavated, so earlier remains are still here.

The houses were figure-of-eight houses (see Fig. 28), each with one large room with a central hearth, and a smaller room leading off this, like the houses in the latest, pre-Viking Age occupation of *Dun Mhulan* (Dun Vulan) and *Beirgh* (Site 78). The architectural form is like the contemporary architecture in Orkney, which was part of the Pictish kingdom. However, whether the occupants here would have thought of themselves as Pictish is unclear.

A reconstructed house at the head of the beach can be visited and gives a very clear feeling of how spacious these buildings were.

82. *Dun Charlabhaigh* (Dun Carloway)   NB 1899 4122

Park in the parking area at the foot of the hill and walk 240m uphill following the track to the broch.

Dun Charlabhaigh (Plate 5) is one of the most intact brochs in Scotland, and it gives a wonderful chance to understand their construction. The building has collapsed and been cleared on the northern side, leaving a cut-away which shows the double, concentric walls, tied together with long stones, and the intramural staircase which would have provided access to the upper storeys. The low doorway is typical; suggested reasons include keeping the warmth in the building and forcing those entering the building to bow down low, so they were vulnerable to attack. The so-called guard cell, immediately beside the door and opening into the entrance passage, might have been a dog kennel.

Little excavation has been carried out here, but a small-scale dig in one of the side cells suggested that the building had been occupied throughout the Iron Age, and then possibly reused later. It is said to have been intact until the 16th or 17th century AD, when it was damaged in a clan conflict.

83. *Barabhas* (Barvas) Machair   NB 348 518

Park at the modern cemetery and walk south and west around the fence towards the sea through the eroding remains of the prehistoric landscapes.

As you walk around the machair to the south and west of the modern cemetery at *Barabhas*, you enter an area where a multi-period prehistoric landscape has been exposed by wind and animal erosion and is now progressively stabilising and being re-covered with grass. Small-scale excavations and systematic field walking and artefact collection have taken place here ever since the 1970s.

The Bronze Age occupation of this landscape is also discussed in Chapter 3, but many of the visible remains date to the Iron Age (Fig. 37). Along the northern edge of the erosion areas, nearest the modern cemetery, are the remains of field walls, and small buildings can still be traced even though the erosion area is beginning to grass over.

At NB 3513 5176 are the ruins of a small oval building, which has been partially excavated. This had a central hearth, so it must have been occupied at some point, but it was used and reused after the hearth went out of use. Just west of this is a cairn, covered in quartz beach pebbles. This was the burial place of a woman, buried in a stone-lined grave, or long cist. She was buried with a beautiful iron

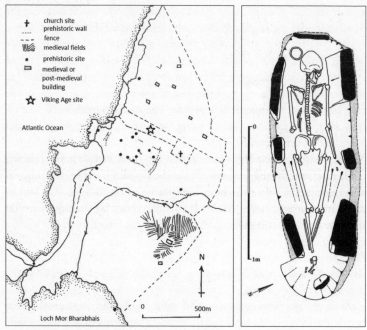

Fig. 37. *Left.* Plan of *Barabhas* (Barvas) Machair
Fig. 38. *Right. Barabhas* (Barvas) burial, with bracelet (© Alan Braby)

and bronze bracelet behind her head (Fig. 38), and radiocarbon dating showed that she had died around the 3rd or 4th century AD.

84. *Eilean nan Luchruban, Nis* (Ness)   NB 5078 6601

Park at the lighthouse and walk 1.4km west along the waymarked route, to overlook the site from the adjacent cliff-top.

Eilean nan Luchruban ('the island of the little people') is also discussed in Chapter 2, as it is one of the sea stacks that was first occupied in the Neolithic Period and then reoccupied in the Iron Age. There has been no excavation on this site since the 19th century, but surveys carried out in the early 2000s indicate that the hollows which are visible on the landward side of the island are probably part of the remains of a large Iron Age roundhouse, possibly even a broch.

5. *Innse Gall* and the Scandinavians
AD 800–1266

Migrating Scandinavians

Monks, writing their chronicles in English monasteries in the late 8th century, stated for the year AD 793 that 'ravages of heathen men miserably destroyed God's church on Lindisfarne, with plunder and slaughter'. This dramatic note, followed soon afterwards by records of similar incidents in Irish annals, gives the historical date that began the Viking Age, marking the start of Scandinavian influence in the British Isles. For the next 250 years, the British Isles and the North Atlantic were subject to piracy, raiding and colonisation by incomers speaking Scandinavian languages, with the Hebrides becoming part of the kingdom of Norway. During this period, the Outer Hebrides were referred to, in Irish sources, as *Innse Gall*, 'the islands of the foreigners'. It wasn't until AD 1266, following a battle at Largs in Scotland, that the Treaty of Perth transferred the Hebrides from Norway to Scotland, after 450 years of Scandinavian domination.

Archaeologists and historians assume that Scandinavian settlement in the Outer Hebrides started in the 9th century, or possibly a bit earlier. It has been suggested that the early recorded Viking raids in Ireland could have been carried out by ships whose crews had overwintered in the Hebrides, or Orkney or Shetland. So far, however, there is no definite archaeological evidence for Scandinavian settlement in the Outer Hebrides any earlier than the 10th century, so the question of exactly when Scandinavian raiders might have started to settle in the islands remains unanswered.

The Scandinavian Period of northern Scottish history is normally divided into two parts, the first being the Viking Age, characterised by raiding, pagan religion, and small local political units, from the beginning of the 9th to the mid 11th century. It was succeeded by the Norse Period, as Scandinavia and the North Atlantic islands converted to Christianity, joined the Catholic Church, and cohered into feudal states. Inevitably, this is an oversimplification of a complex process that varied from place to place. The Outer Hebrides were a long way from centres of power, and we still know little about the local impact of large-scale political decisions, like conversion, on the islanders.

Scandinavian influence, colonisation and trade links extended throughout northern Europe during the Viking Age, from Greenland in the north, to the Mediterranean in the south, the east coast of North America to the west, and the Russian rivers and the Black Sea in the east. Within this wider maritime network, the Outer Hebrides were strategically placed on the direct route from Norway to the Irish Sea, controlling the west coast sea routes to Dublin, north-west England and Wales. There are hints in Irish and Scandinavian sources that the islands were semi-independent, with their own rulers, presumably because of their distance from centres such as Dublin, the Isle of Man, and Orkney, although at various points in time each of these political centres claimed the Outer Hebrides.

Climate and the environment

During the Viking Age, the climate was relatively warm and settled, a climatic optimum, meaning that travel was relatively straightforward in the North Atlantic. Sea ice in the Arctic broke up at predictable times, and there were fewer storms. This would have made settlement easier, as livestock could be out-wintered in Scotland, and harvesting enough hay to feed in-wintered stock in Iceland and Greenland would have been relatively easy. It is important to remember that all these travellers needed to find ways to survive as they moved into new areas, so even pirates, raiders and traders were also, of necessity, farmers, and the availability of farmland, timber, wild animals and fish was a very important incentive to travelling and settling.

However, from the 11th century onwards, the climate started to deteriorate, sliding into the Little Ice Age, a period of colder, stormier, less predictable weather that continued until the 19th century. This shift in climate changed the viability of agriculture in the North Atlantic, and therefore the conditions of the Scandinavian settlements in the Outer Hebrides and other Atlantic islands. The settlements in Greenland increasingly shifted to keeping goats rather than sheep or cattle, and became more dependent on hunting seals. In Iceland, there were problems with soil erosion, and throughout the North Atlantic, including the Hebrides, gales and storms caused difficulties in travelling, eroded land, and damaged crops.

Architecture, settlements and farming

It was during the Viking Age, in the years up to AD 1066, that rectangular architecture for houses was introduced into the islands. The brochs, which had been the focus of power throughout the Iron Age, were abandoned, though other, lower-status Iron Age settlements continued to be used, for example at *Bostadh* (Bosta) on *Bearnaraigh Mor* (Great Bernera) (Sites 81 & 97). The architectural change makes it easy to distinguish between prehistoric settlements, which had curved or round buildings, and historic settlements later than the 9th century, which had rectangular buildings. High-status, important Viking Age buildings, such as those excavated at *Bornais* (Bornish) in *Uibhist a' Deas* (South Uist), mimicked the architecture of important buildings in Scandinavia, with slightly curved long walls, curved ridge lines, long central hearths and aisles (Fig. 39). Evidence from Icelandic sagas, written down in the 13th century but referring back to the

Fig. 39. Reconstruction of *Bornais* (Bornish) Viking Age hall (David Simon, © Comhairle nan Eilean Siar)

Viking Age, indicates that these large buildings were used as halls for feasting and gathering, and had pagan religious functions as well as being the homes of important people.

The use of Scandinavian architecture was important in maintaining cultural links and identities between important families in the Outer Hebrides and the distant Norwegian political power. Smaller Viking Age and Norse farms, such as those excavated at *Cille Pheadair* (Kilpheder) in South Uist and *Barabhas* (Barvas) in *Leodhas* (Lewis), were simpler and more functional structures – small, rectangular buildings, generally with a central hearth.

Excavated evidence from Viking Age farms in northern Scotland suggests that new breeds of sheep were introduced in the 10th or early 11th century, which were significantly larger than the earlier Soay-type that had been kept throughout prehistory. The bones of these sheep are very similar to those of modern Shetland sheep, and they are part of a genetically related group of traditional sheep breeds including the Icelandic, Faeroese and Norwegian *vilsau* sheep, which are found in the former Scandinavian colonies.

Boats and deep-sea fishing

The mobility and expansion which defined the Viking Age were facilitated by sophisticated shipping technology; good examples of ships preserved from this period include the Gokstad ship from Norway, a 9th-century, ocean-going ship, and *Roskilde 2*, an 11th-century warship built within the Irish Sea area, but found in Denmark. Ninth-century ships, at the beginning of the Viking Age, were already specialised, with designs for ocean travel, for trade and moving goods, and for transporting soldiers rapidly for war, and this specialisation in design and form increased throughout the period, as the biggest ships also got larger.

At the beginning of the Viking Age, ships could be beached on any shingle beach and dragged up onto the shore. By the end of the Norse Period, nearly 500 years later, trading ships required specialist wharfs and harbours with jetties, as they could no longer be beached. As a result, trading came increasingly to be focused in larger settlements and towns with deep-water harbours. In the Outer Hebrides, by the end of the Norse Period, there was increasing settlement around

PLATE 1. (*Left*) *Gearrannan* (Garenin) axe

PLATE 2. (*Below*) *Calanais* (Callanish) Stone Circle, *Leodhas* (Lewis) (© Historic Environment Scotland)

PLATE 3. (*Above*) *Clach Steineagaidh, Borgh* (Borve), *Na Hearadh* (Harris)

PLATE 4. (*Right*) Hair ring from *Cladh Hallan*

PLATE 5. (*Below*) *Dun Charlabhaigh* (Dun Carloway), *Leodhas* (Lewis)

PLATE 6. (*Above*) *Stac a' Chaisteal, Gearrannan* (Garenin), *Na Hearadh* (Harris)

PLATE 7. (*Left*) Reconstructed Iron Age house at *Bostadh* (Bosta), *Bearnaraigh Mor* (Great Bernera)

PLATE 8. *Stac Dhomhnuill Chaim, Mangarstadh* (Mangersta), *Leodhas* (Lewis)

PLATE 9. Churches at *Tobha Mor* (Howmore), *Uibhist a' Deas* (South Uist)
(© Historic Environment Scotland)

PLATE 10. (*Above*) Prehistoric and Viking Age cemetery at *Cnip* (Kneep), *Leodhas* (Lewis)

PLATE 11. (*Left*) Joan Blaeu's map of the Outer Hebrides (detail) (Trustees of the National Library of Scotland)

PLATE 12. Cleared landscapes in Uig, *Leodhas* (Lewis)

PLATE 13. Lady Matheson's Seminary, *Steornabhagh* (Stornoway), *Leodhas* (Lewis) (© Crown copyright: HES)

PLATE 14. Eilean Glas lighthouse, *Scalpaigh* (Scalpay)

PLATE 15. Lews Castle, *Steornabhagh* (Stornoway)
(© Crown copyright: HES)

PLATE 16. (*Above*) *Gearrannan* (Garenin) Mill,
Leodhas (Lewis)

PLATE 17. (*Right*) Our Lady of the Isles,
Ruabhal (Rueval), *Uibhist a' Deas* (South Uist)
(© Crown copyright: HES)

An t-Urramach Maighistir Ailean 'us am Pobull, an deidh n' aifrionn, an Eriskay. (Copyright.)

10·3·06. Population is 540, all catholics except one man. Ł.C.M.

PLATE 18. St Michael's of the Sea, *Eirisgeigh* (Eriskay)
(© Historic Environment Scotland)

PLATE 19. St Kilda Gun, *Hiort* (St Kilda) (© Crown copyright: HES)

the natural deep-water harbours on the eastern coastline, in places like *Steornabhagh* (Stornoway).

The maritime culture of the incoming Scandinavians was also reflected in their diet. The Iron Age occupants of the Hebrides ate little sea fish; this was probably a cultural preference. However, the incomers ate large amounts of sea fish, and actively fished in deep waters offshore. Initially, this difference in diet can be seen in the different chemical makeup of the skeletons of locals and incomers, but, over a relatively short period of time, everyone came to eat fish. Metal fishhooks and huge volumes of discarded fish bones are also found on Viking Age and Norse settlement sites. In the Hebrides, this was the period in which eating herring became very important, and preserved herring and white fish were traded in increasing amounts from northern Scotland, to supply the demands of the European church for fish to eat on fasting days.

Language and relationships

Although the initial relationship between locals and incomers is still a matter of active debate, recent archaeological and linguistic research suggests that throughout this period the population was ruled by an upper class who thought of themselves as Scandinavian. Clearly, however, the two populations mixed and intermarried from early on, as we have records which refer to individuals who are named with a mixture of Gaelic and Old Norse personal and nicknames, for example Grimr Kamban, who settled in the Faeroes.

Many place names in the islands date from this period, and lots of township names are derived from Old Norse, including elements such as -bost, from Old Norse *bolstaðir*, meaning 'farm'. Words from Gaelic, for example *airidh* ('milking place', or 'shieling'), were borrowed into Old Norse, becoming *aergi*, and appear in place names in other areas of the North Atlantic such as the Faeroes, while Old Norse *garðr*, meaning 'garden' or 'yard', becomes *garadh* and *gearraidh* in Gaelic, words describing cultivated enclosures of land.

The mixture of the languages indicates that the population was largely bilingual. It also tells us that the Scandinavian incomers probably came largely from Norway, as the forms of the names and loan words are of the western Old Norse dialect. The Old Norse language was dominant, particularly in the naming of settlements, as might be expected if it were the language of the ruling class and therefore of law and status.

Religion

As discussed previously (Chapter 4), the local population were largely Christian by this time, with churches, chapels and monastic sites spread throughout the islands. As the incomers arrived and renamed the landscape they were encountering, their place names reflect the landscape that they found. Christian or monastic sites often have place names including the Old Norse element *papar*, meaning 'priests', as discussed in the previous chapter, or preserve pre-Scandinavian saints' names, for example *Tarasaigh* (Taransay) in Harris. This suggests that Christian practice probably continued throughout the Viking Age.

The incoming Scandinavians practised a polytheistic religion with many gods. This was expressed in a variety of ways: large, high-status halls were places of ritual feasting and ceremonies, as shown at Hofstaðir in Iceland and Tjølling near Kaupang in Norway. Various burial practices were used, including both inhumation and cremation, with sacrifices of animals and people, and the burial of grave goods such as weapons, jewellery and tools, representing the status and activities of the person being buried or their family. Burials were often marked by cairns or stone settings of various shapes with round, triangular, or boat-shaped being common forms.

Farm burial grounds are found next to Viking Age farms in Norway, and this may have been the pattern in the Outer Hebrides as well. A small, Viking Age cemetery at *Cnip* (Kneep) in Uig, Lewis, is located immediately next to the visible remains of a Bronze Age cemetery (Site 47). The large, round mound of the main burial cairn, visible on a headland above an area of rich farmland by the shore, surely determined the location of the Viking Age cemetery. Norwegian farm cemeteries are often focused around a large Bronze or Iron Age burial mound, and this site would have looked very familiar to incoming settlers. It would also have provided a visible link to the history of their new homeland.

In a religion with many gods, the adoption of a further god was easy, and the Scandinavians soon started to practice Christianity or variants of it. In *Landnamabok*, the record of the settlement of Iceland, the author describes Helgi the Lean, a Viking raised by Hebridean foster parents, who believed in Christ on land and Thor at sea, or when he was in trouble. In the Outer Hebrides, evidence of conversion and Christian practice is best shown by the carved stone cross dating to the 10th century (see Fig. 43) from *Cille Bharra* (Kilbar) on *Barraigh* (Barra) (Site 86), which has an interlace-decorated cross in a local style on one side and a runic inscription on the other. It seems to be an epitaph to a woman with a Scandinavian name, perhaps Thorgerðr, the daughter of a father also with a Scandinavian name.

When the Earldom of Orkney officially converted to Christianity and joined the Catholic Church in the 11th century, the Outer Hebrides were probably controlled by Orkney. This was when a parish system was first established and more churches were built. No church excavations have taken place in the islands, but new church building and re-dedication of churches can be seen by the number of churches which have dedications to Catholic saints and the apostles, such as Peter, John, Clement, and Olaf (a sainted Earl of Orkney); an example is *Cille Aulaidh* at *Griais* (Gress) (Site 99), on the eastern coast of Lewis, north of *Steornabhagh* (Stornoway). The present ruinous building is 16th century, but the dedication cannot be earlier than the date of the death of St Olaf in 1030.

Once the islands became part of the Catholic Church there was a change in their political and trade links. The Church, focused around the Mediterranean, formed an organisational superstructure across Europe, using Latin as a common language, moving people, goods and ideas from country to country. This southern influence is noticeable in the introduction of more plant-based ornament in decorated manuscripts, on wood and bone artefacts, and in carved details on buildings. At first, the archbishop for Scandinavia was based in northern Germany, at Hamburg and Bremen, but soon a new archiepiscopate was created at Trondheim in Norway, which covered the North Atlantic colonies, including the Hebrides. This continued to be the archiepiscopate for the whole North Atlantic area for some years after the Treaty of Perth in AD 1266, maintaining links between Norway and the Outer Hebrides even after the islands became part of Scotland.

It may well be in this context of shifting and divided religious and political loyalties that the Lewis Chessmen arrived in the islands. Although they probably post-date the islands' becoming part of Scotland in the 13th century, it is important to discuss them here, in the context of the Norse Period, because they are clearly Scandinavian in origin. Regardless of whether they were produced in Iceland, as suggested by some historians, or in Trondheim in Norway, their design and style, and the fact that they are made of walrus ivory and whale teeth, makes it clear that they were the products of a workshop in the Scandinavian North Atlantic area.

Physically, the chess pieces use a mixture of Scandinavian and Catholic ecclesiastical styles and iconography (Fig. 40). They are full of references to a Viking past, with some of the warders shown biting their shield edges like battle-crazy, berserk warriors, and some of the queens shown with drinking horns in their hands, reflecting women's role in hospitality. But there are also Catholic bishops, with Bible and crozier in their hands and mitres on their heads. A similar piece, part of a queen, was found beneath the floor of the cathedral in Trondheim during renovations in the 19th century; it has since disappeared, but a drawing survives, and this, together with the excavation of a mediaeval ivory-working workshop in the city, tends to tip the balance of probability towards their being produced in Trondheim, which was, after all, the seat of the islands' archbishop. The fact that the Lewis

Fig. 40. Lewis Chessmen

pieces are parts of five sets, of varying quality, makes it possible that they were brought as gifts to reinforce links between the islands and their archbishop, and went astray before reaching their destination.

There are local stories about the finding of the chessmen, and over the years these have probably changed and developed, influencing each other as they were retold and published, but the story most commonly told in the area of Uig where they were found is that, in the early 19th century, a local farmer from *Eadar Dha Fhaoil* (Ardroil) went out on a stormy night to find his missing cow. In the darkness and wind he finally located her, trapped with one leg in a hole by the shore of the Uig Sands. After pushing and shoving, he got her free, and then bent down with his lamp to the hole in the ground, only to see dozens of small faces staring back at him! The chessmen were sold on to a merchant in Stornoway, who further sold them to the Societies of Antiquaries in London and Edinburgh, resulting in the collection being divided between the British Museum and the National Museum of Scotland. In recent years, the British Museum has loaned a selection of pieces to Museum nan Eilean in Stornoway, where they can now be seen.

The end of an era

The Outer Hebrides, then, were part of Norway until 1266, when the Treaty of Perth was agreed between the Crowns of Scotland and Norway. The treaty followed on from the Battle of Largs in 1263, which had an indecisive outcome, but resulted in the death of the Norwegian king, Haakon IV, as he travelled home. The treaty reflects this ambiguity in its unusual conditions; the islands were transferred to Scotland, to be ruled by Scots law, but Hebrideans could stay or leave as they wished, taking their goods and people with them, without penalty. We cannot know how many people moved following this, but documentary records indicate that some branches of senior island families, such as the MacDonalds, did move to Norway, presumably taking with them people who were connected to them. Some settlement sites such as *Barabhas* in Lewis (Site 98) and *Cille Pheadair* in South Uist (Site 87) were abandoned around this time as part of a major landscape reorganisation in the islands, and the possible reasons for this will be discussed further in the next chapter.

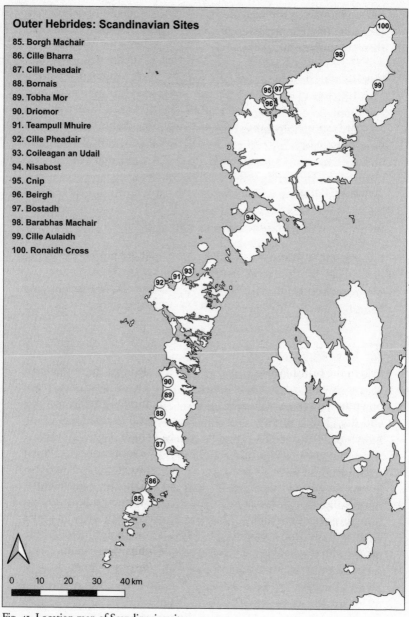

Outer Hebrides: Scandinavian Sites

85. Borgh Machair
86. Cille Bharra
87. Cille Pheadair
88. Bornais
89. Tobha Mor
90. Driomor
91. Teampull Mhuire
92. Cille Pheadair
93. Coileagan an Udail
94. Nisabost
95. Cnip
96. Beirgh
97. Bostadh
98. Barabhas Machair
99. Cille Aulaidh
100. Ronaidh Cross

0   10   20   30   40 km

Fig. 41. Location map of Scandinavian sites

GAZETTEER

Few Viking Age sites have been excavated in the Outer Hebrides and almost nothing remains to be seen of most of these sites. Some have been destroyed by coastal erosion, others by development. Visiting the sites gives an impression of their location and surrounding landscape and how different it was to that of the present day, but is an exercise best combined with visits to other, more visible, sites of earlier or later periods.

Barraigh (Barra)

85. *Borgh* (Borve) Machair standing stones   NF 6527 0144

Situated 100m west of the A888 circular road around Barra, on the machair at *Borgh*.

There are two Neolithic standing stones on *Borgh* Machair, one of which is still visible (Site 6). A strong local tradition links these with a Viking woman's grave found in Barra in the second half of the 19th century. Initially this was identified as a man's grave, as a sword-like object was found within it. However, re-examination of the finds, held in the British Museum in London, revealed that the object is, in fact, a weaving sword, used to beat the weft (cross-thread) into place on an upright loom. Weaving swords were normally made of wood and don't often survive in archaeological sites, but metal ones are sometimes found, and are probably a sign of high status.

The woman was buried wearing a pair of oval brooches, which would have held the shoulder straps of her woollen pinafore dress, worn over a wool or linen underdress (Fig. 42). These suggest that she was buried in a traditional Scandinavian woman's outfit, emphasising her Scandinavian links. She was also accompanied by an antler comb and two iron combs for combing flax or wool, which told the people who saw her buried that she was Scandinavian in culture, and a woman with wealth and responsibility for textile making.

Fig. 42. Finds from Viking Age woman's burial at *Borgh* (Borve), *Barraigh* (Barra)
(© British Museum)

86. *Cille Bharra* (Kilbar)   NF 0551 0738

Situated on the main road at the northern end of Barra. Park in the
cemetery car park.

A group of three mediaeval chapels, within an enclosing graveyard,
is known collectively as *Cille Bharra*, the church of St Barr. The name
of the saint is preserved in the Old Norse name of the island, *Barraigh*,
which suggests that the original church here was Late Iron Age.
However, the surviving buildings are mediaeval in date and are
discussed in Chapter 6 (Site 104).

This churchyard houses a copy of the *Cille Bharra* (Kilbar) Stone,
now in the National Museum in Edinburgh. This is a standing slab
of local stone, which has an interlace cross in a local, Late Iron Age
style of carving on one side, and an Old Norse runic inscription on
the other side (Fig. 43). The inscription says something like: 'this cross
was raised after (to the memory of) Thorgerðr, Steinar's daughter'.
This is important because it states that a person with a Scandinavian
name and father's name was a Christian, probably in the second half
of the 10th century. This shows that there was a process of cultural

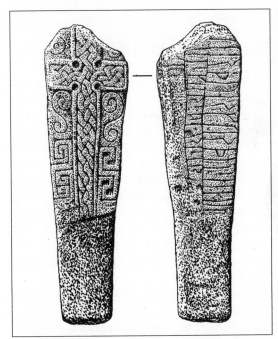

Fig. 43. The *Cille Bharra* (Kilbar) Cross (© Crown copyright: HES)

mixing going on during the Viking Age between the local Christian population and the incoming pagan Scandinavian population. By the 10th century in Barra, it was clearly acceptable to be an important person of Scandinavian descent as well as an open and practising Christian.

Until the 19th century there were four churches on the site, but one was demolished during the construction of the road past the graveyard. The largest surviving building, which is dedicated to St Barr, has two standing walls. There is a door in the north wall, and three windows, all of which are rounded arches on the outside, but have internal triangular points formed by two lintels leaning against each other. This building is thought to be 12th or 13th century in date which, if true, would mean that it was constructed during the Norse Period, perhaps when parishes were established across the Outer Hebrides. The dedications and dates of the other chapels are not known, but one of them has been reroofed and houses some interesting mediaeval grave slabs.

Uibhist a' Deas (South Uist)

87. *Cille Pheadair* (Kilpheder) Viking Age farm NF 7292 1979

Park where the *Cille Pheadair* machair road divides north and south and walk 660m south-west along the track over the machair to the edge of the shore. The site has been destroyed by erosion.

During the mid 1990s, excavation took place at *Cille Pheadair* on a coastal site which was threatened by erosion. The total excavation of the site was completed in 1996; the remainder of the site was destroyed during a terrible storm in 2005. This is, therefore, not a site where there is anything to see on the ground, but it is an enjoyable walk along the beach and allows you to understand something of the archaeological wealth of this area, as it is very close to the *Cille Pheadair* wheelhouse (*Bruthach a' Sidhean*, Site 56) and to where the Late Iron Age square cairn burial of *Cille Pheadair Ceit* (Kilpheder Kate) (Site 57) was found.

The farm started in the late 10th or early 11th century. Small stone and turf buildings were built and rebuilt on the same site, sometimes with additional outbuildings, until the farm was abandoned in the late 13th or early 14th century. Despite the small size of the buildings, there were signs of wealth in the finds from the farm, including fragments of gold from a hair ornament, and a couple of silver coins. Perhaps the household had income from other sources than farming, such as trading.

The end date of this farm is very similar to that of the similar small farm at *Barabhas* (Barvas) in Lewis (Site 98), and they both fit into a pattern of small farms built on existing farmland in the middle of the Viking Age, which were probably never very rich or very important settlements. The complex social, political and economic changes in the islands at the end of the Norse Period may all have contributed to the reorganisation of the landscape and the abandonment of these small independent holdings.

88. *Bornais* (Bornish), Mounds 2 & 3 NF 729 302

Follow the *Bornais* machair road until you get to the bend just north of *Loch Bornais*. Park and walk north following the fenceline along a rough track for about 500m, before turning west for 100m. Make sure that you walk along the boundaries between the strips of cultivation, and don't cross a crop.

The core of the Viking Age and Norse settlement at *Bornais* was on what the excavators of the site called Mound 2, north of the Iron Age site (Site 60). This settlement mound, built up from the remains of houses and rubbish accumulated over around 500 years, was first occupied in the Late Iron Age Period.

Geophysical surveys of the site showed a concentration of large building remains on Mound 2 and smaller buildings on adjacent Mound 3. Excavation started in 1994 and continued for more than six years; it is now the largest published excavation on a Viking Age and Norse settlement in the Outer Hebrides.

The earliest Scandinavian-style building on the site was built in the 900s AD, about 100 years after the beginning of the Viking Age. This was a large, wooden hall, traced by its floor layer and the pits that remained from the posts which had held up the roof. This kind of timber building was not a Hebridean tradition, but timber building was very common in Scandinavia. Mediaeval sagas talk about settlers taking structural posts with them when they moved, a symbolic way of linking their new home to the place that they came from, and this may have happened here. Interestingly, however, the house was semi-sunken into the soft machair soils – a type of building which is typical of Hebridean machair settlement, but not typically Scandinavian. Perhaps it was constructed by local workmen, despite the unfamiliar materials. The finds from the house, which include pots made both of soapstone and of pottery, and a small lead cross, also suggest a kind of blending of local and imported cultures and traditions.

The size of this building shows that this was an important settlement from its earliest establishment. The name of the township, *Bornais*, meaning 'fort headland', refers to the Iron Age broch of *Dun Mhulan* (Dun Vulan) (Site 59), which would have been visible from the settlement and would have been a very important sea mark for ships sailing down the western coast of Uist.

This building was replaced in the 11th century by a large, semi-sunken stone hall with curved long walls. The curvature of the long walls means that the ridge of the house would also have probably been curved (see Fig. 39). The hall measured 19.3m long, orientated east to west, and a maximum of 5.8m wide, giving an approximate floor area of around 100m². Although larger halls are known in Scandinavia, this is a substantial building, reinforcing the importance of the site in the local community. A long hearth stretched down the centre of the building, with raised areas to either side, where people could sit, work or sleep. The whole house was occupied by people; there was no housing for animals inside the building. The large building and many finds of butchered bone emphasise the importance of hospitality for building and maintaining relationships and alliances during the Viking Age.

When this building went out of use it was replaced by a rectangular stone building (Fig. 50), orientated north to south, at right angles across its eastern end. This house didn't have the characteristic Scandinavian bowed long walls, or a long central hearth, and it was smaller, though still substantial, at 12m x 5.4m. Finds from this building, including a bronze or brass buckle and a comb, show that it was occupied into the late 13th or early 14th centuries, to the end of the Norse Period or a little later.

These buildings weren't alone. Excavation on Mound 3 revealed contemporary, smaller buildings, which appeared to have been both workshops and domestic buildings at different times. Evidence was found for ironworking, needed for making and repairing tools and weapons. Antler waste from making combs was found in later layers, and glass beads, ivory, whalebone, bronze and lead objects were also amongst the finds. A grain-drying kiln was also excavated; in the damp weather of northern Scotland, grain must be dried before it can be ground into flour. Charred grain from the kiln showed that the occupants of the settlement were preparing oats and barley towards the end of the life of the settlement. Analysis of the bones from the rubbish layers show that fish had become a very important food source, much increased from the Iron Age, and that herring may have been exported. These activities and objects give a picture of the variety of things that went on around an important centre like *Bornais*, and the mixture of resources that were brought into such a settlement and redistributed from it.

89. *Tobha Mor* (*An t-Hogh Mor*, Howmore)   NF 7579 3643
churches

Park in the parking area at the west end of the *Tobha Mor* road, by
the modern parish church. Walk east along the road for 60m and turn
left (north) just past the thatched cottages along a path to the gate to
the mediaeval churches.

This site is a cluster of Norse and later churches and chapels, like
Cille Bharra (Kilbar) in Barra (see also Chapters 6 & 7) (Plate 9, Fig.
44). There are two large churches and two smaller chapels on the site,
along with a couple of post-Reformation (17th or 18th century) burial
aisles. In the 19th century another chapel was visible, but this no longer
survives above ground. The two churches are *Teampull Mor* (or *Teampull Mhoire*, St Mary's Church), which was the parish church, and
Teampull Chaluim Chille (*Caibeal Dhiarmaid*), both of which survive
only at their eastern ends. The two chapels are *Caibeal Dubhghaill*
and *Caibeal Clann 'ic Ailean* (Clanranald's Chapel).

The place name, which means 'the burial mound', suggests that
this site was the location of a prehistoric or Norse burial mound. Such
mounds, significant enough to form a place name, were often used
as gathering places in the Scandinavian areas, and this is therefore
likely to have been an important early political centre. A Late Iron

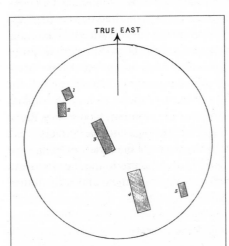

Fig. 44. *Tobha Mor* (Howmore)
churches, *Uibhist a' Deas*
(South Uist) (MacGibbon &
Ross, *Ecclesiastical Architecture*)

Age/Early Christian grave slab of local stone, carved with an equal-armed, outline cross, is amongst the grave markers at this site. It has probably been reused, but its presence here strongly suggests that this was also a pre-Viking Age Christian site.

Recent survey suggests that *Caibeil Clann 'ic Ailean* is the earliest surviving building here. It has at least three different phases of construction, two of which pre-date the 13th-century chancel arch, which is decorated with dog-tooth moulding. This chapel was built during the Norse Period and might have been constructed either as part of the establishment of parishes in the 11th century or as a private chapel. *Teampull Mor* is also probably 13th century or earlier, dated by the shape of the windows in the gable, and comparison of the four buildings suggests that *Teampull Mor* might be the latest of them. If correct, this would mean all the church buildings on the site were constructed under Norwegian rule, before the island became part of Scotland.

There is little doubt that *Tobha Mor* was an early and important focus of Christian belief. It may give a glimpse of the early organisation of the Catholic Church, from the 11th century onwards, and could help to inform us about the relationship between the Catholic Church and the earlier Christian establishments in Uist.

90. *Driomor* (Drimor) Viking house   NF 7564 4096

Follow the *Groigearraidh* (Grogarry) road to the shore and then walk north along the path behind the dunes for 1.3km, turning inland (east) for the last 200m. Note that this walk takes you into the active firing area of the rocket range, and you should not go into the area if the warning flags are flying.

Little remains to be seen at this site, where one of the few early Viking Age sites in the Outer Hebrides was excavated during the 1950s. Preparation for the rocket range involved a campaign of archaeological excavation in this area, including a souterrain and roundhouses 200m south of the Viking Age house. Finds from the house are held in the Kelvingrove Museum in Glasgow. The excavation was not recorded in detail, due to pressure of time, and it is only in retrospect that archaeologists have come to realise how important this building might have been.

The building was an irregular rectangle about 15m long, with curved sides and a rounded end, and had been built and rebuilt, probably using parts of the walls of an earlier Iron Age house. It had a long central hearth in the classic Viking Age architectural pattern, and this had also been rebuilt at least once. The finds from the building date to the 9th and 10th centuries, and although no scientific dating has been carried out, it seems entirely possible that this may have been the earliest dated Viking Age house that has yet been excavated in the Outer Hebrides.

Uibhist a' Tuath (North Uist)

91. *Teampull Mhuire* (Church of St Mary),   NF 7858 7638
    Bhalaigh (Vallay)

The tidal island of Vallay is accessible by walking across the sand from from *Cladach Bhalaigh* on North Uist. The walk is nearly 3km across the sand, and great care must be taken to allow enough time to avoid being caught by the tide. Check tide times locally and take advice on the safest route across the sand, aiming for the large house visible at the centre of the island on the other side. Cattle graze the island; do not visit with dogs, particularly during the calving season.

Walk past Vallay House and then turn east for 1.6km to reach the site of the remains of this early chapel.

The remains of the mediaeval church of *Teampull Mhuire* (Church of St Mary) are barely visible within the churchyard that surrounds it. The upstanding building in the churchyard is a much later burial aisle and may have been constructed on the remains of a second chapel, dedicated to St Ultan, which is also reputed to have been in this cemetery.

This was an early church site; two stone crosses stood here, one of which was moved in the 19th century to Lochgilphead, where it stands in the church of St Margaret. The other, now broken diagonally, has been reused to mark a 20th-century burial, and can still be seen here (Fig. 45). Both crosses date to the 10th century at the latest, indicating an active Christian community on Vallay during the Viking Age.

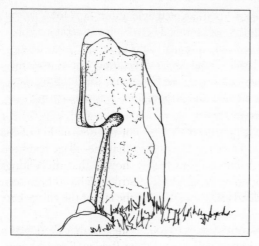

Fig. 45. *Bhalaigh* (Vallay) Cross, *Uibhist a' Tuath* (North Uist)

A rectangular slab of stone with two incised crosses on it is also in the churchyard. This slab was meant to be viewed horizontally, as the long leg of each cross points towards the centre of the slab. It may originally have been the top of an altar in one of the churches.

92. *Cille Pheadair* (Kilpheder) Cross   NF 7260 7439

Park beside the road and cross the fields to the west of the road to the cross, which is visible on a ridge overlooking the machair to the south. This cross was re-erected to the north of its original site in the 1830s by the tenant of the farm. It was originally in the cemetery of St Peter's Chapel, *Cille Pheadair*, which stood south of the outcrop where the cross now stands. The remains of the church and graveyard were destroyed by ploughing, but its dedication suggests that it was a medi-aeval, Catholic foundation. However, the cross is probably of the Viking Age or earlier, suggesting an early chapel on the site.

93. *Coileagan an Udail* (the Udal) settlement   NF 8249 7830

Park at the picnic area on the *Grenitobht* (Grenitote) road and follow the track north onto the machair headland for 3km, bearing west after 2.5km. Visit Outer Hebrides produces a walking leaflet for this route.

Although the visible remains at this site are Iron Age, it was also the largest excavated Viking Age and Norse settlement in the Outer Hebrides, dug between the 1960s and 1997. This was a key site for discussion amongst archaeologists about the relationship between incoming Scandinavians and local people at the beginning of the Viking Age because it produced evidence for the destruction of the Late Iron Age village. The excavator argued that the village had been burnt by incoming Vikings and that this showed that the Vikings took over the islands violently. However, destruction hasn't been seen at other sites in Scotland and it may be that the fate of the village here was unusual.

Interim excavation reports for the site suggest that there was a group of Viking Age houses here, perhaps like *Bornais* (Bornish), with a main hall and subsidiary buildings. However, the site hasn't been published, so detailed comparisons between the sites are not possible.

Na Hearadh (Harris)

94. Nisabost Viking burials   NG 0401 9658

Park in the layby above *Traigh Iar*, Horgabost, and walk 50m along a narrow path towards the beach, or park in the campsite parking area at Horgabost and walk over the headland.

Two Viking Age burials have been excavated next to the path that leads from the road down to *Traigh Iar* (the West Beach) on the Nisabost headland. This may be the site of a small Viking Age cemetery like that at *Cnip* (Kneep) (Site 95). The headland of Nisabost has archaeological remains from the Neolithic Period onwards and only small areas have been excavated, most often in response to the exposure of archaeological remains by wind or sea erosion.

The two burials here were excavated 15 years apart. The first was a person who lay on their back in a grave that had been cut into the clean sand and marked by a layer of stones on the surface of the ground. The body had been buried with something made of iron, possibly a spear head or knife, and with a small, typically Scandinavian whetstone for sharpening blades.

The second burial was laid within a stone-lined grave, called a cist, cut into the sand, and covered with cover slabs, in the local Late Iron Age tradition. A scatter of stones found over the grave suggests it might also have been marked on the surface of the ground in a similar way to the first. The lower half of the body had been destroyed by erosion and the upper half was in poor condition, and no artefacts were found in the grave, but the fact that the burial was on the same south-west to north-east alignment as the first one, and only 2.5m away from it, suggests that both were visible on the surface of the ground at the same time. They were probably broadly contemporary.

The name Nisabost, which used to apply to a township stretching across Harris from this headland, means 'the farm of the headland' in Old Norse. The adjacent name to the north, Horgabost, means 'the farm of the burial mound', probably referring to the Neolithic chambered cairn here (Site 27). These and the other Old Norse farm names along the western coast of Harris, for example *Sgarastadh* (Scarista) and *Borgh* (Borve), show where Viking Age and Norse farms were on the machair and indicate the importance of the area at the time.

Leodhas (Lewis)

95. *Cnip* (Kneep) cemetery and naust, Uig   NB 099 396

Park at the campsite parking area and walk 500m north along the beach to the headland. The cemetery is enclosed by a fence. The naust, or boathouse, is at the edge of the headland.

The Neolithic and Bronze Age burial ground on *Cnip* headland (Site 47) was also the location of the only known Viking Age cemetery in the Outer Hebrides (see Fig. 21 and Plate 10). The earlier cairns were almost certainly visible on the headland when the incoming Scandinavians decided to bury here, and the setting and earlier burial mounds would have been very similar to burial grounds in mainland Scandinavia at this time. In Scandinavia, a farm would have its own cemetery, normally close to the settlement. This would typically have a large Bronze Age or Early Iron Age mound or cairn at its centre, surrounded by smaller, later burials.

Four adult and two children's burials have been found here. The adults were in a clustered group to the west of the prehistoric burial mounds and the children were further away, one in the hollow to the north of the main exposure. One of the adult burials was of a woman buried in her best Scandinavian clothing, with oval brooches for her dress, a belt with bronze mounts, beads, sewing kit and a sickle to demonstrate her responsibility for the farm (see Fig. 42). The other adult burials were not accompanied by any objects, and it has been suggested that they could have been slaves. However, it is equally possible that their plain burials reflect religious and cultural changes in the community.

The farm which they came from is probably nearby but has yet to be discovered. However, next to the headland at the northern end of the beach, immediately below the cemetery, are the walls of a large naust. This would have accommodated a very big boat, indicating how important this area was in the Viking Age maritime economy.

96. *Beirgh* Viking Age farm   NB 105 351

At the far, southern end of the beach from *Cnip* (Kneep). Park beside the road and walk 200m south through the fields, staying to the east of the large drain.

As you walk across the fields towards the site of the Iron Age broch (Site 78), try to imagine that you are on the shores of a fresh-water loch as it was 1,000 years ago. At the right time of year, slight variations in the surface of the field and in the growth of the grass clearly mark the location of a group of large, bow-sided buildings (Fig. 46). This characteristic form is a marker of Viking Age architecture. This hall and farm buildings were built within sight of the broch remains on the fertile machair next to the loch, like *Bornais* (Bornish) (Site 88), which may have shown that it was an important Viking Age farm. The site has not been excavated.

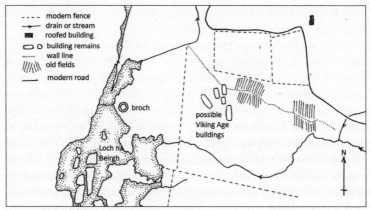

Fig. 46. Plan of *Beirgh* (Berie), Uig, *Leodhas* (Lewis), showing Viking Age halls and Iron Age broch

97. *Bostadh* (Bosta), *Bearnaraigh Mor*   NB 137 401
(Great Bernera)

Park at the cemetery and walk north 250m around the graveyard wall to the Iron Age site.

The Iron Age settlement here (Site 81) was followed by a small farm with a building in which Viking Age artefacts were used. However, by the time that excavation took place here, the building had been largely destroyed by erosion, and what remained were the rubbish layers that had built up next to it. These showed that, as at all the other Viking Age settlements in the Hebrides, there were cultural changes here in the Viking Age. Fish became a more important part of the diet of the occupants of the farm, and soapstone (steatite) pots were used as well as pottery.

Nothing of the Viking Age farm remains to be seen, but the site is worth visiting for its lovely setting. The place name, *Bostadh*, is a simple Old Norse name meaning 'farm', suggesting that it was important enough on the island that it didn't need any other description. At the southern end of the island is a settlement called *Circebost* (Kirkibost), which means 'church farm' in Old Norse. It gives a picture of a time when there were two big farms on the island – the Farm and the Church Farm.

98. *Barabhas* (Barvas) machair   NB 350 520

Park at the modern cemetery and walk south and west around the fence towards the sea through the eroding remains of the prehistoric landscapes.

At the northern edge of the *Barabhas* machair, where the ground levels out directly to the west of the modern cemetery, is a large sand extraction site. This area was where a small Viking Age to Norse Period farm, very similar to that at *Cille Pheadair* (Kilpheder) in South Uist (Site 92), was located. A small-scale evaluation of the site in the 1970s found that the farm began in the 11th century and continued until the late 13th or early 14th century. Only part of the site was excavated, and it has now been lost to sand quarrying. Survey and stray finds show that the Norse and mediaeval settlement was further back from the sea than the prehistoric settlement (Sites 50 & 83), which stretches down the slope to the south towards the *Abhainn Thanndaidh* (Handay River).

This settlement and *Cille Pheadair* in South Uist (Site 87) were probably secondary settlements, filling in gaps in the Viking Age landscape as the population grew in the good environmental conditions of the 10th and 11th centuries.

99. *Cille Aulaidh, Griais* (Gress)   NB 4901 4155

Park at the layby outside the cemetery wall and walk 40m across the graveyard.

The roofless church at *Griais* (Fig. 47) is probably post-mediaeval in date; you can see a date stone above the door with the eroded date of 1681 and initials IB/MK. Given its small size and very simple structure, however, this might be the date of a post-Reformation renovation or remodelling of an earlier mediaeval church.

The church stands on a raised area of the modern cemetery, where centuries of burials have built up the surface of the ground. It is dedicated to St Olaf, a king of Norway who died in the early 11th century when the Scandinavian world had just converted to Christianity. The Roman Catholic Church was establishing a parish system across the northern world, and it would have been politically important for the

Fig. 47. *Cille Aulaidh* Church, *Griais* (Gress), *Leodhas* (Lewis)

Scandinavian countries to have their own saints. Olaf, who died in AD 1030, was canonised locally the following year, and the great archiepiscopal cathedral at Trondheim (also called Nidaros) was built over his burial and dedicated to him. Nidaros was the archdiocese which had spiritual control over the Scandinavian North Atlantic, including northern Scotland and the Hebrides.

We don't know whether *Cille Aulaidh* was a parish church, but it was a pre-Reformation sanctuary, so it was a church of some importance. Its dedication demonstrates the relationship between the islands and Norway, and it suggests that there was probably an important settlement nearby. The township name, which means 'grass' in Old Norse, reflects the high quality of the grazing and arable land here.

100. *Ronaidh* (Rona) Cross

NB 5006 6164

The *Ronaidh* Cross is now held in the museum of *Comunn Eachdraidh Nis* (the Ness Historical Society) at Cross Old School.

This local museum is worth visiting for its fascinating collections of local memorabilia and artefacts and its comprehensive collections of genealogical materials relating to the community of Ness. The *Ronaidh* Cross was brought here in 1992 from *Teampull Mholuaidh*, to which it had been moved before 1936 from the island of *Ronaidh* (North Rona).

The dating of the cross is uncertain, but its style is clearly either Late Iron Age or Viking Age, more probably the latter (Fig. 48). It

Fig. 48. *Ronaidh* (Rona) Cross, *Leodhas* (Lewis) (© Crown copyright: HES)

was a standing cross slab, perhaps originally a grave marker though it could have been a sanctuary boundary marker. It shows the body of a naked man and has three holes bored through it, through which people are said to have looked at the sanctuary of the church.

The original context of the cross is the small ruinous settlement on *Ronaidh*. The numbers of cross slabs found here show that this settlement had an early Christian population; it has been suggested that it may have been a monastery. Two drystone chapels survive on the island, one a tiny oratory only 3.4m x 2.2m internally, and the other larger. The oratory is built of corbelled drystone, in the local Iron Age tradition, with the walls getting closer and closer together at the top until the gap can be spanned by large, flat lintels. This type of construction can also be found on Late Iron Age Christian sites in Ireland.

Comparing this stone with the cross from *Cille Bharra* (Kilbar) (see Fig. 43), and with the pagan burials from the islands, gives an idea of the variety of cultural influences which were active in the Hebrides during the Viking Age and Norse Period, and the diversity of religious practice in the community.

6. The Lordship of the Isles:
Mediaeval Sea Lords AD 1266–1560

Sources of information

The later Middle Ages, from the later 13th century to the mid 16th century, were a time of change in the Outer Hebrides. As there are documents from this period, we have a variety of sources of information with which to explore the islands' role in the wider kingdom of Scotland. However, documents and archaeology tell us different kinds of things, and we must consider why this might be and find ways to relate them to each other.

It is worth considering who requested, created and preserved documentary records. Literacy was not widespread, so documents were prestigious, rare things, written by specialists for powerful people. A lot of professional scribes were churchmen, and the language of most Church documents was Latin. The Church kept records for various reasons: they were landowners, who recorded land transfers, rentals and land management; they had pastoral and legal responsibilities, of which they kept records; and they preached and taught, creating Bibles, prayer books, liturgies and music. Church clerks might also work for landowners and aristocrats, creating land records, recording marriages, deaths and births, writing letters and legal documents and sometimes histories. Within the Gaelic-speaking areas of Scotland, including the Outer Hebrides, there were also hereditary professional families, including doctors, teachers and historians, who had high levels of literacy.

It is evident, therefore, that most records relate to the aristocracy and upper classes of society and particularly to their interests in land, law and power. Most people lived their lives unrecorded in any way. In addition, while the written record contains fascinating information, it is a record of the thoughts of individuals. These may or may not have been true; there could have been sleepy or slightly deaf scribes who misheard or miswrote, or recorded an error that was passed on to them by someone else and, of course, there were as many reasons then to falsify records deliberately as there are today.

Complementing the documents, the archaeological evidence focuses on the material stuff of life; the remains of houses, pots, fields, roads and human beings are the evidence of archaeology. This is a different kind of information, reflecting different aspects of peoples' lives. Archaeology rarely gives insight into the thoughts of an individual, but it does tell us what meals they ate, or perhaps their state of health in life or death.

Balancing these two sources of information becomes the concern of the historian and archaeologist of the Outer Hebrides from the 13th century onwards. However, given the relatively poor survival of documentary records for the islands, due to the vagaries of conflict, fire, damp and deliberate destruction, archaeology remains key to creating any coherent picture of life in the islands during the later Middle Ages.

Changing physical and social environments

The environmental changes that started towards the end of the Norse Period in the islands continued. As the climate shifted from the relatively stable and warm weather patterns of the Viking Age towards cooler, stormier, and less predictable weather, the more marginal parts of Scotland, amongst them the Outer Hebrides, were particularly affected. This change was relatively abrupt, and it persisted throughout the 1300s and 1400s. The wind, rainfall, and increased salt blown in from the sea had impacts on crops and increased the amount of coastal erosion. There were years of famine and storm damage recorded in monastic records. Scientists and archaeologists studying the changing coastline of the Outer Hebrides have been able to date evidence of sand blow at sites such as *Coileagan an Udail* (the Udal) in *Uibhist a' Tuath* (North Uist) to this period of environmental change and deteriorating local climate.

This was also a time of epidemics, the most famous being the Black Death, the great plague that spread through Western Europe in the 14th century, moving along the trade and shipping routes, and in some areas reducing the population by as much as 60%. Initially, the plague came to Scotland in 1349, spread by an invading English army on the southern border, and it recurred throughout the 14th and 15th centuries. The relatively low density of population in the Highlands means that it appears to have spread more slowly in the northern parts of the country, and there are almost no known surviving documentary records of what its impact might have been in the Hebrides, with the sole exception of a brief reference saying that the islands were laid waste. We don't, therefore, know much about what happened to the population of the islands, but elsewhere in Scotland the population fell sharply as a result of the disease, and we must assume that this happened in the Hebrides as well.

Epidemics also affected animals in the 14th century and, given the importance of cattle to the economic system of the Hebrides, this would have caused social and economic problems. The dairy-dependent diet typical of the Viking Age and Norse Period would have been undermined by the fall in the numbers of cattle, and people's ability to pay rents to their lords would have decreased. Both human and animal epidemics would have had their greatest impact on populations that were already weakened by poor nutrition caused by crop failures so are likely to have hit the poorer members of the community most heavily.

Lordship, clans and feudalism

The Middle Ages in northern Scotland were the age of the Clans. In the Hebrides, the great families of the MacDonalds, MacLeods, Morrisons, MacAulays and MacNeils were already warlords and landlords by the time of the Treaty of Perth. The most powerful local family, the MacDonalds, descendants of the powerful 12th-century lord Somhairle (Somerled or Sorley) MacGilleBrigte, is relatively well documented. Somerled's extensive territories were split between his sons at his death in AD 1164, so that much of the west coast of Scotland and all the Inner and Outer Hebrides were under the control of related MacSorley clans. The mediaeval Lordship of the Isles continued to be held by members of this family until the end of the 1400s.

In Uist, from the 12th century onwards, the MacRuari branch of the MacDonalds were lords, owing their allegiance first to the Norwegian Crown and later to the Crown of Scotland. The MacNeils were probably established in *Barraigh* (Barra) by the early 14th century at the latest, as were the MacLeods in Lewis and Harris, though these clans are much less well documented than their superiors and they may also have been in the islands at an earlier date.

As the archipelago became part of Scotland, the local powers had to deal with a new and different legal system, feudalism, and had to give allegiance to a different Crown. However, it is important to realise that the islands remained very independent in many ways. The power of the MacDonald Lordship of the Isles, recognised by the Scottish Crown, was based on shipping and boats. The theoretical basis of feudalism, which stated that the Crown owned all land, and all people of all ranks were vassals holding their land at the pleasure of the king, was based on land-based military power. It was difficult for the Scottish kingdom to exercise effective power in the Highlands generally, and in the Hebrides in particular, and the relationship between the Crown and the Lordship was never very comfortable. This is visible in the highly militarised landscape that developed on the western coast of the mainland and in the Inner and Outer Hebrides, where castles overlooking transport routes and harbours were constructed for defence, offence, and the demonstration of status, throughout the Middle Ages. Good examples of this are *Caisteal Chiosamuil* (Kisimul Castle) at *Bagh a' Chaisteil* (Castlebay) on Barra (Fig. 49) and *Caisteal Bhuirgh* (Borve Castle) on *Beinn na Fhaoghla* (Benbecula).

Fig. 49. *Caisteal Chiosamuil* (Kisimul Castle), *Barraigh* (Barra) (MacGibbon & Ross, *Castellated Architecture*)

In 1493, James IV of Scotland made the Lordship of the Isles forfeit, bringing an end to the relatively unified power on the west coast of the mainland and the islands. This move left a power vacuum in the islands and some areas became extremely unstable. While the southern part of the Outer Hebrides continued to be held by the MacDonalds and MacNeils, in Lewis the MacLeods gradually lost control, to be replaced later by the MacKenzies after nearly 100 years of civil war in the island. Without the intervening power of the Lordship of the Isles, the Crown was able to extend its influence and control to the Outer Hebrides, ending the semi-independence of the Middle Ages.

The mediaeval landscape

The political and legal changes associated with the transfer of the Hebrides from Norway to Scotland, and the environmental and population shifts, probably explain the mediaeval changes in the settlement pattern of the islands. The architecture of houses changed, as it had at the beginning of the Viking Age, and the location of settlements started to move away from the prehistoric foci on the machair.

Excavations at *Bornais* (Bornish) and *Cille Pheadair* (Kilpheder) in *Uibhist a' Deas* (South Uist), *Coileagan an Udail* (the Udal) in *Uibhist a' Tuath* (North Uist), and *Barabhas* (Barvas) in *Leodhas* (Lewis) all showed either temporary or permanent settlement abandonment in the 14th century. Some of this may relate to the movement of people to Norway at the time of the Treaty of Perth, as has been argued for *Barabhas*, but the restructuring of the landscape seems to have been more comprehensive than can be accounted for by a small level of emigration. At *Barabhas*, the south-facing machair slope, which had been the focus of settlement since the Late Bronze Age, was abandoned at the end of the 13th or beginning of the 14th century in favour of settlement on higher land to the north and south of the area. At *Bornais*, and more widely in South Uist, there was a clear movement in the 14th century away from the machair to the higher land on the edge of the moor to the east. In both cases, though, the boundaries between townships remained stable, following natural topographical features. One possible explanation for the shift could be that when or if the population dropped due to plague, earlier settlements and houses were abandoned due to fear of infection. If an epidemic coincided with coastal erosion and sand blow over the machair, the physical and psychological impacts on the population must have been severe.

Shifting settlement patterns could also reflect the change in the way that land was held, and a new relationship between farmers and the aristocracy. The introduction of feudal law would have created a landlord and tenant relationship, albeit one probably modified by a perception of kinship and family links between the two. The free-holding farmers who existed under Norse Udal law would have legally disappeared, and this change opened the way for landholders to plan and reorganise settlements as they wished, a change that would have very long-term effects in the Outer Hebrides.

Change also affected the architecture of individual buildings. *Bornais* is a good example of this, as the characteristically Norwegian architecture that had been used for the main hall at the site was replaced in the 13th or early 14th century by a rectangular stone house, possibly of more than one storey (Fig. 50). Interestingly, the types of pottery and food debris found associated with the new house did not change, including the use of the Norse baking plates for making hard bread, which suggests that even if the external look of the house had changed, the people living in it had not.

Another way in which the local aristocracy emphasised their new Scottish identity was to reoccupy Iron Age fortifications. *Dun Mhulan* (Dun Vulan) in South Uist (Site 106), *Dun an Sticer* in North Uist (see Fig. 35, Site 68), *Dun Loch an Duna* in Lewis, and many others, have mediaeval rectangular buildings constructed within the circuit of the Iron Age broch. The remains of the brochs were not removed but left clearly visible, seemingly providing a signal of continuity with prehistory, and local, non-Norse identity.

We have, unfortunately, little evidence for the houses in which the ordinary people of the islands were living. Excavations at *Druim nan Dearcag* and *Loch Olabhat* (Fig. 51) in North Uist of late mediaeval or post-mediaeval houses revealed very small, turf and stone structures, internally only 10 or 15m² in floor area, with earth floors and hearths. Pottery was used to date these structures to the Middle Ages, but their very small size and relatively marginal locations make it uncertain whether they were occupied year-round or seasonally. They are on

Fig. 50. *Right. Bornais* (Bornish) mediaeval house

Fig. 51. *Below. Loch Olabhat* late mediaeval houses

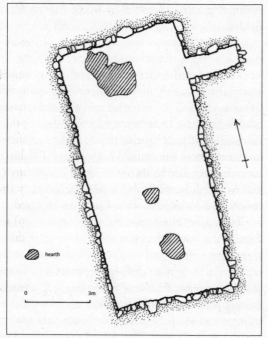

hearth

0   3m

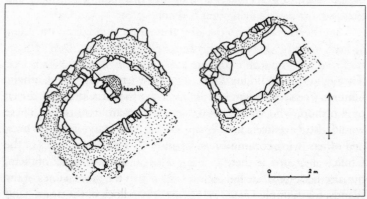

hearth

0   2m

peaty land, and there is no surviving animal bone on the sites, which makes it very difficult to determine what the occupants were doing there and how they were surviving. The excavator believes the sites to have been small farms, but they could also have been shielings for summer grazing of cattle or sheep, or huts for shepherds or cattle herders.

South Uist is the best understood of the islands in the Middle Ages as a result of archaeological work by the SEARCH Project. It has a long, continuous machair band along the west coast, with freshwater and brackish machair lochs forming a near-continuous line orientated north to south along the flat machair plain. Many of the islands on these lochs were occupied during the Middle Ages. The ruins of churches, chapels, castles and houses are still visible, and there are areas where the canals and waterways linking some of the lochs to each other and to the coast are visible. Many of these sites can be visited, as landscape mobility and 17th-century and later drainage has meant that lochs have silted up or disappeared. The religious centre at *Tobha Mor* (Howmore) (see Fig. 44, Site 89) is a good example of a site where boat access was possible in the Middle Ages. A local tradition states that it was possible to sail a boat from the southern end of the island to the north without leaving this inland waterway and, although this is probably an exaggeration, it was certainly possible to travel from one loch to another, and from some lochs to the western or eastern coast of the island, by boat. This reinforces the importance of shipping and water routes, both inland and at sea, in the millennia before the creation of a road network in northern Scotland.

Religion and ritual

Throughout the Middle Ages the islands were part of the Catholic Church. Each settlement was part of a parish with a priest, overseen by a bishop, who was, in turn, overseen by an archbishop. There would also have been monks and nuns, some living itinerant lives, and others living communally. We know that these structures of the Church all existed, as there are fragmentary historical records of them, but also because references to them survive in the place names of the islands, for example *Cnoc an t-Sagairt* ('the hillock of the priest') and *Baile nan Cailleach* (Nunton) in Benbecula.

The Church provided social welfare, such as medical services, hospitality for travellers, and education; for the aristocracy, many of whom were illiterate, they provided scribes and record keepers. The Church was also a large landowner and took a tax from every household for the support of the local priest and the wider church. Land was often given to the Church in order that perpetual prayers or masses should be said for the donor, and therefore church assets accumulated over time. It was also a powerful political institution, linking the islands and Scotland to other European countries, and church representatives travelled widely, forming a network via which news, money and political influence were transmitted.

The archaeological remains of the mediaeval church in the Outer Hebrides are fragmentary, due to neglect following the Reformation in the 16th century. There were parish churches in each parish, and other chapels as well, some of which had much earlier, pre-Viking Age origins. Most parish churches would have been dedicated to the saints of the Catholic Church, the Apostles, or the Virgin Mary. *Colm Cille* (St Columba) and Saint Brid (Bridget) were earlier saints, but were brought into the Catholic Church, and such dedications are also very frequent in the islands, for example *Cille Bhridge* at Sgarastadh (Scarista) in *Na Hearadh* (Harris) (Site 115).

Ruined mediaeval chapels can still be seen in some of the coastal graveyards of the islands. These graveyards are often some distance from modern settlements, on the coast, where churches or chapels were built when settlement was coastal in the Viking Age and earlier. Where erosion damages historic coastal graveyards, or where there is still active burial, there is often evidence of prehistoric settlement underneath the cemetery, for example at the mediaeval chapel on Manish Strand on *Ensaigh* (Ensay), in the Sound of Harris, and at *Sheabie* in *Bearnaraigh* (Bernera).

Changing times

The end of the Lordship of the Isles in 1495 marks the end of the Middle Ages in the islands. From this time forward, with the fragmentation of this formidable west-coast power block, and as transport, politics and technology changed, the islands became progressively more a part of the larger polity of Scotland, more focused towards the mainland. The change happened gradually and was not smooth; it progressed at different rates in different parts of the islands, but it was irreversible, and we will consider it in the next chapter.

GAZETTEER

We know unfortunately little about the Middle Ages in the Outer Hebrides, due to the lack of documentary evidence and very limited archaeological excavation. During the extensive archaeological surveys carried out in Barra and Uist over the 1990s, little evidence of mediaeval settlement was discovered. The sites of this period that we can identify tend to be those of the Church and aristocracy; churches and castles were built of stone and lime and tended to survive.

Barraigh (Barra)

101. *Caisteal Chiosamuil* (Kisimul or Kiessimul Castle) NL 6651 9791

This property is run by Historic Environment Scotland and open to the public from April to September. Catch a boat from Castle Slip Landing in *Bagh a' Chaisteil* (Castlebay), 5 minutes across the harbour to the island on which the castle stands.

This MacNeil castle (see Fig. 49) in Barra is the most dramatic surviving castle in the Western Isles and well worth a visit. The building was extensively renovated in the mid 20th century, incorporating the then-ruinous remains of the buildings, but enough survived of the original plan and structures that the castle gives a good impression of what it would have been like in the 17th century.

Limited archaeological excavation was carried out within the castle in 2000–1, when the MacNeil family leased the building to Historic Environment Scotland on a 1,000-year lease (for an annual rental of £1 and a bottle of whisky). The evidence suggests that the earliest part of the castle dates from the 15th century in the late Middle Ages, and that it was occupied until the 18th century, when it was abandoned and destroyed by fire. The construction date of the castle is debated; some authors have set it as early as the 13th century but, as yet, little evidence supports this, and the only earlier mediaeval evidence from the excavations was a single, gold lace-tag. The excavations also showed that the island was occupied in the Neolithic and Bronze Age, but the excavation area was small and didn't provide detail about the prehistoric settlement.

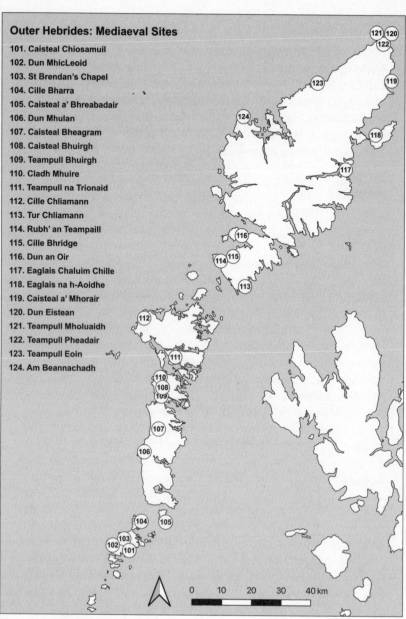

Outer Hebrides: Mediaeval Sites

101. Caisteal Chiosamuil
102. Dun MhicLeoid
103. St Brendan's Chapel
104. Cille Bharra
105. Caisteal a' Bhreabadair
106. Dun Mhulan
107. Caisteal Bheagram
108. Caisteal Bhuirgh
109. Teampull Bhuirgh
110. Cladh Mhuire
111. Teampull na Trionaid
112. Cille Chliamann
113. Tur Chliamann
114. Rubh' an Teampaill
115. Cille Bhridge
116. Dun an Oir
117. Eaglais Chaluim Chille
118. Eaglais na h-Aoidhe
119. Caisteal a' Mhorair
120. Dun Eistean
121. Teampull Mholuaidh
122. Teampull Pheadair
123. Teampull Eoin
124. Am Beannachadh

0 10 20 30 40 km

Fig. 52. Location map of mediaeval sites

The 15th-century castle consisted of an enclosure (curtain) wall around the island with a keep tower and hall. The early castle had two entrances, one on the eastern side which was later blocked by construction of the Watchman's House, and a small gate on the northern side. In the 16th century, the tower and the enclosure wall were all raised, and in the later part of the 16th century or early 17th century, the present main gate was constructed. Further 16th-century alterations probably included the round tower in the northern corner, the Watchman's House, the Tanist's (Heir's) house, and the boathouse (or crew house) outside the curtain wall. In the 17th century the hall was raised and extended, blocking the small northern gate.

The changes in the castle reflect the changing society of Barra and the Isles. The earliest form of the castle is like the castle of *Breachacha* on the Inner Hebridean island of Coll, probably reflecting their similar political context as a local clan leaders' military base within the overarching Lordship of the Isles. The castle is the physical expression of the military mediaeval clan society in the islands. However, as society changed over time, becoming less military, more buildings were constructed within the curtain wall, providing more comfortable and increasingly private accommodation for the family. Eventually the MacNeils built a private house on Barra and abandoned the castle, which was destroyed by fire and then robbed of stone to provide ballast for ships and boats using the harbour during the height of the herring industry. Then, in the 20th century, the ruins were purchased by an American descendant of the chiefly family, who reconstructed and reoccupied the buildings for several decades prior to their handover to Historic Environment Scotland.

102. *Dun MhicLeoid* (Castle Sinclair),   NL 6475 9960
    Loch Tangasdail (Loch Tangasdale)

The site is visible from the main road, on a small island in the loch.

This small, mediaeval tower is said to have been three storeys in height, though it is now only about 4.5m high. The tower itself is just over 5m square, similar to the small tower built on *Dun Eistean* in Lewis (Site 120). Local tradition has it that it was built for the brother of one of the MacNeil chiefs of Barra in the 15th century.

The island on which the tower is built was occupied by an earlier, probably Iron Age, stone roundhouse and may have had a causeway linking it to the south shore of the loch. This earlier occupation under mediaeval reoccupation is similar to several other Iron Age fortified sites in the islands, for example *Dun Mhulan* (Dun Vulan) (Site 59) and *Dun an Sticer* (Site 68) on Uist, and *Dun an Oir* (Site 73) on *Tarasaigh* (Taransay). Some sites appear to have had towers or castles built onto them around the 13th century, when the islands became part of Scotland, while others seem to have been refortified in the period of instability towards the end of the 15th century when the Lordship of the Isles ended. In both cases the reuse was probably tied as much to questions of identity and land claiming as it was to a need for defence.

103. St Brendan's/St Michael's Chapel,   NF 6477 0168
   Borgh (Borve)

Park just off the main road and walk about 720m west on the machair track towards the cemetery, which is visible on the southern coast of the headland

The first edition of the Ordnance Survey map of Barra identifies this chapel as dedicated to St Brendan, but there is an earlier 19th-century reference to St Michael's church here. It is possible that there may have been two chapels at this site, only one of which is now visible.

The remains of the chapel are a rectangular outline of grass-covered stone, slight, but clearly visible, in the south-eastern corner of the graveyard. The walls show a typical mediaeval chapel shape – rectangular – orientated east to west, with the chancel divided from the nave. The wall dividing the chancel from the nave is clearly visible and not covered in grass.

This is a particularly interesting site, despite its denuded remains, because it is clear if you look at the outside of the cemetery enclosure wall that the church was built on the top of the remains of a broch. The curved cemetery wall in this corner reflects the line of the Iron Age broch wall underneath it, an example of the continuity or reuse of Iron Age settlement sites for churches. A group of cist burials were uncovered by erosion nearby in the early 20th century, but the discovery record is insufficiently detailed to be sure of whether these were associated with this site.

104. *Cille Bharra* (Kilbar) churches

NF 0551 0738

On the main road at the northern end of Barra. Park in the cemetery parking area.

There are three surviving mediaeval churches in the graveyard at *Cille Bharra*, the largest and probably earliest of which is dedicated to St Barr and is likely to date to the 12th or 13th century (Site 86). Originally there were four churches, one of the others dedicated to St Mary; the remains of the fourth church were demolished in the 19th century. The Viking Age and other crosses of Late Iron Age date on the site indicate that this was an important early religious site. The author Compton Mackenzie, who lived on Barra, stated that there was a ruinous priory here in the late 17th century, and it may have been a monastic site before the Reformation.

The roofed chapel was originally a burial chapel for the MacNeil chiefs of Barra, probably built late in the Middle Ages or around the time of the Reformation. It became derelict and was reroofed in the 1970s to shelter three fine, late mediaeval grave slabs, probably of MacNeil chiefs (Fig. 53). These are like other chiefly memorials on the west coast of Scotland, decorated with foliage and symbols of aristocratic power, including swords, animals, and a typical west coast mediaeval ship, called a birlinn. There were at least two different styles or schools of carving, one of which was based around Iona, the other around *Oronsaigh* (Oronsay), and both are represented here.

The third chapel, of which little survives, is to the south of the other two. It has one surviving round-headed window, which suggests that it may also have been, perhaps, 13th century in date.

This site is very like *Tobha Mor* (Howmore) in South Uist (Site 89). It was a chiefly religious centre, with multiple chapels, and the architecture of the buildings suggests it was a religious centre before the Treaty of Perth in AD 1266. The carved stones on the site indicate that this was an established Christian centre in the Late Iron Age, continuing as an active church site through the Viking Age.

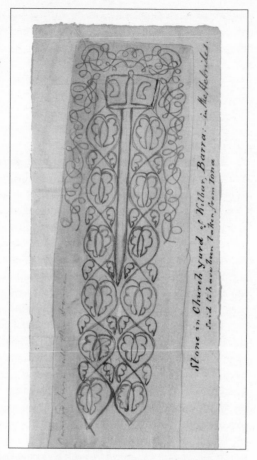

Fig. 53. Mediaeval grave slab at *Cille Bharra* (Kilbar), *Barraigh* (Barra) (Courtesy of HES (Society of Antiquaries of Scotland Collection))

105. *Caisteal a' Bhreabadair* (*Caisteal an Reubadair,* Weaver's Castle), *Na Stacanan Dubha*   NF 7859 0717

The ruins of this castle can be seen from the ferry travelling between Barra and South Uist, on a group of small islands immediately south of *Eirisgeigh* (Eriskay).

This ruined, small tower house, by comparison with other similar sites, probably dates to the late Middle Ages at the latest. It was once a stronghold of the MacNeils of Barra, who also held the southern end of South Uist and Eriskay, but oral tradition has its last occupant as one Reubadair Stache, a notorious wrecker and pirate. The modern name Weaver's Castle is a translation of the Gaelic *Caisteal a' Bhreabadair*, but this is a corruption of an earlier name which meant Reiver's Castle.

Uibhist a' Deas (South Uist)

106. *Dun Mhulan* (Dun Vulan)   NF 7140 2980

The machair road is suitable for vehicles, but you must stop at the parking place before the promontory begins, as the road thereafter has been very severely damaged by storms and is only passable by foot.

The Iron Age broch, which had been abandoned around AD 800 (Site 59), was reoccupied later in the Middle Ages. The date of this reuse is not entirely clear but, judging from pottery finds, it may have been in the 14th or early 15th century. A rectangular building was constructed on the outside of the broch, on its north-eastern edge. During excavation a part of this building was investigated to the original floor level, but no further. As a result, little is known about the building and what it was used for.

Although the use of the broch is poorly understood, it fits into a wider picture of the reoccupation of brochs after the end of the Scandinavian Period. *Dun an Oir* on Taransay (Site 73) and *Dun an Sticer* on North Uist (Site 68) are amongst the many brochs which were reused in the Middle Ages. Typically, a secondary, rectangular structure – a small tower or building – was built inside the curving wall of the broch, with other rectangular buildings on the outside. The curve of the broch wall was normally visible under or around the later building.

107. *Caisteal Bheagram*   NF 7610 3711

This site is visible from the *Druimisdal* (Drimsdale) road, on an island in the loch to the north of the above site.

The remains of a 15th-century castle are located on an island in a loch north of *Tobha Mor* (Howmore) (Site 89). Documentary evidence from royal records names a man called Ronald Alanson, a Clanranald chief who lived here in the early 16th century, but the buildings are probably earlier.

An underwater causeway leads to the island across the loch, and survey and aerial photographs show that the whole island was enclosed with a stone wall with buildings against it on the inside. The two-storey remains of a lime-mortared tower, the castle keep, are on the northern wall. Survey also revealed that, although the island is probably largely natural, it has been modified and may have had earlier occupation.

Together with the churches at Tobha Mor, this castle was the heart of mediaeval South Uist, and of the Clanranald landholdings. The association of secular and ecclesiastical power would have reinforced community control by the landowner and, in the Middle Ages and later, landowners often had either influence or control over local church appointments.

Beinn na Fhaoghla (Benbecula)

108. *Caisteal Bhuirgh* (Borve Castle)   NF 7733 5050

In croft land to the north of the B892. Visible from the road.

The looming ruins of a mid 14th-century tower house can be seen in a croft in *Borgh* (Borve), to the north of the road (Fig. 54). The construction of the castle is attributed to Amie MacRuarie, wife of John of Islay, a Lord of the Isles. She is also reputed to have ordered the building of *Teampull na Trionaid* in North Uist (Site 111).

The building originally stood on either an island or a headland in a machair loch. Sea-level rise, pushing the machair sands ahead of it, and extensive 17th- and 18th-century drainage, have removed all trace of the loch in which it stood, and there is now no evidence of the outbuildings and walls which probably surrounded the tower.

The castle was occupied by the MacDonalds until the early 17th century, if not a little later. Only three walls are now standing, as the northern wall has collapsed, but in the early 20th century it stood to a height of three storeys.

Fig. 54. *Caisteal Bhuirgh* (Borve Castle), *Beinn na Fhaoghla* (Benbecula) (MacGibbon & Ross, *Castellated Architecture*)

109. *Teampull Bhuirgh*   NF 7693 5027

On the opposite side of the B892 from *Caisteal Bhuirgh* (Borve Castle), this site is in the middle of an area of cultivated machair strips. Park clear of the gate to the machair at NF 7711 5050 and walk 290m down the diagonal track towards the mounds, then carefully pick your way across the strips to the site. Don't cross any crops.

In the 1920s, the walls of a large church could be seen in the centre of the eastern of two settlement mounds on the *Borgh* (Borve) machair. They are partially obscured now by tumble and blown sand, but the structure can still be made out. It is a rectangular building, orientated east to west, and measuring internally 14m east to west and 5m north to south. It was mortared with lime mortar, as is typical of mediaeval chapels and churches in the islands; the brightness and whiteness of this would have provided a marked contrast with much of the other architecture, emphasising the importance and special nature of the building. Two windows at the eastern end of the long walls would have lit the area around the altar.

The mound on which the church sits has produced Iron Age pottery, suggesting that this was an earlier, prehistoric settlement, and there may have been a Late Iron Age church or chapel here before the mediaeval building was constructed. It is tempting to associate the building of the church here with the construction of the nearby castle, as the church is also clearly mediaeval, and the association of an important church with a centre of secular power is to be expected.

110. *Cladh Mhuire, Baile nan Cailleach* (Nunton)   NF 7664 5379

The ruins of this mediaeval chapel are in the old Nunton cemetery. Park beside the road and go through the gate.

The place name 'Nunton' suggests that this was the location of a pre-Reformation convent and Martin Martin, writing in the 17th century, commented that a building was locally believed to have been a nunnery dedicated to the Virgin Mary. The foundation was understood to have been a daughter house of the convent in Iona. Unfortunately, no evidence of the convent, its form or location, survives, unless the chapel is its last remains, and local tradition has it that the stone from the nunnery buildings was used to construct Nunton House and Steading, which stand to the south of the cemetery (Site 135).

The late mediaeval church stands to its full height, though roofless. In the early 20th century there were two carved stone crosses here, one in the graveyard and one within the chapel, but these are no longer visible. A late 19th-century source also reported the finding of a 'Celtic bell' at the site which, if true, would imply that there might have been a Late Iron Age chapel on the site, but the present location of the bell is unknown.

Uibhist a' Tuath (North Uist)

111. *Teampull na Trionaid, Cairinis* (Carinish)   NF 8162 6028

Park by the roadside, use the croft gate entrance and walk 220m along the southern boundary of the croft to reach the monument.

Teampull na Trionaid is a 14th-century church, with an adjoining 16th-century chapel, linked by a barrel-vaulted passage (Fig. 55). This was not a parish church; it is said to have been a monastery and educa-

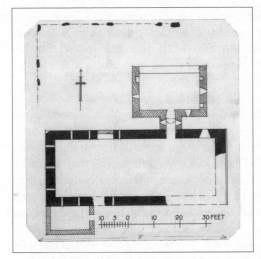

Fig. 55. *Teampull na Trionaid, Cairinis* (Carinish), *Uibhist a' Tuath* (North Uist) (© Crown copyright: HES)

tional establishment prior to the Reformation. A local tradition states that the mediaeval theologian John Duns Scotus was educated here.

The building of the church is attributed to Amie MacRuari, who is also said to have built *Caisteal Bhuirgh* (Borve Castle) (Site 108), and a 14th-century date is compatible with the architecture of the large building. As excavation on the site found Middle Iron Age pottery, it is likely that there is a prehistoric settlement beneath the church, and the church itself may be a renovation or rebuild of an earlier structure.

The building has been robbed of stone over the years, and although carved stone detailing and figures survived in the early 20th century, they are now lost. There are square sockets built into the western wall, which may have supported a wooden gallery.

112. *Cille Chliamann/Kilchalma* (St Clement's   NF 7114 7279
    Chapel), *Taighgearraidh* (Tigharry)

Park at the entrance to the machair at NF 7211 7273 and walk west and then south following the machair tracks for 1.1km, south of the beach, to the western side of the western headland. This area of machair is often under cultivation so be careful of crops.

This beautifully located chapel is shown on Joan Blaeu's map of 1654 as *Kilchalma*, so the dedication could as easily be to St Colman as to St Clement. The implications of the two dedications are rather different; Colman was a 6th-century Irish saint, and a dedication to him might imply that this was a Late Iron Age, pre-Roman Catholic foundation. However, dedications to St Clement in the British Isles are often associated with Scandinavian communities and might imply that this was a Viking Age or Norse foundation.

The monument is the remains of a very small rectangular building, only about 4m x 3m internally, within a rectangular enclosure wall. The enclosure wall may mark a surrounding graveyard, but there are no visible grave markers and the ground is not built up to the extent that might be expected if it had been used as a burial ground. The slight remains of a second building are visible within the enclosure adjacent to the north-west wall. It is possible that the chapel and building together might have been a monastic or private chapel, rather than being a community church.

Na Hearadh (Harris)

113. *Tur Chliamann* (St Clement's Tower   NG 0475 8318
    or Church), *Roghadal* (Rodel)

Park by the churchyard gates and walk up the paved path to the church. Managed by Historic Environment Scotland.

This splendid church (Fig. 56) was built in the early 16th century by the laird of Harris, Alasdair 'Crotach' MacLeod of Dunvegan in Skye, and it is said to have been built on the site of an earlier church or monastery. It is the largest surviving mediaeval church in the Outer Hebrides and contains a wealth of symbolic sculpture reflecting the interests and priorities of this powerful family.

The building of the church probably started in the 1520s or 1530s, soon after the end of the Lordship of the Isles, at a time when many of the clan leaders whose families had previously buried their dead in Iona constructed their own family mortuary chapels in their territories. It is included as a mediaeval monument because it illustrates the mediaeval relationship between the Church and secular power before the

Fig. 56. *Tur Chliamann* (St Clement's Tower or Church), *Roghadal* (Rodel),
Na Hearadh (Harris) (MacGibbon & Ross, *Ecclesiastical Architecture*)

Reformation. The MacLeods of Harris had their main seat at the castle of Dunvegan in Skye but had also held Harris for at least two centuries by this time, in a lordship that was linked, rather than divided, by the water between the two islands. The outside of the church displays symbols of the family's power; above the main door to the cruciform building is a bull's head, and on the tower, four panels show the figure of a bishop, probably St Clement, a further bull's head, two fishermen in a boat, and a 'Sheela na gig' (a naked female figure) similar to that on the nunnery on Iona. In addition, there are two male figures on the tower, one in a kilt and the other half-naked. Local stories have it that the latter was dismembered in the 19th century when the wife of the landlord felt it was indecent.

Within the church, at the eastern end, is the arched, highly decorated tomb of Alasdair Crotach (Fig. 57). The carvings around the tomb highlight his Catholic faith, with the Crucifixion on the keystone of the arch, and the Virgin and Child in the centre of the back panel. Two bishops stand either side of the Virgin, one of them St Clement, carrying a skull. Around them are secular and religious symbols, the Apostles are represented, but so also is a beautiful hunting scene, a castle, and a ship (a birlinn) representing power over the seas. The effigy of the dead man shows him in European-style armour, rather than Highland clothing, displaying his national and international significance and sophistication.

Fig. 57. Tomb of Alasdair Crotach, *Tur Chliamann* (St Clement's Tower or Church) *Roghadal* (Rodel), *Na Hearadh* (Harris) (MacGibbon & Ross, *Ecclesiastical Architecture*)

On one of the window ledges towards the rear of the church is the broken head of a free-standing mediaeval cross, with a crucifixion scene on it, which probably stood in the churchyard or at the gate, marking the entrance to the sanctified ground. In the two chapels to north and south of the nave are further mediaeval tombs and grave slabs for the MacLeod family. The burial ground has been continuously used; outside the eastern end of the church is an unusual iron-framed grave marker.

The church fell out of use after the Reformation in 1560 and became derelict. It was renovated twice in the 18th century by Captain Alexander MacLeod, and extensively repaired in the 19th century by Lady Dunmore, the wife of the then landowner. It is now in the guardianship of Historic Environment Scotland, who maintain it.

114. *Rubh' an Teampaill, Taobh Tuath* (Northton)   NF 9701 9134

Walk 2.5km from *Taobh Tuath* along an unpaved machair path.

Walking along the southern coast of *Gob an Tobha* (Toe Head), past the remains of the multi-period site of *Baile Deas* (South Town)

(Site 1), you will see a roofless building silhouetted against the sea and sky on a headland. This is the remains of a late mediaeval chapel, possibly dedicated to St Luke. It measures only 7m x 3m internally, and at the eastern end are the remains of the footings of the altar, two niches and a small stone shelf for communion vessels or statues. There are patches of lime plaster on the internal walls and the walls were bonded with lime mortar, making it relatively light and bright both inside and out. At the western end are the remains of a small loft. Building survey shows that the present structure is all of one period, dating to the end of the Middle Ages, but it contains some shaped stones which have been reused from an earlier structure, so there may have been an earlier church or chapel on the headland.

Inside the building, two later burial enclosures have been constructed; the chapel continued to be an important site for a local family or families after it became derelict and roofless, presumably following the Reformation.

The chapel is surrounded by the remains of a graveyard, and its western end is on top of the edge of the footings of an Iron Age broch (Site 71). The stone from the walls of the broch has been used to construct the chapel and probably other buildings in the area. There are large enclosure walls, visible as turf-covered ridges partially obscured by blown sand, around the landward side of the site. Survey and geophysical survey on this headland produced evidence of extensive settlement on the landward side of the chapel site and possible further burials. However, these sites remain unexcavated and we cannot know what period they date from. Clearly this was an important, long-term settlement, from at least the Iron Age.

115. *Cille Bhridge* (Kilbride), *Sgarastadh*   NG 0070 9282
(Scarista)

There is a car park by the 19th-century church.

The remains of the old parish church of Harris are probably in the centre of the mounded, crowded old burial ground at *Sgarasta Mhor* (Fig. 68). However, as the ground level has built up with burials, nothing is now visible of the church.

Two mediaeval grave slabs have been found at this site. A cast of one of them can be seen in the parking area by the 19th-century church, showing a foliated (leafy) cross, scrolling plant, a lion, a sword and a heraldic shield. This style of carving is of the Iona school, emphasising the links and cultural continuity of the islands under the Lordship of the Isles. The second slab was more worn and appears to have been of the Oronsay school of carving. It was made of the same stone as many of the carvings in *Roghadal* (Rodel) church.

Tarasaigh (Taransay)

116. *Dun an Oir* (*Dun Clach*)   NG 0358 9961

If you follow the line of the old township road about 350m northeast along the coast from the landing place, you will come to the remains of this fort.

The Iron Age broch at *Dun an Oir* (Site 73) was reoccupied in the Middle Ages. A small rectangular building was constructed into the circular broch wall, with a narrow entrance from the landward side. The township head dyke runs up to the broch, dividing the settlement from its outfield grazing land, and the strategic location of the site overlooking the township and the water between the island and Harris would have been as important in the Middle Ages as it was in the Iron Age.

Leodhas (Lewis)

117. *Eaglais Chaluim Chille* (St Columba's Church)   NB 3858 2104

Park at the end of the Crobeg farm road before the cattle grid and walk along the road, turning west (right) onto an unsurfaced track just before the house. Follow the track to the shore and the causeway across to *Eilean Chaluim Chille*. This causeway is only passable at low tide, so check the tide tables and keep an eye on water levels. On the other side, turn west (left) along the shoreline for 450m until you come to the graveyard. Total walk 1.2km one way.

Eaglais Chaluim Chille is located on a strategic island at the entrance to *Loch Eirisort* (Loch Erisort), a deep-water loch on the eastern coast of Lewis that was important in the maritime mediaeval world. Its strategic location is one of the reasons that it was a very important early church foundation, and its dedication to St Columba could reflect links to the early Christian monastery on Iona. Before the Reformation, this was the main place of worship in the area of Lochs.

The visible ruins of the church are mediaeval and it was later reused as a private burial aisle, at which time the south-eastern window was blocked. The ground around the church is built-up from years of burials, and evidence for any earlier church or chapel on the site is probably concealed within and under the graveyard.

Outwith the cemetery, the ruins of old houses and fields are visible, showing that the island was densely occupied and intensively farmed until the 18th or 19th centuries. The island is very fertile, and in 1549, when Sir Donald Munro carried out his survey of the islands, he reported that there was an orchard here.

118. *Eaglais na h-Aoidhe* (*Eaglais Chaluim Chille*, St Columba's Ui Church), *Aoidh* (Ui)   NB 4846 3226

Park in the parking places by the main road and walk 170m, following the path north across the peninsula to the gate of the churchyard.

This 14th-century church was the parish church for Stornoway in the Middle Ages and the burial place of many of the MacLeods of Lewis, who controlled the island until the 1500s. It may have been founded on the site of an earlier church, dedicated to St Catan, and there are the remains of an Iron Age settlement immediately next to and under the church, suggesting that it was originally a Late Iron Age foundation. It was last used for regular worship in 1829.

Inside the church are two late mediaeval grave slabs. One of these shows a knight in Highland dress with a pointed helmet, said to be Ruairidh the 7th chief of the MacLeods of Lewis, who died around the end of the 15th century. The use of Highland military dress, which consisted of a padded, quilted tunic with a helmet and mail coif, is a contrast to the later memorial to Alasdair Crotach at *Roghadal* (Rodel) (Site 113), emphasising a more regional and Highland identity. The other grave slab shows an interlaced cross with animals and leaves, and has an inscription to the memory of Margaret Mackinnon, daughter of Ruairidh.

Recent survey has shown that the church was built and rebuilt at least seven times, with extensions and additions to serve succeeding generations. The initial simple rectangular plan was modified with a new sacristy aisle to the south, later removed, and a large chapel was added to the west. The roof was removed from the main church, presumably well after the Reformation, and the chapel continued in use until the 19th century, when the building was abandoned. The graveyard continued to be used into the 20th century.

The church was within a circular graveyard in the Middle Ages, but erosion on the northern side has removed all the land to the north of the building. It continues to be threatened by coastal erosion and sea-level rise.

119. *Caisteal a' Mhorair, Traigh Ghearadha* (Garry Beach) NB 5368 4970

Park in the parking area by the beach and walk south and east 510m along the machair and the cliff-tops until you can overlook the site.

Caisteal a' Mhorair ('the castle of the nobleman') is the remains of a small rectangular building on the top of a pinnacle of rock above this beautiful beach. A wall encloses the summit, forming a building with two rooms, which would have had open views to the north and east. Its location, rectangular shape and orientation towards the Minch, the waterway between the island and the mainland, make it clear that this was a mediaeval fortification, reflecting a period when larger and heavier ships needed to use the deep-water ports on the eastern coast of Lewis.

120. *Dun Eistean, Nis* (Ness) NB 5355 6501

Park by the road in the layby at NB 5340 6415 and walk 1.2km north and west following the track across the moorland. You can cross to the site over a footbridge.

Dun Eistean is another late mediaeval fortification overlooking the north-eastern coast of Lewis. It is built on a large sea stack, defended on the landward side by a steep, tidal ravine. Excavations on the site showed that it was fortified in the 15th century, and local traditions describing it as the fort of the Clan Morison of *Nis* were accurate. There was no prehistoric occupation on the sea stack, nor any evidence that it ever had an ecclesiastical use, both of which interpretations had previously been suggested.

The top of the stack is enclosed by a turf and stone wall forming a rectangular bailey, with the remains of a two- or three-storey keep on the seaward side and further buildings including a corn-drying kiln within the bailey and against the wall. A pond to collect rainwater was formed by damming a hollow on the stack, providing a water source.

The fort and the keep were occupied and altered at least twice, and had also been attacked, as the excavation found musket and pistol balls that had been fired, and gunflints. The 15th and 16th centuries in Lewis were unstable; the ending of the Lordship of the Isles caused one hundred years of civil war on the island, known as the 'Evil Trubles of the Lews'. The location of this fort, with its mainland-orientated outlook as well as the defensive ravine and wall on the landward side, makes it clear that threats were all around.

121. *Teampull Mholuaidh / Teampull Mhor* NB 5194 6516
(St Moluag's Church), *Nis* (Ness)

Park at the side of the road and follow the fenced and signposted path 220m north to the church.

The church of St Moluag (Fig. 58) was restored in the early 20th century, having been derelict since the Reformation. It is T-shaped in plan, with a small chapel and a sacristy on either side of the eastern end of the church. The wall around the church dates to its restoration, and it was probably originally within a much larger enclosure; the first edition of the Ordnance Survey map of the area, from the mid 19th century, shows an irregular, roughly rectangular enclosure around the roofless building.

The age of the building is debated. Some have suggested that its

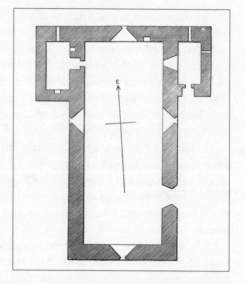

Fig. 58. *Teampull Mholuaidh* (St Moluag's Church), *Nis Teampull Mhor*, (Ness), *Leodhas* (Lewis) (MacGibbon & Ross, *Ecclesiastical Architecture*)

simple form might be of 13th-century date, whilst others compare it to *Tur Chliamann* in *Roghadal* (Rodel) (Site 113) and propose that it should be dated to the 15th century at the earliest. Archaeological excavation around the church in 1977 did not provide any evidence to date the building.

Following the Reformation, when the island suffered from a lack of ministers, the church became the focus of various festivals and practices, including a festival relating to the sea-god Shony, recorded by Martin Martin in the early 18th century as having stopped around 30 years earlier. The name of the sea-god is very similar to one of the Gaelic forms for the name John, Seonaidh, and it would seem likely that this might have been a modified version of earlier Saints' Days festivals, which were celebrated without church oversight in the century after the Reformation.

122. *Teampull Pheadair, Nis* (Ness)   NB 5085 6383

Park by the modern *Nis* cemetery at NB 5120 6404 and walk 560m south-west, following the unpaved machair track, through a gate, to the old graveyard.

Little remains of the original parish church of *Nis*, save a large, rectangular, east to west orientated hollow, with part of the east gable standing and the footings of the south wall. The valley surrounding the church, now divided between the townships of *Tabost* and *Suainebost*, was an important settlement in Ness from the Iron Age onwards. The mediaeval *Taigh Mor* ('big house') of the Morrisons of *Nis* was to the north of the township wall, though there is little to see at the site now. Settlement mounds on the opposite site of Abhainn Shuainebost from the old graveyard, to the south-west, have produced evidence of Norse and mediaeval occupation. The ridge and furrow of old cultivation can be seen over the slopes surrounding the valley, which was clearly intensively farmed.

The importance of the area is reflected in the size of the church, which was around 19m in length. It was used until the 18th century, when it was replaced as parish church by the church of St Mary at *Barabhas* (Barvas).

123. *Teampull Eoin, Bragar* NB 2882 4890

Follow the machair road down to the shore and turn north-west along the shoreline until you reach the cemetery, which is still in use.

The church of St John the Baptist was listed as a pre-Reformation sanctuary by Martin Martin in the early 18th century. It is a much smaller building than was *Teampull Pheadair*, and it seems likely that some of the pre-Reformation churches may have been subsidiary to larger parish churches.

The remains of the church stand on a knoll in the more extensive cemetery; the knoll is a prehistoric settlement mound, finds from which appear occasionally in rabbit burrows. The church was a two-room building, with a nave and chancel, and the chancel arch survived until the mid 20th century. Although the standing building appears to be made of dry stone, it was probably mortared with clay and lime, which has been lost to weathering. Three of the grave markers to the north of the church are small stone slabs with holes in them, which are probably slates from the mediaeval roof of the church.

Around the church and graveyard is a wonderful landscape palimpsest of mediaeval and post-mediaeval cultivation and buildings.

The footings of buildings, enclosures and field walls are crossed by, and cross, earlier and later ridges and furrows of *feannagan* ('lazy bed' cultivation). *Bragar* was not cleared, and the landscape still shows evidence of the hundreds of years of use focused around this area of shoreline settlement.

124. *Am Beannachadh*, Uig   NB 0386 3791

Park at NB 049 380, in *Aird Uig*, opposite the restaurant. Walk past the houses and polytunnel westwards on the moorland road that leads up to the buildings on the top of the hill. Continue west past the end of the road for another 650m, crossing a wall to the south of a small loch, until you reach the site.

This small ruinous church building is called *Taigh a' Bheannaidh*, which means 'the house of blessing', and the area around it is called *Am Beannachadh*. The building itself is a simple rectangular structure, about 5m long internally, built of stone bonded with clay. East of the church are various small hut circles and cairns, which have led to the whole site being interpreted as an early monastery. However, the church building itself appears to be later than the other remains in the area. A spring, originally covered by a building and now filled in, is to the south-west of the church building.

This site has no documentary history at all, but the archaeological remains clearly show that it was used and reused over a long period of time. The presence of the spring may be, in part, an explanation of this long use. Springs and holy wells were often important in local landscapes as a source of healing and blessing; they are often dedicated to saints, or have crosses carved near them, perhaps to bless and christen important pre-Christian landscape features. The chapel is clearly mediaeval or later, but the earlier buildings and cairns suggest that this was a mediaeval or earlier sacred site.

7. United Kingdoms:
The Post-Mediaeval Period AD 1560–1900

Historical sources

Increasingly, from the end of the Middle Ages, we have more documentary sources about the islands. At first these were descriptive; Donald Munro, for example, a cleric of the Archdeaconry of the Isles, wrote a description of the Outer Hebrides on behalf of the Bishop of the Isles, based on a trip around 1549. His was the first systematic description of the islands, and it gives us a useful picture of the islands' economy and culture at the end of the Middle Ages. He focused particularly on the rents people paid and on customs and beliefs because he was reporting on behalf of the Church, which had both landowning and religious responsibilities in the archipelago.

A later description of the islands came from Martin Martin, a native of Skye, who published *A Description of the Western Islands of Scotland* in 1703. His interest was ethnological; after the union of England and Scotland, he wrote his book to represent the islands to the wider world. Indeed, Samuel Johnson and James Boswell, travelling in northern Scotland later in the 18th century, took copies of the book with them, though they did not reach the Outer Hebrides.

The first maps of the islands date to the seventeenth century (Fig. 59, Plate 11). These are based on a 16th-century survey, but they do not give a geographically accurate picture of the topography of the islands. Accurate mapping only extended to the Hebrides in the second half of the 18th century, largely as a result of the need for military maps after the final Jacobite Rebellion in 1745–6.

Estate records are increasingly common from this period as well, although their survival is patchy. Damp, fire, war and tidying-up have all taken their toll; for example it seems very likely that most, if not all, of the early records for the Isle of Lewis Estate were destroyed during the 1745 Rebellion, when they were being held on mainland Scotland. Estate records, of course, are concerned with rentals and

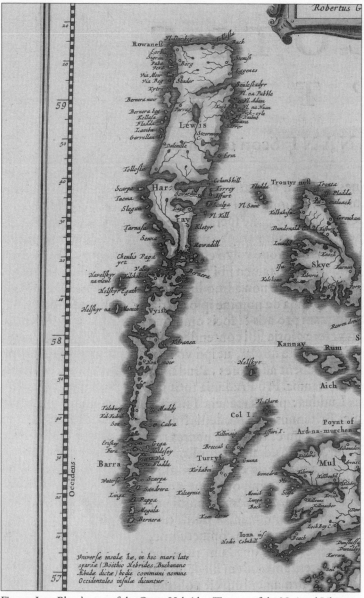

Fig. 59. Joan Blaeu's map of the Outer Hebrides (Trustees of the National Library of Scotland)

land transfers, but also give fascinating glimpses into people's lives, particularly in records of complaints and disputes.

National records, both secular and ecclesiastical, also increased during this period. With the forfeiture of the Lordship of the Isles, land transfers and inheritances began to be recorded by the Crown. When rebellion led to the government seizing many island estates in the first half of the 18th century, factors (estate managers) working for the government surveyed their new landholdings by creating detailed rentals to record tenancy arrangements. These are sometimes the earliest surviving written rentals for estates, for example the Isle of Lewis Forfeited Estate Rental in 1726.

In the late 18th century, driven by ideas of scientific understanding and political progression, a national survey of Scotland was organised by Sir John Sinclair of Ulbster in Caithness. He circulated a long list of questions to each parish minister in the country and, between 1791 and 1799, accumulated a picture of each parish in Scotland, known as the Old Statistical Account. Between 1834 and 1845 a second survey was carried out – the New Statistical Account. These are important historical sources for Scotland, particularly for areas like the Hebrides, which were otherwise poorly recorded.

From the second half of the 18th century onwards, some parish records in the islands survive. In *Leodhas* (Lewis), *Steornabhagh* (Stornoway) records started in 1762, but elsewhere in the islands parish records began around the 1830s. In 1801 the national census started, but it wasn't until 1841 that it included names and occupations, providing personal information about Hebridean individuals. In 1855 civil registration of births, deaths and marriages was introduced, and the numbers of personal records increased once again.

By the end of the 19th century, the population of the islands, their lives and politics, were as well recorded as anywhere else in Great Britain. The development of high-speed printing presses led to the increasing availability of information through newspapers, linking the different parts of the country more closely, and reducing differences between communities, influencing local and national politics and economies. Not only were the islands aware of the life of the mainland, mainlanders became increasingly aware of the life of the islands.

We can create a national and a local historical framework from the sources, which we can then use to inform the changing archaeology and material culture of the islands. History and archaeology do not provide the same type of information, and sometimes they do not tell the same story, but the differences allow us to understand more about how people led their lives. Ironically, as documentary sources become more common, there is less archaeological information; less research and excavation has been carried out on post-mediaeval sites than has been on prehistoric sites.

Reformation and Union

In 1500, islanders living on most of the islands of the Outer Hebrides would still have thought of themselves as being within a clan, and as having land rights in return for rent in kind, such as cloth, cattle, cheese and butter, and service, often military, to a clan chief. That clan chief and landlord would have had judicial rights of life and death over his tenants. The Catholic Church ruled matters of religion, morality and education, providing education and welfare as well as religious sacraments and services. Although the Lordship of the Isles had been made forfeit, and there was civil disruption to a greater or lesser extent in the islands associated with manoeuvring for power amongst the aristocracy, nonetheless life was very much as it had been since the 13th century. However, this was not to last.

In 1560, the Reformation Parliament in Edinburgh abolished the Catholic Church, and adopted a Protestant, Reformed confession of faith. At a stroke, this dismantled the legal authority and structure of the Catholic Church and started the process of dismantling its physical structure. Although in some areas of Scotland, for example Orkney, most priests seem to have adopted the Reformed faith and stayed in post, in the Hebrides there were too few ministers available to serve the area. The southern part of the islands, particularly South Uist and Barra, remained strongly Catholic, but the northern part of the islands, particularly Lewis, which was moving into nearly a century of civil disruption over estate inheritance, had very little church influence for the following century. As a result, church buildings fell into ruin, and local religious beliefs and practices became increasingly unorthodox.

Forty years after the Reformation, in 1603, James VI of Scotland united the Crown of England and Wales. The mainland of the British Isles had one monarch, which opened the border between Scotland

and England, increasing trade with the south. James moved immediately to London, to return only once to Scotland in the rest of his life, but he continued to have an interest in the 'civilisation' of the Hebrides, and the Highlands more widely. In 1609, the Statutes of Iona were introduced, requiring clan chiefs to educate their heirs in English-speaking, Protestant schools, to support Protestant ministers, and limiting the right to bear and use arms in northern Scotland. This was the start of a series of laws which, over the next 150 years, progressively eroded the rights and customs of the Highlands, with the intent of making the region more like the rest of mainland Britain and eradicating the use of Gaelic.

Civil war and rebellion

Following the execution of James' son, Charles I, the country was ruled first by parliament and then by Oliver Cromwell, succeeded by Richard Cromwell, from 1649–59. Although this was a short period of time, it had an important impact on the Highlands and Islands, as Cromwell introduced a standing army of professional soldiers for the first time. To secure the north of Scotland from incursions by the Dutch, with whom the country was at war, large forts, called citadels, were built at important harbours, including Inverness, Lerwick and *Steornabhagh* (Stornoway), and barracks were built on the mainland, to house soldiers. A sketch of the fort in *Steornabhagh* (Fig. 60) shows it was built around existing buildings in the town centre, including the church and manor house, and this is discussed in more detail in the gazetteer.

In 1688, Catholic James II was removed from the throne, in favour of joint monarchs William and Mary. Particularly in Scotland, this triggered nearly 60 years of Jacobite risings, with two major rebellions in 1715 and 1745–6, with the intent of returning the Stuart line to the throne. Although James II was Catholic, the population of the country did not divide on straightforwardly religious lines, and Catholics and Protestants were to be found on both sides. In Scotland, the risings provided a political and military outlet for Highland aristocratic families who hoped that support for the Stuarts would return the legal privileges that had diminished since the Union of Crowns.

The Act of Union, joining England and Scotland in 1707, and

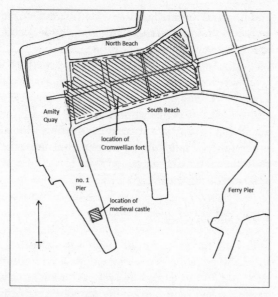

Fig. 60. Sketch of the Cromwellian Fort in *Steornabhagh* (Stornoway)

the failure of the Stuart cause led, however, to more restrictions on Highland customs and legal freedoms, with Acts of Parliament passed in 1716 and 1725 forbidding the carrying of weapons, and in 1746 forbidding carrying weaponry, the wearing of Highland dress, and abolishing hereditary legal jurisdictions. Although the abolition of Highland dress was revoked in 1782, the other changes were permanent, and made the Scottish legal system more like that of England. A further effect of the rebellions was that many estates in northern Scotland were forfeit to the Crown, allowing national auditors to survey and assess them and to start to introduce changes to their management. This period in the hands of national government marked the first time that full, written, estate rentals were created for many estates and, because these were national documents, they survive, giving an important insight into the population and economy of the Highlands in the first half of the 18th century.

Between the 1715 and 1745 Rebellions, the government sent General George Wade to northern Scotland to advise on infrastructure development, resulting in the construction of roads linking the military barracks. This was the start of the Highland road system and marked a move towards greater use of land transport in the region, initially for military purposes. It opened the area up to increasing numbers of visitors and trade and linked the society of the Highlands and Islands more closely to the Central Belt and England.

Clearance and Empire

The long period of rebellions, following so quickly after the Commonwealth, had left many areas of the Highlands poor and underdeveloped and, in the century following the Jacobite defeat in 1746, efforts were made to improve this situation. The Scottish Society for Propagating Christian Knowledge (SSPCK) was founded in 1703, and by 1758 it had 176 schools in the Highlands and Islands and had provided a parallel Gaelic–English translation of the New Testament. Until the Education Act of 1872, it was the largest provider of schools in the Hebrides.

Many parishes in the Highlands and Islands had neither church nor manse in the late 18th century, and in 1823 an Act of Parliament was passed allocating a sum of money to provide them. The Scottish engineer Thomas Telford provided designs (Fig. 61) for economical churches and manses that could be built at a cost of no more than £1,500 and £750 respectively, and 32 were constructed in the following decade, including a number in the Outer Hebrides. Providing facilities for worship and religious education of adults, in addition to the SSPCK schools, was an important strand in the national programme of 'civilising' the Highlands and Islands.

In this context of poverty and instability, emigration increased in northern Scotland. As cultural ideals moved away from the clan feudalism of the later Middle Ages, and Enlightenment ideals of rationality and control spread amongst the Lowland-educated Highland aristocracy, estate reorganisation became increasingly common. The 17th- to 18th-century move from a concept of power as personal military might, towards power as cash-based wealth, created a tension between landowners' desire for increased wealth and the poverty of the tenants of their overpopulated estates. While there was military instability in the region, the inevitable conflict was deferred, but the second half of the 18th century saw widescale estate reorganisation in the Highlands and Islands, with tenants being removed from traditional settlements in the Clearances. When and how Clearance happened, and

HIGHLAND CHURCH AND MANSES.

Plans and Elevations of a Church.

Plan of Gallery Floor.

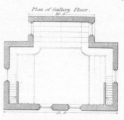

West Elevation.

Ground Plan.

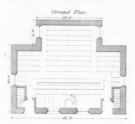

South Elevation.

Plan and Elevation of a Manse of one Story.

Ground Floor.

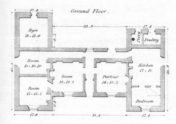

Elevation.

Plans and Elevation of a Manse.

Ground Floor.

Elevation.

Ground Floor.

Second Floor.

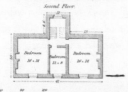

Scale of Feet.

the outcomes for the tenants, varied widely from estate to estate, depending upon the priorities of the landowners.

Meanwhile, the expansion of the British Empire provided opportunities for migrants, both voluntary and involuntary, and we know that individuals, families and sometimes whole communities from the north of Scotland left for North and South America and other colonies. Military service, and service in the trading companies, such as the Hudson Bay and East India Companies, also took individuals overseas and fed money and new cultural influences back into the region.

The short-lived industry of kelp-manufacturing, burning seaweed to provide alkali for industry, boomed in the late 18th century, providing work for coastal communities and keeping people on estates. It then collapsed after the end of the Napoleonic Wars in 1815, when cheaper alkali once again became available from the Mediterranean, and unemployment and poverty soared as a result. As rent arrears became more common amongst tenants, Clearance and estate re-organisation also rose.

The mid 19th century was a hard time in the Scottish Highlands, as potato blight spread from Ireland. When we think of the Potato Famine, Irish starvation and emigration come to mind, but the northern Scottish population was also largely dependent upon the potato as a staple food and suffered from the crop failures. This was mitigated by the fact that much of the inland settlement in the Highlands had been Cleared by this stage, and most people lived close to the shore, where wild food could be gathered. However, once again, tenants across the region fell into rent arrears, as their cash income was spent on food. Some landlords provided work in return for food, for example in road building, which helped avoid outright starvation, but the programmes of work were not universal, and they did not make a significant difference to the economic problems caused by the famine. The decade of 1855–65 saw the last large-scale Clearances in the Highlands and Islands, particularly the removal of tenants in favour of sheep farming.

The Clearances were the last wave of a process of landscape

Fig. 61. Parliamentary church and manse designs (Courtesy of HES (From 'Atlas to the Life of Thomas Telford')

re-organisation that had started as early as the 14th century in the south of England. One of the great differences, however, was that Clearance in the Highlands and Islands took place in the full view of the media – newspapers. Journalists reported on individual Clearances, for example at Croick in Glencalvie, and on the situation of crofting tenants remaining on estates, who had no security in their tenancies, high rents, and lived in poverty. In the 1870s and 1880s, there were demonstrations and riots in Wester Ross, Lewis and Skye, raising public awareness of the situation, which resulted in the appointment of a Royal Commission in 1883. The Napier Commission took personal testimony from landlords, factors, ministers, doctors, crofters and many others at hearings across northern Scotland and the islands, and was published the following year. Overwhelmingly, the evidence suggested local populations wished for security of tenure and for rent control; the Crofters' Holdings Act 1886, resulting from the work of the Commission, provided security of tenure for existing crofters for the first time and created a land court to arbitrate between landlords and tenants. This set the landholding pattern that has shaped the landscape of northern Scotland since then.

In the islands

Today we think of the Outer Hebrides as one geographical unit, but throughout the Post-Mediaeval Period the islands were divided polit-ically, with a regional boundary between *Leodhas* (Lewis), and *Na Hearadh* (Harris) and the Southern Isles – *Uibhist a' Tuath* (North Uist), *Uibhist a' Deas* (South Uist), *Beinn na Fhaoghla* (Benbecula), *Barraigh* (Barra). In more recent times, this boundary was between Inverness-shire to the south, and Ross and Cromarty-shire to the north, along the Lewis/Harris border. There is some evidence that at earlier times the boundary may have been along the southern edge of the Sound of Harris, the islands in the Sound being part of the parish of Harris then, as they still are. The island groups had different histories.

Leodhas (Lewis)

Sixteenth-century Lewis was a hotbed of rebellion, as the MacLeod chiefs of the island supported attempts by the descendants of the last

Lord of the Isles to regain his title. By the middle of the century, this was made worse by a disagreement about inheritance between the many legitimate and illegitimate sons of Ruairidh MacLeod. Three successive wives, each of whom had had sons, and each of whom were related to different and important mainland families, resulted in total chaos, which spread outwith the island to adjoining areas of the mainland and Inner Hebrides. This unstable situation was part of the reason that, at the end of the 16th century, James VI of Scotland insisted that all Highland chiefs and landowners produce documentary evidence of their entitlement to their lands. The MacLeods of Lewis failed to do this and, in 1597, the estate was made forfeit; shortly after, rights in it were transferred to a group of gentlemen from Fife, known as the Fife adventurers. The adventurers had the commission to civilise the island, by whatever means necessary, and were given total judicial authority. However, their three attempts to settle in *Steornabhagh* (Stornoway) and extend control over the island to the hinterland failed utterly; their settlement in *Steornabhagh* was sacked, and local tradition has it that they retreated to a small fort constructed on *Eilean nan Gobhair* (Goat Island) in *Steornabhagh* harbour. In 1609 or 1610, the Isle of Lewis was sold to the MacKenzies of Kintail, the family of the first of Ruairidh's wives.

The Mackenzies initially met significant resistance from the islanders; their first foothold in the island is said to have been at Seaforth Head in Lochs, from which they took their title. By the 1630s, however, the island had been pacified, and MacKenzie connections held most of the land. Sometime in the late 17th or early 18th century, the family constructed a house on the opposite site of the Inner Harbour from the town of *Steornabhagh*. The remains of this house were revealed in recent renovations of Lews Castle, encapsulated within the 19th-century building. They pushed the Crown to recognise *Steornabhagh* as a royal burgh, with special trading rights, to exploit the developing fisheries around the island. Documentary records from both England and Scotland emphasise the huge value of the fisheries as new markets opened up following the Union of Crowns, and they also record local difficulties between incoming Englishmen, Dutch fishermen based in *Steornabhagh*, and the local populace. Theft of ships, equipment and cargoes, violence and false imprisonment are all recorded.

In 1653, Cromwellian troops were sent to garrison *Steornabhagh*, where they built two forts, one in the centre of the town (see Fig. 60) and another on Goat Island, in the outer harbour. Neither survive; they were rapidly demolished following the Restoration of the Stuart monarchy in 1660, and their stone is probably built into the older houses in the centre of the town. The western wall of the town fort was recently discovered near Amity House in the centre of the town.

Kenneth MacKenzie, Earl of Seaforth, spent much of the Commonwealth in prison for his Royalist sympathies, after attacking *Steornabhagh* fort. His son and grandson were also involved in the Jacobite cause in the early 18th century, and the estate was made forfeit; this is the period from which the earliest estate documents survive. By the beginning of the 19th century, however, the family estate and title had been reinstated, and the family remained owners of the island until the mid 19th century when, due to financial difficulties, it was sold to Sir James Matheson.

The first half of the 19th century in Lewis saw major changes in the estate, as financial difficulties and social shifts caused pressure to generate more cash income. The earliest surviving estate map of the island, Chapman's survey of 1807, was created to provide a record of land management and a basis for change. The rental documents show the disappearance of the landholding middle class of tacksmen, with more small tenants paying rent directly to the landowner. As these small tenants slipped into arrears in their rents, due to lack of opportunities to earn cash, there were Clearances, with townships being made into farms. Good examples of Cleared landscapes can be seen at *Beirirho* and *Eadar Dha Fhaoil* (Ardroil) in Uig (Plate 12), but many other areas were stripped of the remains of earlier buildings by the farmers who moved into them.

When Sir James Matheson, merchant and banker (Fig. 62), took over the island in 1844, landscape reorganisation and emigration increased. He instituted a variety of estate projects in the 1850s, providing work for tenants destitute as a result of the Potato Famine. Several important buildings in *Steornabhagh* were constructed, including Lews Castle on the site of Seaforth Lodge, and the Female Industrial School (Lady Matheson's Seminary – Plate 13), to train girls in reading, writing and needlework. The road network in the island also developed at this time, with the completion of an east–west road across the centre

Fig. 62. Sir James Matheson
(Henry Cousins, Oxford
Dictionary of National
Biography – public domain)

Fig. 63. Land War monument, *Aignis* (Aignish),
Leodhas (Lewis)

of the island, from *Steornabhagh* to *Barabhas* (Barvas).

Throughout the second half of the 19th century, with a rising population, Lewis saw regular land disputes, rooted in the demand for security of tenure and for more land for crofters, as the townships that had not been Cleared became ever more congested and overpopulated. The most notable of these are now marked by monuments (Fig. 63) commemorating the land raids and battles that raised the profile of the crofters in the national press and led eventually to the legal recognition of crofting.

Na Hearadh (Harris)

Harris continued to be owned by the MacLeods of Skye until the late 18th century and thus had more internal stability than Lewis. It largely bypassed the disruptions of the 16th century, following the end of the Lordship of the Isles and, in the 17th century, as the MacLeods were Royalist supporters, their estates were secure following the Restoration.

Fig. 64. The
Factor's House,
Roghadal (Rodel),
Na Hearadh
(Harris)

The MacLeods of Dunvegan then supported the government, rather than the Jacobites, in the 18th century and retained their estates. This did not, however, stop them getting into financial problems, and Harris was sold in the late 1770s to a relative, Captain MacLeod.

Although the main seat of the MacLeods of Harris was always in Skye, their centre in Harris was at *Roghadal* (Rodel), on the east coast. This is a natural harbour and, in the 16th century, a church dedicated to St Clement was built here by Alasdair Crotach as his burial place, probably completed just before the Reformation. Following his purchase of the island in the 18th century, Captain MacLeod started a programme of improvements, amongst which were probably the two other major buildings in *Roghadal* – the girnal or store house called the Factor's House (Fig. 64), and the Laird's House (Fig. 65).

The continuity of ownership in Harris is probably the reason that, in the late 18th century at the time of the first Statistical Account, the tenancy pattern of middle-class tacksmen, with sub-tenants, had not changed. The account states that, in 1792, the whole of Harris, barring four small farms held by MacLeod, was in the hands of eight 'gentlemen farmers', who sublet land to smaller tenants. By the time of the second account, less than 50 years later, the estate had been sold on again, to the Earl of Dunmore, and most arable land had been converted into sheep farms. The population had doubled and had been Cleared from the fertile machair of the west coast, to settle along the eastern, less fertile coast, on small patches of arable land around the Bays.

Fig. 65. The Laird's House and the harbour, *Roghadal* (Rodel), *Na Hearadh* (Harris), in the 18th century (© Historic Environment Scotland)

The two Statistical Accounts make it clear that the mid 19th-century depression, Clearance and congested townships were as severe in Harris as in Lewis. In Harris, Lady Dunmore, the wife of the local landowner, encouraged the development of textiles as a local industry, particularly the weaving of traditional woollen cloth, tweed. The contemporary fashion for all things Highland meant that the industry was hugely successful. The tweed was woven at the homes of the weavers, and many houses were extended to accommodate a loom. Around 1900, the Hattersley company of Keighley in Yorkshire developed a mechanised, foot-treadled loom, which sold extensively on the islands (Fig. 66).

Uibhist (Uist) and *Beinn na Fhaoghla* (Benbecula)

In the Middle Ages, North and South Uist, and Benbecula, had been part of the core power base of the Lordship of the Isles. The islands were held by MacDonalds and these families continued in power after the forfeiture of the Lordship, as late as the 19th century in South Uist. However, this continuity did not prevent changes in the manage-

Fig. 66. The
Hattersley loom

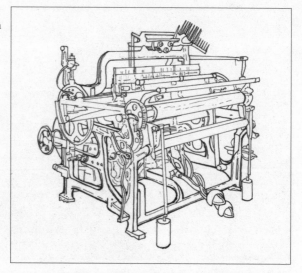

ment of the estates and in the settlement patterns of the landscape.

The population of the islands rose throughout the Post-Mediaeval Period, pushing the boundaries of sustainability on the marginal landscape, and it became increasingly important for landowners to generate a direct cash income from their tenants in the 18th century. The growing population cultivated more land, with fields spreading into higher, peaty soils, worked as lazy beds using spades rather than ploughs. The machair was overcultivated and not allowed to rest and revegetate between crops. This overuse of machair is one explanation for the devastating impacts of a series of storms in the late 17th and 18th centuries, when blown sand engulfed fields, and extreme coastal erosion reputedly destroyed whole townships.

Excavations at *Airigh Mhuillinn* (Milton) (Site 130, Fig. 67) in South Uist give a picture of life in the southern part of the islands in the late 18th to 19th centuries. The houses were thatched, with little or no evidence of windows, orientated downslope, with the lower part of the building used as a byre for animals. The hearth was in the middle of the floor. The walls were very thick, constructed of dry stonework, with a core of clay and peat. In Uist by this time, local pottery was not produced, and finds from the houses included factory-made English and Scottish pottery and fragments of wine bottles.

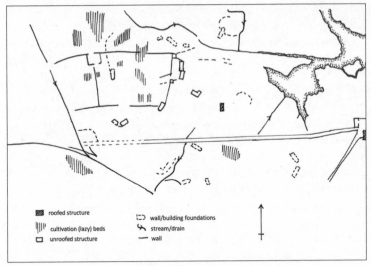

Fig. 67. *Airigh Mhuillinn* (Milton), *Uibhist a' Deas* (South Uist)

Most of the pottery was bowls, reflecting a diet based on porridge and potatoes, and much of it was the very cheapest pottery available from Stoke on Trent, Edinburgh and Glasgow, often imperfect seconds. Despite this, several pieces showed evidence of being repaired, indicating how important it was to its owners.

Airigh Mhuillinn was excavated because it was linked to Flora MacDonald, the famous Jacobite heroine, who was reputedly born there, as daughter of the local tacksman. However, the excavated settlement dates to long after her birth in 1722, and the earlier location of the settlement is not known. The Outer Hebrides, despite having links to both sides of the Rebellion, was a safe haven for Prince Charles Edward Stuart. He landed in *Eirisgeigh* (Eriskay) in 1745 and, fleeing with a £30,000 bounty on his head, returned to the islands after Culloden in 1746. Flora MacDonald is famed for rescuing him ahead of the government forces by disguising him as her Irish maid and travelling with him from Uist to Skye.

There was emigration from Uist from the 18th century onwards, initially voluntary. For example, in 1772, a community of 100 Catholics from *Baghasdal* (Boisdale) left for North America, with their tacksman, after their Protestant landowner threatened to evict them if they did not convert. Economic and political pressures also drove individual migration, but, despite this, the population of the islands grew, largely because of an increasing dependency on the staple crop of potatoes. Potatoes were adopted late, and reluctantly, by a population who were too close to the edge of subsistence to risk trying anything new. In 1743, Macdonald of Clan Ranald is said to have forced his tenants to grow potatoes, which they then dumped on his doorstep in Benbecula, stating that he could force them to grow the things, but he couldn't force them to eat them! However, the success of the crop, which provided over fivefold the calorie yield of barley or oats, soon meant that they became the staple food of the islanders.

An early estate map of South Uist – Bald's map of 1805 – was surveyed to provide the basis of changes in land management, like Chapman's map of Lewis. Clan Ranald reorganised South Uist townships near good kelping shores, such as *Cill Donnain*, dividing land into small crofts whose tenants had to work burning the seaweed, in return for their tenancies. The success of these tiny landholdings was dependent upon cultivation of potatoes for food, and external work to provide cash for rents and other necessities.

However, the kelping industry collapsed in the 1820s, South Uist was sold to a mainland landowner, Gordon of Cluny, in 1838, and the potato crops failed from 1846 onwards. The townships, which had provided kelp labourers, were Cleared, and people were resettled on the small island of Eriskay, or on the eastern coast of Uist, and, as the catastrophic crop failures set in, Gordon of Cluny Cleared over 30% of the islands' population, exporting them to eastern Canada. The remainder of the population, on poor land, lived lives of grinding poverty, recorded in their Napier Commission testimony in the 1880s, which noted families of eight or more individuals occupying one- or two-room houses, with no furniture, in *Dalabrog* (Daliburgh).

Barraigh (Barra)

The family who held Barra after the Middle Ages were the MacNeils, based at *Caisteal Chiosamuil* (Kisimul Castle) (see Fig. 49) in *Bagh a' Chaisteil* (Castlebay). They had held the island under the Lordship and had a power base which was deeply rooted in shipping, as reflected in their maritime castle on a rock in the centre of the best harbour in the island. At the end of the Middle Ages, the MacNeil of Barra was reputed to have 200 fighting men, whose families would have held land on Barra and the islands to the south. Given that some families would have provided more than one man of fighting age, a reasonable population estimate for Barra at the beginning of the 16th century might therefore be around 500–750 people. By 1750 the population was 1,285, and by the 1830s it was over 2,000.

As with Uist, Barra was held by its traditional landowners up to the middle of the 19th century. The national pressures of social and economic change had a similarly severe impact on Barra. There are few visible remains of the mediaeval landscape because the rapidly growing post-mediaeval population cultivated ever-larger areas, planting over, recycling and building on the remains of earlier settlements and buildings. The population moved away from living on the machair as it grew, to allow the maximum cultivation of the best land, and by the beginning of the Post-Mediaeval Period, most settlements were in the areas where they are now, set back from the shoreline on the boundary between hill grazing and the coastal plains. Although in the 1500s shielings and moorland grazing were still in use on Barra, seasonal transhumance stopped by, at the latest, the early 19th century. This may reflect the shift from grazing cattle, which need active herding, to grazing sheep, which need less attention when they are out on the hill.

Excavations at post-mediaeval settlements in Barra have given us a glimpse of everyday life on the island. At Gortein there were three generations of small turf and stone houses dated to the 18th and 19th centuries, and at *Buaile nam Bodach* the township was occupied from the early 19th century to the early 20th century. Finds from these sites included local handmade pottery, but also included imports of colourful bowls from Scottish and English potteries. The dominance of bowls over plates reflects the diet of potatoes and porridge, served communally in a large dish, and eaten by hand or with a horn spoon. The importance of small imported luxuries is marked by broken clay pipes for smoking tobacco, and pieces of teapots and teacups.

In the 1820s, the Barra estate was in financial trouble, and the landowner embarked upon major changes to attempt to revive its fortunes. Large-scale Clearance saw tenants moved from the more fertile western townships to the east coast and replaced by cattle and sheep farms. A factory (Site 126) was built to process kelp, to keep the industry going. However, by the 1830s, the investment had bankrupted the estate, and it was sold to Gordon of Cluny in 1840, who thus became landlord of the whole of the southern part of the Outer Hebrides. His solution to the problems caused by the collapse of the potato harvest in the 1850s was the same as in Uist; between 1850 and 1851 over 30% of the population were removed from the island and sent to mainland Scotland or North America. Oral tradition in the islands tells of violence and force used to remove people, often with nothing but the clothes on their backs and at the cost of splitting families, so that some who were away from home remained, while others were dragged to the ship and disappeared to Quebec. This was when the township at *Buaile nam Bodaich* was Cleared, and the crofting tenants replaced by fishermen and a mainland farmer. The population of the island did not start to recover for another 20 years.

Changing landscapes

The end of the 19th century, then, saw a very different landscape in the islands to that of the 16th century. The multitude of small settlements, variously organised as communal farms, tacks and sublets, had disappeared. Large farms and occasional planned crofting townships covered the whole of the islands, occupied by a population who were densely packed into relatively small areas of the landscape. The machair was relatively unoccupied, and the poorer areas of land densely cultivated with potatoes. In the northern part of the islands, families still went to the shielings on the moor each year from May to September, to maximise the use of grazing.

Island estates had established building standards as part of their leases, and most people in the southern part of the islands lived in houses with chimneys and with walls separating the animals from the people. This was an innovation that was adopted late in Lewis, where many houses at the turn of the 20th century were still without chimneys and had a central hearth on the floor.

Public buildings, including churches and chapels, Protestant in the north and Catholic in the south, and state schools, were frequent throughout the islands. Small shops had started to appear in most districts, but families were still largely self-sufficient in basic foodstuffs, and in Lewis, handmade local pottery was still being produced.

The islands were still amongst the poorest areas in the British Isles, however. Houses were small, families were large, and malnutrition and endemic illnesses, particularly tuberculosis, were significant problems. Cash incomes were typically earned by working away from the islands and seasonal migration was very common, with people working in the herring fleets, or in service in big houses or hospitals on the mainland. In many ways, the late 19th-century Hebrideans were materially less well-off than their mediaeval predecessors.

Religion and ritual

The impact of the Reformation in the islands was dramatic. Although there are few pre-Reformation documents relating to the islands, there were probably priests in most parishes. Monastic foundations were scattered throughout the islands, helping to provide social services, such as medical provision, education and hospitality. However, from the 16th century, for at least 100 years, the islands had very few clergy. There may have been ministers in Harris, *Barabhas* (Barvas) and possibly *Steornabhagh* (Stornoway). Elsewhere, there was a gap of between 100 and 200 years before there was wider provision of ministers in most parishes.

At the Reformation, education and social care provision devolved to the parishes of Scotland. In areas with no minister, these aspects of life would have largely collapsed, except for the wealthiest classes. In the landscape, this is visible in the dereliction of mediaeval churches. Those that survive today, such as *Roghadal* (Rodel) in Harris, St Moluag's in *Nis* (Ness), Lewis, and *Cille Bharra* (Kilbar) in Barra, were renovated and reroofed in the 19th century. Elsewhere in the islands, the mediaeval churches fell into disrepair. Their ruins and foundations can be seen in the older cemeteries, many of which are still in use, at places like *Gabhsann* (Galson) on the west coast of Lewis and *Tobha Mor* (Howmore) in South Uist.

Another side effect of the lack of ministers was the development of unorthodox religious practice. In the 18th century, ministers recorded local traditions, such as an annual celebration in Ness, in Lewis, when beer would be brewed and poured out as a sacrifice to a sea-god called Shony, culminating in a feast and party around the ruins of St Moluag's Church. This was probably a relic of the feast of St John, which falls close to midsummer, but after a century and more of ecclesiastical neglect it had developed a local character. The ruins of the mediaeval churches and holy wells also served as places for healing, frequently for toothache, madness or infertility, complaints which reveal a great deal about the nature of life at the time. This might involve a ritual, for example walking around the ruins of a church three times in a clockwise direction, and then sleeping in the ruins overnight, or praying and leaving a stone or pebble on the site of the ancient altar.

In South Uist and Barra, Catholicism continued after the Reformation, reflecting the Catholicism of the landowning MacDonalds and MacNeils. This was a stronghold of the Counter-Reformation, with priests sent from Ireland and France in the 17th and 18th centuries to provide for the islanders, and to serve as missionaries to the northern part of the islands. However, as the ban on Catholics in public life continued into the 18th and 19th centuries, landowners converted and began to put pressure onto their tenants to do likewise. In the late 18th century and 19th century, Protestant Macdonald landowners in Uist started to dispossess tenants who would not convert, and similar pressure was put on tenants in Barra in the first half of the 19th century. However, it is noticeable that in Uist, Benbecula and Barra mediaeval stone crosses and the ruins of many mediaeval churches still stand. North of the Sound of Harris, in Lewis and Harris, this is not the case, and the Catholic population of the Southern Isles probably protected and respected the remains of their religious past, even while they did not have the resources to maintain their religious life.

Following the 1745 Rebellion, as part of the campaign to 'civilise' the Highlands and Islands, Parliamentary churches and manses were built in the islands. *Sgarastadh* (Scarista) Church in Harris is a fine example of this; the church stands behind the ruins of its mediaeval predecessor, which is beneath the centre of the old graveyard, and adjacent to the manse (see Fig. 68). While the size of the new churches and manses typically reflected the population of an area, the enormous manse at *Cuidhir* in Barra (Site 127, Fig. 70) must instead have reflected the status of the landowner; it is very hard to believe that there were ever large numbers of Protestants resident in Barra.

Fig. 68. *Sgarastadh* (Scarista) Church, behind the site of *Cille Bhridge, Na Hearadh* (Harris)

Moving into the 20th century

The period between the 1500s and the beginning of the 20th century was not long, in archaeological terms; compare this period of 500 years to the 3,500 years of the Neolithic Period, for example! However, it saw huge change in the islands' landscape, subsistence and culture, and included long periods of terrible disruption, civil unrest and uncertainty, resulting in a community which was amongst the poorest in Great Britain. This time of change shaped the culture and society of the modern period in the islands. Clearance and the cultural and physical distancing of landowners from their tenants led to a 20th-century community where a typical crofter might never meet or speak to the person who owned their land and would therefore have no real relationship with them. Insecurity of tenure, mobility and loss of land led to a sense of helplessness before the wishes and whims of landowners, and to the demands made by crofters on the Napier Commission for, above all else, security of tenure. The late provision of state education led to a huge demand for learning and teaching, but poverty restricted many from taking advantage of its benefits. Above all, though, coming into the 20th century, the legacy was the feeling tha, in order to succeed you had to leave; there was little hope of advancement, security or change to be had at home. We will discuss the impacts of this in the next chapter.

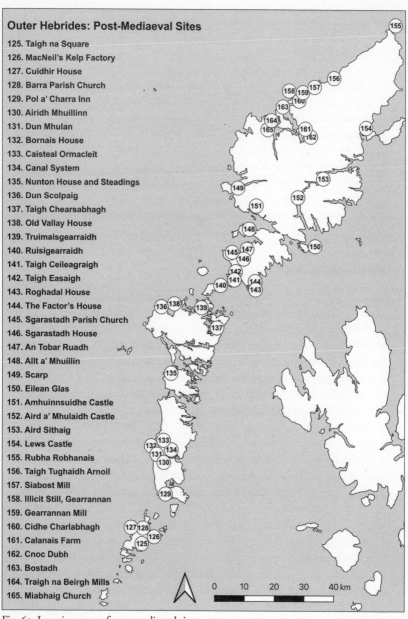

Outer Hebrides: Post-Mediaeval Sites

125. Taigh na Square
126. MacNeil's Kelp Factory
127. Cuidhir House
128. Barra Parish Church
129. Pol a' Charra Inn
130. Airidh Mhuillinn
131. Dun Mhulan
132. Bornais House
133. Caisteal Ormacleit
134. Canal System
135. Nunton House and Steadings
136. Dun Scolpaig
137. Taigh Chearsabhagh
138. Old Vallay House
139. Truimaisgearraidh
140. Ruisigearraidh
141. Taigh Ceileagraigh
142. Taigh Easaigh
143. Roghadal House
144. The Factor's House
145. Sgarastadh Parish Church
146. Sgarastadh House
147. An Tobar Ruadh
148. Allt a' Mhuillin
149. Scarp
150. Eilean Glas
151. Amhuinnsuidhe Castle
152. Aird a' Mhulaidh Castle
153. Aird Sithaig
154. Lews Castle
155. Rubha Robhanais
156. Taigh Tughaidh Arnoil
157. Siabost Mill
158. Illicit Still, Gearrannan
159. Gearrannan Mill
160. Cidhe Charlabhagh
161. Calanais Farm
162. Cnoc Dubh
163. Bostadh
164. Traigh na Beirgh Mills
165. Miabhaig Church

0   10   20   30   40 km

Fig. 69. Location map of post-mediaeval sites

GAZETTEER

Barraigh (Barra)

125. *Taigh na* Square, *Bagh a' Chaisteil* (Castlebay)   NL 6663 9829

In the main square in *Bagh a' Chaisteil*, on the main road.

    This rather splendid, large, plain building is one of the older buildings in *Bagh a' Chaisteil*. It was probably built as a kelp store, with accommodation upstairs, serving the kelp trade in the late 18th or first half of the 19th century. The ground floor was later adapted as a shop and used until recent years.

126. MacNeil's Kelp Factory, *Thiarabhagh*   NF 7082 0313
    (Northbay)

This site is north of the A888, in *Thiarabhagh*. Park by St Barr's Church and walk along the lane leading to the church house.

    In 1828, General Roderick MacNeil built a factory at *Thiarabhagh* to process kelp for a higher alkali content, adding value. At the time, the business employed 500 people, including the kelp gatherers, so would have been the largest source of employment in Barra. Unfortunately the venture failed, undermined by cheaper imports of alkali from the Mediterranean following the end of the Napoleonic Wars.

    Although the factory has been largely demolished, and the church house with a walled garden stands on the site, if you walk along the shore you can see that the sea wall is the wall of the former factory, with blocked sea doors for loading the kelp from boats at high tide. The sea wall continues to the east of the site as a wharf for shipping.

127. Cuidhir House   NF 6683 0361

This house in *Cuidhir* is in private hands, but can be viewed from the A888 road.

    Cuidhir House is the former Church of Scotland manse for Barra (Fig. 70). It was designed by John Loban of *Steornabhagh* (Stornoway)

Fig. 70. Cuidhir House, former Church of Scotland manse, *Barraigh* (Barra)

and is very like the former manse at *Sgarasta* (Scarista) in Harris, which was also designed by Loban (see Site 146). The house was built in 1814–16 as part of the push to provide ecclesiastical services throughout the Highlands and Islands, and its grandeur and fine architecture reflect the desired status of the national church. However, Barra was, and is, overwhelmingly Catholic in faith, and the Protestant congregation was never large.

128. Barra Parish Church, *Cuidhir* NF 6707 0340

The Church of Scotland parish church is a couple of hundred metres east along the road from the manse.

This building has been heavily renovated, and it is not obvious that it is early 19th century, designed by Alexander Robertson in 1825 and built about 10 years after the construction of the manse, above. It is a simple, relatively small, rectangular building, but the western wall was left deliberately blank to allow it to be easily extended into a larger T-plan church if required. The Protestant burial ground for Barra is to the north and east of the church.

Uibhist a' Deas (South Uist)

129. Pol a' Charra (*Polochar*) Inn   NF 7467 1441

On the southern end of South Uist, at the end of the road along the west coast.

There has been an inn here since the 17th century or earlier, serving the ferry routes into Uist before the construction of the Eriskay Causeway and ferry harbour. The eastern end and northern range of the present buildings are shown on the first edition of the Ordnance Survey in the 19th century, so are at least 150 years old, and they may contain the remains of earlier structures. A slipway leading from the parking area into the small natural tidal harbour in front of the building, and two nausts, or boathouses, in the headland to the west, emphasise the connection between the building and the sea.

130. *Airigh Mhuillinn* (Milton)   NF 7410 2691

The site is signposted from the A865.

As early as the first Ordnance Survey in this area, in 1878, one of the ruinous buildings in *Airigh Mhuillinn* (Fig. 67) was identified as the birthplace of Flora MacDonald (born *c.* 1722, died 1790) of Jacobite fame. A large memorial cairn stands in one of the ruins at the site, stating that the lady spent her early life in the building there, though the local story has it that this was the building in which she was born.

On this basis, archaeological work was carried out on the house and settlement in the mid 1990s. It became immediately evident that the building reputed to be her birthplace was built later than her childhood; its construction could be dated by pottery finds and a militia belt-buckle to about 1790, and it continued in use until around 1830. However, although this specific building was not tied to the life of the Jacobite heroine, her father was the tacksman of the township for a time during her childhood, so it is probable that she did live in the area.

The remains of the late 18th-century township are interesting to visit, regardless of their associations. The footings of several houses with their adjoining stackyards, a corn kiln and fields are visible, carefully located in relation to the local landscape for dry ground, light and shelter from the wind, giving an impression of the organic settlement pattern that was common in the islands before the agricultural changes of the 19th century.

131. Kelpers huts, *Dun Mhulan* (Dun Vulan),　　　NF 7170 2987
　　　Bornais (Bornish)

The machair road is passable by vehicles, but you must stop at the parking place before the promontory begins, as the road thereafter has been very severely damaged by storms and is only passable by foot.

On the northern edge of the peninsula which leads to *Dun Mhulan* are the remains of 24 small huts which were used by people cutting and burning kelp on this coast. The bothies are arranged around a rectangle, open towards the west, and would have provided accommodation and shelter for people whose homes were probably well away from the west coast.

There has been some excavation on this site, which showed that each hut was constructed of a circular mound of sand, with a rectangular room in the middle, formed by building cobble walls against the surface of the sand. They were entered from the east, the direction away from the prevailing westerly wind, probably to keep them warm, but possibly also to avoid the noxious smoke that would have been created by the kelp burning along the shoreline.

Most of the huts had small hearths, and pieces of pottery bowls, clay pipes, buttons and a broken mirror give a glimpse of daily life. A very early photograph shows the site in use, with thatched and turfed roofs on the huts, and local people and estate records suggest that the accommodation may have been built as late as the 1870s, as kelping remained an active industry in South Uist until the end of the 19th century.

132. Bornais House, *Bornais* (Bornish)   NF 7363 3003

Turn west off the A865 following signs for *Bornais*. The house is to the north of the road, just before you reach the machair. The house is in private ownership but can be seen from the road.

Bornais House may be the earliest of the large farmhouses on the South Uist machair. It is the physical representation of the process of Clearance which so changed the landscape of the islands in the late 18th and 19th centuries. The very plain architecture of the building, with relatively small windows in relation to the walls, suggests an early date, possibly in the late 18th century, before the large-scale reorganisation of the estate that was carried out under the ownership of Gordon of Cluny in the first half of the 19th century.

The farmhouse stands to the front of, and forming one side of, a steading around a square courtyard, following a typically symmetrical, 'improved' form of architecture markedly in contrast to the earlier forms used in the surrounding landscape. Its location on a knoll overlooking the surrounding landscape also emphasises the dominance of the building and its occupants over the land around.

Similar, though probably slightly later, farmhouses can be seen at *Airigh a' Mhuillin* (Milton House) and *Aisgernis* (Askernish House); these, together with Bornais House, formed the heart of the scheme to convert South Uist Estate to sheep farming in the 1830s.

133. *Caisteal Ormacleit* (Ormiclate/   NF 7399 3180
    Ormaclate Castle)

Turn west off the A865 to *Ormacleit*, then south at the crossroads towards the castle, which can be seen behind the farmhouse. Do not go into the building, as it is not safe. It can be observed from the road leading through the farm towards the machair.

Caisteal Ormacleit (Fig. 71) was built between 1701 and 1703 in a substantial township which was a gathering place for cattle for trading. It was constructed by Allan Macdonald of Clanranald for his wife, Lady Penelope, who is reputed to have told him that her father's henhouse was finer than the 16th-century Clanranald house that was on the site previously. The new castle, which was a fine, French-style

Fig. 71. *Caisteal Ormacleit* (Castle Ormiclate), *Uibhist a' Deas* (South Uist)

chateau, was only occupied for 12 years; it was destroyed by fire the day that Allan Macdonald was killed at the Jacobite Battle of Sherrifmuir in 1715.

The house is T-shaped in plan, and survey and excavation on the site has shown that it probably incorporates the remains of the earlier house. The ranges of service buildings to the east and west of the house may be part of the earlier building, and the western range contains an arched fireplace that may date to the late 16th century.

There are many local stories about this building, amongst them that it was roofed with marble. Recent excavations at the site found fragments of greenish stone slabs, which were probably used for the roofing and may explain this story. This stone could come from *Stulaidh*, an island on the east coast of Uist, or it may be from the west coast of the mainland or Inner Hebrides. Recent surveys suggest it was probably moved across the island using the canal system (Site 134) linking the east and west coast of South Uist. Little archaeological evidence survived within the building, however, where most of the finds were 19th and 20th century. It seems likely that anything which was reusable was taken from the house, including the worked stone around the windows and doors.

134. Canal system   NF 7662 3002

Take the road to *Loch Aineort* (Loch Eynort) west off the main road
and pass the first track to the left. Stop by the croft fence on the left
and follow it north to the loch. A footbridge crosses the canal at the
grid reference above.

Recent research has suggested that the canalised drains which link
Loch Aineort to the freshwater lochs to the north and west may be
18th century in origin. In the 1740s, machair drainage on the west
coast was started, but the proximity of the western end of this system
to *Caisteal Ormacleit* (Ormiclate Castle) may indicate that this system
was primarily for transport of goods from the sheltered, relatively deep
harbours of the east coast through to the settlements of the west coast.

This is only one of the possible canal systems in South Uist. A
later 18th-century canal was built to link *Loch Dalabrog* to the coast,
and local stories and early maps suggest that waterways were kept
open between some of the machair lochs during the Middle Ages for
movement of boats from one loch to another up the western coastline.

Beinn na Fhaoghla (Benbecula)

135. Nunton House and Steadings, *Baile*   NF 7644 5353
     nan Cailleach (Nunton)

On the B892, on the west coast of Benbecula. The house is in private
hands but can be seen from the road.

Nunton House was built in the early 18th century as the seat of
the Macdonalds of Clanranald, following the destruction of *Caisteal
Ormacleit* (Ormiclate Castle) (Site 133) in South Uist. It is now divided
into three houses and parts are derelict, but the arrangement of the
L-shaped building, with ranges to the south-west and north-west,
walled gardens to the front and rear, and two small formal pavilions
either side of its entrance, are still clear. In the late 18th century, the
gardens were said to contain many varieties of fruiting trees.

To the north of the house, the remains of a road lead south-east
into the heart of Benbecula, towards and crossing the large, 18th

century, north–south drain, and continuing to emerge at Griminish. To either side of this route, as far as the drain, the remains of field boundaries can be traced, marking the fields belonging to Nunton House.

One hundred metres to the north of the house is Nunton Steadings, now renovated as office space and a visitor centre by the Uist Building Preservation Trust. This is the earliest steading building in the Outer Hebrides; it was built in the late 18th century to serve Nunton Farm, and originally faced west. Alterations in the 19th century, when the western range was built, changed its orientation. A bell which originally hung in the bellcote is inscribed with the name of Ranald Macdonald of Clanranald, and the date 1776.

Uibhist a' Tuath (North Uist)

136. Dun Scolpaig Tower
NF 7310 7503

Park on the edge of the main road and walk north-west for 200m down the road towards Scolpaig Farm. Turn west onto the grassy remains of an old track towards the southern edge of the loch, where you can view the tower.

The island in this loch is said locally to have been a crannog, but nothing visible remains of its early origins. Instead, it is now the location of a folly, built by local doctor Alexander MacLeod around 1830. Survey of the site in 2008 confirmed that it is linked to the loch edge by a causeway constructed of rough stone, which has been damaged by erosion. As there were no finds made during the survey, the question of the date of the causeway remains unanswered.

137. *Taigh Chearsabhagh, Loch nam Madaigh* (Lochmaddy)
NF 7496 7528

Near the ferry terminal in *Loch nam Madaigh*, and a good place to get a cup of coffee while waiting for the boat.

Taigh Chearsabhagh (Fig. 72) has been a merchant's house, factor's office, and inn. It was built in 1741, on the site of a former salt house

Fig. 72. *Taigh Chearsabhagh, Loch nam Madaigh* (Lochmaddy), *Uibhist a' Tuath* (North Uist)

for the fishing trade. It has a separate external stable and storehouse, across the car park from the main building, and its own pier, contemporary with the building. The 18th-century building has been extended twice since 1990, and is now a multi-purpose community building, housing a shop, post office, café, museum, art studio and art gallery. It is the oldest building in *Loch nam Madaigh*.

138. Old Vallay House and the Chamberlain's   NF 77438 76005
House, *Bhalaigh* (Vallay)

Vallay island is tidally accessible from *Cladach Bhalaigh* on North Uist. Take local advice about crossing to the island and be extremely careful.

Two roofless 18th-century buildings stand to the east of Erskine Beveridge's Vallay House (Site 171). The older of these two buildings is the tacksman's house, Old Vallay House, built around 1727. This has crowstepped gables, and a carved datestone over the door commemorating the marriage of the tacksman, Ewen Macdonald, for whom the house was built, and Mary MacLean, in 1742. Although

this building was ruinous in the late 18th century, it was clearly renovated and reused, as it later became the servants' house for the adjacent
Chamberlain's House. In the 19th and early 20th century, it was used
as the laundry and had a school upstairs, but it had fallen out of use
by 1940, and is now in very poor condition.

The Chamberlain's House was built at the very end of the 18th
century as the farmhouse for Vallay. In the early 19th century, it served
as the manse for the minister of Bayhead, on North Uist, and it was
the main house on the island at the end of the 19th century, when
the island was purchased by Erskine Beveridge.

139. *Trumaisgearraidh* (Trumisgarry)   NF 8671 7478
Church and Manse

Turn west off the B893 following the signs to *Trumaisgearraidh*. The
church is visible from the main road. The former manse is privately
owned.

This church and manse, built to standardised Parliamentary
(Thomas Telford) plans in 1821, were part of the campaign of church
building of the late 18th and early 19th century, as were Cuidhir
Church and Manse (Site 127) in Barra. After the post-Reformation
ecclesiastical neglect of the islands, these buildings and their new
ministers were the first new churches in the islands for over 200 years.
Trumiasgearraidh Church also served as a school until its closure in
1941. The walls of the church stand to their full height, but it has been
roofless for many years.

Caolas na Hearadh (Sound of Harris)

140. *Ruisigearraidh* (Ruisgarry) Parliamentary   NF 93083 82027
Church, *Bearnaraigh* (Bernera)

This building is a private house now but can be seen from the road.

Like *Trumaisgerraidh*, Bernera also had a Parliamentary church
and associated manse, to Telford designs. The church was built in
1829 and still in use in the early 20th century, but by the 1960s it was

roofless and disused. The decline and disuse of these large churches in the 20th century was a physical reflection of a sharp decline in the islands' population, which fell by nearly 50% between 1901 and 2001.

141. *Taigh Ceileagraigh* (Killegray House),　　　　NF 9769 8414
　　Ceileagraigh (Killegray)

The island of Killegray was a wealthy tack (rented farm) in the Middle Ages and later, and a large 18th-century farmhouse stands on the island. The house was completely renovated in the 1990s for its present owner.

142. *Taigh Easaigh* (Ensay House), *Easaigh* (Ensay)　　NF 9808 8651

As with Killegray, Ensay was an important tack in the Harris Estate, and from the 18th century onwards probably a single farm. Ensay and Killegray were both famed for the quality of their farmland, and this is reflected in the size of the two farmhouses. *Taigh Easaigh* was updated in the 19th century as a sporting lodge, but the building itself is certainly 18th century, and may be earlier at its core. A small, late mediaeval chapel stands to the north of the house. It was restored in 1910 and renovated in 1979, and services are held in it by the Episcopal Church each year.

Na Hearadh (Harris)

143. *Roghadal* House (formerly Rodel Hotel)　　NG 0477 82906

This former hotel, now being renovated as a private house, is on the A859 road through *Roghadal* (Rodel).

Roghadal House (see Fig. 65) was the late 18th-century or earlier Laird's House for the Harris Estate. It is part of the complex of estate buildings based round the natural harbour in *Roghadal*, including the Factor's House (overleaf) and the church (Site 113). From the A859 road towards *Roghadal* from *An t-Ob* (Leverburgh) you can see on the southern side of the valley the line of the original road which linked the two harbours and their settlements.

The house was certainly in place at the end of the 18th century, when it was painted by William Daniell in his tour around the British Isles. It may include parts of earlier structures; there was an inn in *Roghadal* at an earlier date, and there must also have been some estate accommodation. However, the late 18th century saw an expansion of facilities under the ownership of Alexander MacLeod of Bernera, who also constructed the harbour walls in front of the house, which are still in use. On the harbour wall, a 19th-century iron hand crane, for unloading cargo, can be seen.

In 1850, this house was the location of a violent and romantic episode, the Balranald Elopement, when a young couple from Uist were forced to land in Harris because of bad weather. The young woman, niece of the occupant of *Roghadal* House, was imprisoned by her uncle, and her lover stormed the house with a group of his friends, successfully freeing her and fleeing to the mainland. The couple were married in Gretna and emigrated to Australia.

The house was extended with a single-storey wing in the 19th century, and was used as a sporting lodge by Earl Dunmore, before it became a hotel in the 20th century. It was extensively renovated, with much loss of character, in 2001, and has recently been restored as a private house.

144. The Factor's House   NG 0461 8330

This building is also on the A859 road in the centre of *Roghadal* (Rodel). It is in a dangerous condition so should not be entered. It can be seen from the road, or the back of the house can be viewed from the opposite side of the bay.

Although locally called 'the Factor's House', this building probably started its life as a girnal, or grain store, for the estate. It may date to the same period of estate development as *Roghadal* House (Site 143) – the late 18th century – but both buildings could well incorporate parts of earlier estate buildings.

The building is of two storeys, the lower being a storehouse, opening with three doors to the rear into an enclosed yard with a high stone wall for security. The yard has a cart entrance built into the wall. Domestic accommodation was on the second storey, entered by a forestair at the front of the building.

145. *Sgarastadh* (Scarista) Parish Church   NG 0075 9278

On the A859 at *Sgarastadh Mhor*. Parking is available outside the church.

The present church was built in 1840 to replace a church which had been constructed in the 1780s by Alexander MacLeod of Bernera, but which was ruinous by 1839. There had been at least three earlier churches on the site; the ancient graveyard just to the north of the present church was the location of one of these, which has been covered over by generations of burials.

The church is a simple building, with no internal gallery. Until recently, it preserved original features including an integrated precentor's box on the pulpit, where the precentor stands to lead the singing, and a sounding board above to help project the unamplified voice of the minister. The pews appear to have been lengthened, and there may originally have been a long communion table down the centre of the church.

146. *Sgarastadh* House (Scarista Manse)   NG 0078 9289

On the A859 at *Sgarastadh Mhor*, now a hotel.

The former manse at *Sgarastadh* (Fig. 73) is virtually identical in its original form to the former manse at Cuidhir in Barra (Site 127). Constructed by John Loban of *Steornabhagh* (Stornoway) in 1827, it is plain and symmetrical. The wing which extends at right angles to the rear of the building may be earlier than the front of the house; it has smaller, fewer, irregularly placed window openings.

The house was used as a manse until the mid 20th century, and then stood empty for some time until revived as a hotel. Many of the interior details, including shutters and chimneypieces, survived, giving a good impression of the status of a 19th-century minister and the public role that their manse was expected to fulfil.

Fig. 73. *Sgarastadh* (Scarista) House, former Church of Scotland manse, *Na Hearadh* (Harris)

147. *An Tobar Ruadh* ('the red well')   NG 0193 9381

Park in the parking area to the west of the road, just south of the site. The well is just off the road, on the northern side of a small burn.

The *Tobar Ruadh* is a typical Western Isles well, consisting of a semi-circular drystone wall constructed around an iron-rich spring, and capped with a stone slab. These wells had local reputations for healing, particularly of illnesses such as toothache and madness, which give interesting insights into the nature of historic life in the islands and the needs of the local population! This well and its healing properties were mentioned by Martin Martin in his early 18th-century description of the Western Isles.

148. *Allt a' Mhuillin* watermill, *Tarasaigh*   NB 0261 0029 (Taransay)

Walk 1.2km up the valley which leads north-north-east from the village on Taransay, following the stream.

The name of the stream leading south from Loch an Duin on Taransay to the village of *Paibeil* is *Allt a' Mhuillin* (Mill Stream). This grid reference will lead you to the well-preserved remains of a mill but, if you look carefully, you will see other, earlier mill foundations along the stream as well. There were often several mills on a stream, and more than one may have been in use at the same time. These are horizontal watermills, where the grinding stones were driven by a small, horizontal waterwheel mounted directly beneath the stone, with no gears. The mills were not very efficient, the grinding stones were relatively small, and a community often needed more than one mill to provide meal.

149. Scarp   NA 9881 1359

This island is just off the west coast of Harris; it is sometimes possible to get a boat over to the island from *Huisinis*.

The settlement on the east coast of Scarp has been abandoned since 1971, but it is worth visiting to get an impression of the layout of an island village at the turn of the 19th to 20th century. At most 213 people lived on the island in the late 19th century, on 16 subdivided crofts. There are remains of a late mediaeval chapel in the burial ground, a late 19th-century school and schoolhouse, and a 19th-century Mission House with accommodation next to it. Some of the houses are still roofed and used by island families as holiday homes, and the remains of traditional thatched houses are still clear, particularly at the northern end of the village.

Scarp was the site of an experiment in providing post by rocket, in 1934, when German emigrant Gerhardt Zucker attempted to send post from the mainland of Harris to the island using gunpowder rockets. Both attempts failed when the rocket exploded. A film called *The Rocket Post* was made about the attempt in 2004. Successful rocket mail deliveries were later made in America, but the service was never economically viable, and the development of airmail made it unnecessary.

150. *Eilean Glas* Lighthouse, *Scalpaigh* (Scalpay)   NG 2474 9471

Follow the road and the peat road toward the Scalpay wind turbine, then turn right before you arrive at the turbine. There are two parking/turning places on the peat road. It is then a walk of 1.5km on a surfaced path to the lighthouse.

Eilean Glas on Scalpay (Plate 14) was one of the earliest lighthouses constructed by the Northern Lighthouse Board. The circular tower, the stub of which is visible at the seaward edge of the complex of buildings, was commissioned jointly between the Lighthouse Board and the local landowner, Captain MacLeod, in 1787. Although the Lighthouse Board wished to use their own design, engineer and masons, Captain MacLeod started building the lighthouse using the local tacksman, Mr Campbell, and local workmen, to a larger scale. Once this work had been inspected, the Board continued the work. The interior of the lighthouse was fitted out by a joiner from North Uist and a house was constructed next to the tower, to house the keepers.

The early lighthouse was used until 1824, when it was succeeded by the existing Robert Stevenson tower. This stands in a group of buildings, including jetties, houses, storage, accommodation for keepers and their families, fields and a walled garden. The buildings are decorated in a Graeco-Egyptian style, including lotus-headed iron washing-line poles. A new keeper's cottage and foghorn were added in the early 20th century, and a helipad and automated light later in the 20th century.

151. Amhuinnsuidhe Castle   NB 4956 7806

Directly on the B887 road to *Huisinis*, which crosses through the front garden, running immediately in front of the house. The house is run as a hotel.

This grand, mid 19th-century house, completed in 1867, was designed in a Scots baronial style for the Earl of Dunmore by David Bryce. It was in the latest fashion, with crowstepped gables and military detailing, reflecting the aristocratic interest in all things Scots and historical, a fashion led by Queen Victoria and Prince Albert at Balmoral. The large ground-floor windows demonstrate, however, that the building was never really built to be defended.

Immediately in front of the house, just across the lawn, is the salmon river that determined the location of the house. It has been landscaped to increase its beauty! The shooting and fishing are still an important source of income for the hotel. The move from an estate centre based on a fine natural harbour, at *Roghadal* (Rodel), to an estate centre based on a salmon river, clearly reflects the social and economic changes that took place in the Highlands and Islands of Scotland between the 18th and 19th centuries.

152. *Aird a' Mhulaidh* (Ardvourlie) Castle   NB 1894 1053

To the east of the A859, next to the border of Lewis and Harris.

This small 'castle' is a shooting lodge built in the 19th century for the Earl of Dunmore. It was effectively a holiday cottage, used particularly for deer hunting in the hills of North Harris. It followed in a long tradition of deer hunting here; Martin Martin's early 18th-century description of the islands notes that this area was reserved for deer hunting by the MacLeods of Harris, as the adjacent *Pairc* area of Lewis was for the MacLeods of Lewis.

The houses which make up the small crofting township around the castle building were originally occupied by the families of estate workers, who provided service in the castle and on the land. A small school was run in the castle for the children of the estate.

Leodhas (Lewis)

153. *Aird Sithaig* (Loch Seaforth Head)   NB 27465 16642

Park at the fank and walk westwards, keeping the fence on your left. You will need to cross two fences to reach the headland.

Aird Sithaig is a small, south-facing headland on the northern shore of *Loch Siophort* (Loch Seaforth). It is covered with archaeological remains of mediaeval and later date, which appear to form at least three successive landscapes.

Most recently, probably in the early 19th century, the headland was used for kelp burning. Across the top of earlier remains, a series of small huts and kilns were constructed. The people who worked at the site would have lived temporarily in the huts while the seaweed was being cut and burned to make alkali. This was hard work, as the kelp was cut by hand in cold tidal waters, then dried, and burned in kilns, continually turned and raked, to produce the chemical. The cold, wet and fumes had serious impacts on the workers' health, but there was little choice of work available locally.

Before this, the headland was occupied by a rectangular house and a shed, the footings of which can be easily seen at the landward end. These buildings, and the field system that surround them, pre-date the clearance of the land in the 19th century. Under the remains of the house you can see the footings of an earlier house, which had curved walls. This architectural form, sub-rectangular with curved long walls, is typically Viking Age, and the earlier building may date to the period when the islands were part of the Scandinavian world.

At the southern, seaward point, a turf-covered wall cuts off the end of the headland, forming a small promontory enclosure. Within this are the footings of two curved, cellular structures and a rectangular stone building. This promontory enclosure may be either prehistoric or late mediaeval. Erosion has reduced its area, which would have been larger in the past. The Mackenzie family built a castle at *Aird Sithaig* in the early 17th century, when they took over the island from the MacLeods, and this may be its location.

154. Lews Castle (Seaforth Lodge), *Steornabhagh*   NB 420 331
    (Stornoway)

Park at the museum car park behind the castle. The ground floor of the castle is open to the public except when booked for private events.

This gothic country house (Plate 15) was built in the mid 19th century by Sir James Matheson, to update and replace the 17th- or 18th-century Seaforth Lodge which had been the centre of the MacKenzie Lewis Estate. It was designed by a fashionable Glasgow architect, and funded by the proceeds of the Far Eastern trading company, Jardine, Matheson & Co., which Matheson had co-founded and developed selling tea and opium during the Chinese Opium Wars. The grandeur of the building reflects Matheson's status as one of the largest landholders in the British Isles in later life.

Recent renovations of the castle revealed parts of Seaforth Lodge encapsulated within the later building, including the full height of one gable wall. The internal plan form of the present building is partly determined by the pre-existing house, which was a much more modest structure of harled local stone. Reused stonework and some late 18th-century illustrations of the town have suggested the possibility that the earliest part of Seaforth Lodge might have been a tower house, and therefore earlier in date than previously thought, but this has not been confirmed.

The entire building has been recently restored and repaired; the service quarters at the back were demolished and replaced by a museum and archive buildings. The ground-floor rooms, which have been decorated in their original style, with as much of the original detail preserved as possible, are open to the public, while the upper floor is let as holiday accommodation.

The surrounding gardens, which are also being restored, were designed and planted by the Mathesons from the mid 19th century on, following the Clearance of the local settlement of *Gearraidh Cruiadh*. An enclosure wall, with gate lodges, was built, an arboretum, terraced gardens, glasshouses and kitchen gardens were laid out, and battlemented sea walls built along the shore. Following Matheson's death, a marble monument in his memory was raised by his widow. It was restored in 2005 and is visible from the town.

The estate and castle were sold in 1891 to Lord Leverhulme, and the castle was given to the people of the parish of *Steornabhagh* in 1923, since when it has been in public hands.

155. *Rubha Robhanais* (Butt of Lewis)   NB 5197 6648
     Lighthouse

Follow the A857 road north, turning north off onto the B8013 or the B8014, and then at their northern end turning onto the unnamed paved road which leads to the lighthouse. There is parking at the end of the road.

The Butt of Lewis Lighthouse (Fig. 74) is one of the many designed and built by the company of D. & T. Stevenson in the second half of the 19th century, constructed by D.A. Stevenson in 1862. It marks the northern end of the Isle of Lewis, and the western side of

Fig. 74. *Rubha Robhanais* (Butt of Lewis Lighthouse), *Nis* (Ness), *Leodhas* (Lewis)

the entrance to the relatively sheltered shipping channel of the Minch. It had a keeper until 1997, when it was one of the last lighthouses in Scotland to be automated.

The tall tower itself is, unusually, of red brick, which was imported to the island, being landed at a small harbour, Port Stoth, less than 1km to the south of the light on the east coast. An enclosed courtyard of keepers' cottages is immediately to the south of the light. In 1940, the light was strafed by German aircraft.

156. *Taigh Tughaidh Arnoil* (Arnol Blackhouse)   NB 31069 49238

Turn north off the A858 into Arnol, following the signs for the black-house. There is parking just to the north of the monument.

The thatched house at Arnol is run as a museum by Historic Environment Scotland. The roofless ruins across the road and the two-room 'white house' are also part of the attraction.

The descriptive term 'blackhouse' has its roots in the derogatory use of the adjective 'black' meaning poor, primitive, bad, as, for example, in 'black magic'. In the 17th and 18th centuries, 'blackhouse' didn't necessarily mean that a house was coloured black. However, the physical contrast between a drystone house, and a house built with mortared walls, which appeared lighter on the outside, reinforced the use of the term, and it is now the name for a house built with unmortared walls and normally a thatched roof.

This house was built at the end of the 19th century and occupied up until 1964. It was not much modernised during its use; the open fire remained in the centre of the floor, and there were no chimneys or gables in the building. The walls are constructed of unmortared, 'dry' stone, with a core of mixed clay, stone and peat holding the stone faces together. The hipped roof has a heavy covering of thatch, which would traditionally have been made from whatever was available but is now of straw. The thatch is held on with ropes weighted with stones, and the rafters of the roof are tied down internally to pegs and iron bars built into the walls. The byre is at the lower end of the house, so that the central drain empties out of the building, and the two living rooms are at the upper end of the house, to take advantage of the rising warmth from the animals in the byre.

The house has internal wooden walls dividing up the rooms, which was a requirement introduced by the estate in the 18th century. There was reputedly some resistance to building dividing walls and shutting the animals away from a view of the fire, which was thought to be good for their wellbeing.

The roofless house across the road shows the many alterations and extensions which were typical of such buildings, reflecting the growth and contraction of the family using them. Quite often a cluster of houses would be built back to back, with separate entrances, as young people started their own families.

157. *Muillin agus Ath Shiaboist* (Shawbost Mill   NB 2444 4633
    and corn-drying kiln)

Park in the small parking area beside the loch, and follow the path for 390m north across rough grazing, to the mill and kiln

This horizontal watermill, a so-called 'Norse' mill, was in use until the 1930s, after which it fell derelict. In the 1960s, the students and teachers at the local school reconstructed the mill and built a corn-drying kiln here. It is a fine example of how one of these mills would have looked when in use. The lade, undercroft, and wooden machinery are all as they would have been in a working mill.

The kiln would not normally have been near the mill or the houses of the township, because of the risk of fire. Typically kiln buildings stood a little separate, but close enough that the drying grain could be watched continually, often by a child, to ensure that it didn't catch fire, as it lay on the grid over the bowl of the kiln, with the warm air from the flue of the fire passing through it.

158. Illicit Still, *Gearrannan* (Garenin)   NB 1925 4513

Follow the signposted coastal footpath north from *Gearrannan* village over the Aird Mhor, for around 950m, and immediately after you leave the first big headland, turn north along the bottom of an outcropping crag forming the south-western edge of a small valley. The footings of the building are about 100m along at the bottom of the crag, amongst tumbled boulders.

Gearrannan was a township with poor land, and densely occupied. In the 19th century, and probably earlier, illicit stills in the immediate area around the settlement generated cash to pay the rent. A small excavation was carried out on this building in the 1990s, which found the remains of the fire which heated the still, and the drains leading from it. Fragments of demijohn jars confirmed the use of the building.

The location of this still, concealed beneath a rock outcrop, close to running water and to an accessible, though dangerous, bay, are typical. Whisky production needed water, the building was difficult to find, and the product could be easily shipped away by people who knew the coast and shoreline.

159. *Gearrannan* (Garenin) Mill   NB 2097 4462

Follow the coastal path west from *Dail Mor* (Dalmore) for 800m, over the first ridge, cross the fence line using the stile near the shore, and then turn north, following the fence line for around 500m to come to the remains of the mill.

The stream which marks the boundary between the townships of *Gearrannan* and *Dail Mor* is called *Allt a' Mhuillin*, the Mill Stream, and this mill (Plate 16) is the best preserved of the many mills along it. This mill was ruinous on the mid 19th-century Ordnance Survey map, but it may have been brought back into use later in the century. There were mills along this stream for several hundred years, as rental documents from the 1700s show the tacksman of *Dail Mor* paying extra rental for a mill or mills.

You can see the two-storey structure of the building, with the lower chamber which would have housed the horizontal waterwheel, and the upper chamber where the grinding stones were. If you walk a little further inland along the valley, you can also trace the covered lade, or aqueduct, which brought the water from the stream to the mill.

160. *Cidhe Charlabhagh* (Carloway Pier)   NB 1923 4224

Turn west off the A858 at *Carlabhagh* Bridge, immediately descending to the lower road beside the river, and following it westwards until it comes to the pier

The district of *Carlabhagh* ('the bay of the men', Old Norse) is named after the sea inlet which stretches in from the western coast. This has been an important harbour for at least 1,000 years. There was originally a fort, probably a broch, on a natural spit of land extending into the inlet at *Borghaston* ('the village of the fort', Old Norse). This was largely demolished when a quay was built in the late 19th century, as part of a planned expansion of the herring fisheries on the west coast of the Isle of Lewis.

There was an 18th-century building on the shore, which had probably originally served as a salt house for the fishing industry. The southern wing of this single-storey stone building, which was originally

T-shaped, still stands as part of the complex of fisheries buildings on the now extended pier. It may be one of the few survivors of an early phase of organised, pre-19th century herring fisheries; documents from the 16th century onwards emphasise the importance of the fisheries and the involvement of both the English and the Dutch in their exploitation.

161. *Calanais* (Callanish) Farm   NB 2134 3278

Follow the signs to the *Calanais* standing stones; the farmhouse stands just between the car park and the visitor centre.

Calanais farmhouse was an inn in the mid 19th century, serving a landing on the shoreline immediately to its east, from which a ferry linked *Calanais* and *Linsiadar* on the other side of *Loch Rog Beag*. It is probably the building shown at *Calanais* on Murdoch Mackenzie's coastal chart of Lewis in 1750, making it one of the earliest surviving buildings on the western coast of the island.

By the end of the 19th century, a post office had been included in the inn, and in the 1930s, a telephone box had been added. It later served as the farmhouse for Calanais Farm.

162. *Cnoc Dubh*, shieling hut   NB 2319 3019

Park on the road and walk 145m east up the track towards the fank, where you will see the reconstructed shieling hut.

The area around the modern fank is a rich archaeological land-scape, used over thousands of years. As you walk up towards the shiel-ing hut, you will notice a large outcrop of white quartz on the crag to your right. This was used as a source of stone for making tools in prehistory.

The shieling hut is shown as a ruin on the mid 19th-century maps. It is a stone-roofed, beehive-shaped building, using a drystone construction technique called corbelling, which was used from the Neolithic Period onwards. The stone walls were kept stable by a cover-ing of turfs, which were replaced yearly. Later shieling buildings often had timber and turf or thatch roofs. Archaeological work in this area has shown that sometimes the land around the shieling was cultivated and at other times not, presumably depending partly on the climate, and partly on the level of population and the demand for land.

Shieling huts, which were normally only used in the summer, can be thought of as stone tents; they were small compared to the buildings on the shore, which were lived in during the winter. They did not accommodate animals, and the people who used them to sleep in were spending most of their time outside, herding cattle and sheep, and doing dairy work.

The remains of thousands of these buildings, of various periods, emphasise the importance of the resources of the moor to the community's survival. Taking animals to the summer grazings allowed the crops to grow undisturbed on the land by the shore, while people hunted and gathered wild food such as berries, game birds, eggs and fish. The animals got new, clean grazing while they were in milk, and butter and cheese were made to store for the winter. Importantly, too, the social connections that people made when they were out on the moor were often different from those they had on the coast; a lot of courting was done out at the summer shielings.

163. *Bostadh* (Bosta), *Bearnaraigh Mor*   NB 138 401
      (Great Bernera)

Park at the parking area near the cemetery, at the northern end of the B8059 *Bearnaraigh* road.

The deserted township of *Bostadh*, at the northern end of Great Bernera, is a lovely site to visit. The scattered footings of the 19th-century houses can be seen in the valleys leading away from the shore. The settlement was occupied at least from the Iron Age (Site 81) but was Cleared when the peat ran out in 1878, leaving the occupants with no fuel. Some people returned to *Circebost* (Kirkibost) in the south of the island, from where they had been Cleared around 20 years earlier, and others moved elsewhere. The village has never been reoccupied, and it is now part of the grazings of Tobson.

164. *Traigh na Beirgh* mills   NB 0995 3551

Park at the campsite and walk 550m around the southern end of *Loch na Cuilc*, sticking closely to the edge of the rocky crags, to avoid the marsh. This brings you to the bottom of *Allt na Muilne*.

The ruins of five horizontal watermills can be seen on this short, steep, 150m length of stream, falling from *Loch Bharabhat* at the top, to *Loch na Cuilc* at the bottom. None of these are shown on the first edition Ordnance Survey map, but the stream was already called the Mill Stream at that time.

Walking to the top of the stream takes you to *Loch Bharabhat*, and an Iron Age roundhouse on a crannog (Site 79).

165. *Miabhaig* (Miavaig) Church,   NB 0869 3480
      Ceann Langabhat

As you leave the *Bhaltos* (Valtos) Peninsula, you will pass the church to the east of the road.

Ceann Langabhat church was originally built as a Free Church in 1843. The then owner of Lewis, Mrs Stewart MacKenzie, refused permission to build a Free Church on her land so, in response, the local crofters built up the shoreline to create new land. This is therefore a very early example of the physical results of the resistance to land-lords' influence over the Church of Scotland which had led to the Church of Scotland splitting earlier that year.

8. The Modern Outer Hebrides:
A Strategic Focus

At the beginning of the 20th century, life for many people in the Outer Hebrides still followed patterns that had been established in the Post-Mediaeval centuries. Most of the islands' population still lived a rural, subsistence farming life. Twenty years of security of tenure for crofters had not eliminated the feeling of insecurity, and there were still many people who had no rights to a croft and squatted on land held by relatives, or on smallholdings won from common grazings. Land hunger persisted, and the islands were amongst the poorest areas of Britain.

The town of *Steornabhagh* (Stornoway) was growing and had a well-established harbour, which was a focal point for the herring fisheries which supported the economy of much of northern Scotland. Herring fleets anchored throughout the islands, and men and women worked with the fleet, with men fishing and women cleaning and packing the fish. Ferry services ran regularly from the islands' ports, and a road network had extended across the landscape, providing land linkages through the islands.

Despite continuing emigration, the islands' population was growing vigorously, and state education in English was universally available, so literacy and English fluency were very widely spread. Hebrideans could be found throughout the British Empire, and bilingual, Gaelic-speaking communities were established in most of the Empire cities. Islanders worked at all levels of society, and particularly served in large numbers in the merchant navy. There was continuous movement between these expatriate communities and the result, in the Outer Hebrides themselves, was a cosmopolitan society, many of whose members were comfortable in multiple languages and cultures, and where families existed in a worldwide network of kinships and friendships.

First World War

In this context, the call-up for the First World War – the 'Great War' – was rapidly responded to. The national government promised that at the end of the war there would be 'a land fit for heroes', which was understood on the islands as 'land for heroes', and of the total population of 29,600 in *Leodhas* (Lewis), 6,700 men, nearly 23% of the population, signed up. There was a widespread assumption that military service would lead to crofting land being made available in post-war years, perhaps because of the traditional link between military service and land tenure, and the promise of a reduction in landlessness and insecurity was undoubtedly an important factor in the high levels of volunteering. Although the death rate was not unusually high, at around 17%, the percentage population loss for Lewis was higher than anywhere else in Britain.

But what happened to the islands themselves during the war? The absence of most of the young, male population had affected crofting and industry, particularly fishing. All over Scotland, fishing boats were laid up during the war as their sailors went to serve, and many of these boats were never used again. The bulk of croft work during the war was done by women and older men. Rationing was not introduced until towards the end of the war, so, during the war, the islanders continued to depend largely upon local production of food.

Steornabhagh harbour was home to a naval yacht during the war and was a strategic port on the western seaboard. That shipping movements and communication along the west coast were strategically important is demonstrated by the U-boat attack on St Kilda in May 1918, which destroyed the military wireless station that had been established there at the beginning of the war. There was no loss of life and little damage; the U-boat issued a warning prior to the shelling, and the residents fled the village for the surrounding hills. As a result of this a gun emplacement was set up on *Hiort* (Hirte) in October 1918, a month before the end of the war, but it was never fired in anger. The gun is still visible at the eastern end of the village.

The sinking of the Iolaire

At the end of the war, Scottish survivors were demobilised in time for them to return home for the New Year celebrations. At that time in Scotland, the New Year was much more widely celebrated as a festival and holiday than was Christmas, and demobilised men from Lewis and *Na Hearadh* (Harris) were eager to get back to the island for the celebrations.

The *Iolaire*, the naval yacht that had been based in Steornabhagh harbour, was sent to Kyle of Lochalsh on the mainland to collect men on New Year's Eve 1918. Official records state that 283 men were passengers aboard the boat, but there is some uncertainty as to the accuracy of the records. Coming into *Steornabhagh* harbour, in deteriorating weather conditions very early in the morning of New Year's Day 1919, the boat wrecked on *Biastean Thuilm* (the 'Beasts of Holm'), a reef at the entrance to the harbour, with the loss of at least 205 lives of passengers and crew. Only 82 of the passengers survived, a devastating blow to the islands of Lewis and Harris, made worse in the context of such terrible wartime losses. Poetry and oral traditions from across the island describe the families collecting corpses and children's toys, gifts for the holiday, from the *Steornabhagh* beaches in the days following the disaster.

War memorials

Travelling around the islands, the visitor will see many war memorials. Some of these, including the tower on *Cnoc an Uan* just outside *Steornabhagh*, date to just after the Great War. The Lewis War Memorial on *Cnoc an Uan* was funded by public subscription and includes the names of the dead of the *Iolaire*, as well as those lost in the conflict. The location was chosen because all the four parishes of Lewis are visible from that spot.

Recently, as the last of the survivors of the Second World War have died and the hundredth anniversary of the First World War has been marked, new memorials have been raised in many individual villages throughout the islands. There is also a memorial to the sinking of the *Iolaire* at Holm, outside Stornoway, and a stone pillar on the reef, which can be seen from ships entering and leaving the harbour.

Migration and movement – the inter-war years

Unfortunately, the promised new crofts for soldiers failed to materialise on the scale required after the war and, during the early 1920s, the government encouraged emigration from the islands. There were better prospects of land and work in the colonies, and the 1920s was a decade of mass emigration from Scotland. The overall population of Scotland fell by nearly 40,000 between 1921 and 1931, a fall of 1%, but the population of the Outer Hebrides fell by nearly 6,000 in the same period, a fall of 12%, despite high birth rates. However, these figures do not capture the true scale of the movement; over 360,000 Scots migrated during this decade, and most of the migrants were young, economically active people, the majority of them men. The social impact of this movement, after the loss of men in the war, was significant.

In the islands, this movement of people was marked by a decline in the land under cultivation, and a reduction in the rural population. There was also a gradual but steady increase in the overall standard of living. The Highlands and Islands Medical Service had been established just before the war and, by the 1920s, had doctors and nurses throughout the islands providing accessible and inexpensive treatment. Provision of hospitals throughout the islands had started in the late 19th century, and the first air ambulance services were established in the 1930s.

One of the ways in which the rise in living standards was visible was the construction of new 'white' houses, of mortared stone. Government grants for crofters to build houses to standard plans meant fewer traditional drystone houses were built, though the new houses were often as densely occupied as the earlier ones. Stories tell of new houses in which each room of a four-room house was occupied by an entire family. Many of these houses are still occupied today, and it is important to remember, when looking at the landscape, that most of the mortared-stone cottages that are visible were built in the 20th century (Fig. 75).

As the Great Depression took hold in the 1930s, there was some return migration, as unemployed islanders came home to live and work on family land, but the overall population trend in the islands continued downwards throughout the 1930s. Crofts were made available in

Fig. 75. Grant-aided house types

a few new settlements during this period, for example at *Sgarasta* (Scarista) in Harris and *Solas* (Sollas) in *Uibhist a' Tuath* (North Uist), but the demand for land continued to be high and unmet. In many townships, related families could be found sharing single crofts. With the Depression affecting the tweed industry, cash was short; Harris author Finlay J. MacDonald wrote a vivid memoir of this period, *Crowdie and Cream*, describing growing up on the islands between the two world wars, through the years of the Depression.

Changing technology

The inter-war years were also characterised by technological changes and developments. One of the most colourful of these episodes was the 1934 experiment with transporting mail by rocket, tested by German rocket engineer Gerhard Zucker, between the offshore island of Scarp (Site 149) and Harris. It failed, and the rocket exploded. However, the same year, and more successfully, the first air flights to the islands heralded the start of what was to become a life-line service with the opening of airports at *Beinn na Fhaoghla* (Benbecula) in 1936 and *Steornabhagh* in 1937. From the beginning, the air service was both military and civilian, and an air ambulance service was introduced in 1936, allowing the medical service to send patients rapidly to mainland hospitals for urgent treatment. Water and electricity services started to spread gradually outwith the main towns.

Second World War

In 1939, the outbreak of the Second World War once again saw significant enlistment from the islands' population. During this war, however, the islands themselves became an important strategic base, and many remains of wartime structures can still be seen. The Royal Air Force, based at Benbecula and *Steornabhagh* airports, expanded the runways and constructed buildings and housing in the surrounding areas. Estates of military housing can be seen to the south of *Baile Mhanaich* in Benbecula, reflecting the continuing military presence here after the war, until the 1990s, while large concrete foundations of buildings, now removed, east of the runways at Stornoway airport remain from the Stornoway base, which continued in operation until the 1980s.

Radar stations were established in *Tabost* (Habost) in *Nis* (Ness), at the northern end of Lewis, and on the west coast of Lewis at *Aird Uig*. Although most of the buildings related to the *Tabost* station and the associated camp at *Eorodail* are no longer visible, some still survive as parts of houses and sheds that are currently in use. This station went out of use at the end of the war, in 1945, but the *Aird Uig* station, at *An Gallan Uigeach* (Gallan Head), continued in use until the 1990s, gradually shrinking in size and personnel.

A Royal Naval gun battery protected the entrance to Stornoway Harbour and can still be seen at *Rubha Airinis* (Arnish Point) (Fig. 76), on the western coast of the harbour. This consisted of two gun emplacements, an observation post, and searchlight emplacements, of poured concrete and brick construction, which were armed with four-inch guns.

Elsewhere in the islands, the remains of smaller military establishments and structures can be seen. At *Mealastadh* (Mealista) (Site 183), at the southern end of the road along the west coast of Lewis,

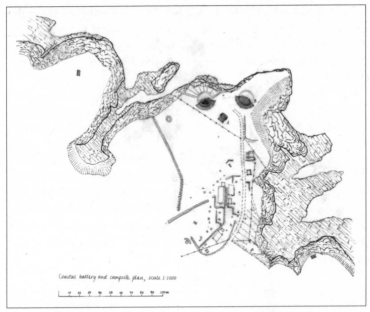

Fig. 76. *Rubha Airinis* (Arnish Point) gun emplacement, *Leodhas* (Lewis)
(© Crown copyright: HES)

the well-preserved remains of an air raid shelter are close to the road, near the footings of buildings and communications masts constructed by the RAF. In *Ness*, at *Carnan a' Ghrodhair* in *Suainebost* (Swainbost), a small lookout post above the western Atlantic coast was inserted into a mound in the machair, breaking through into a well-preserved Iron Age souterrain, or underground passage.

Ceos (Keose) Harbour in Lewis was the site of a particularly interesting military establishment of the Second World War. In the middle years of the war, it was a submarine base where early testing and training on small submarines called the 'Chariot human torpedo' were carried out. These were vehicles on which one or two divers sat, which could be steered and propelled underwater.

Throughout the islands, controls on civilian movements were put in place, and the islands were a 'controlled zone'. This meant that movement to, from, and between islands theoretically required a permit. However, island tradition suggests that movement within the islands continued quite freely, via fishing boats and pleasure craft. This is one of the themes of the famous comic novel *Whisky Galore*, written by the author Compton Mackenzie, who lived in Barra throughout the war, and whose house can still be seen adjacent to the airport in Barra.

Whisky Galore is based on one of the more colourful wartime incidents, the sinking of the *Politician*. The *Politician* was a cargo vessel, heading for America in 1941, which sank near *Eirisgeigh* (Eriskay), between *Uibhist a' Deas* (South Uist) and *Barraigh* (Barra). Her cargo was almost entirely whisky, and when this became known, much of the cargo was removed from the stricken ship by islanders from throughout the Hebrides. Banknotes were also being carried on the ship and these turned up shortly afterwards at banks throughout the sphere of British influence, as far away as Jamaica, Canada and Switzerland, emphasising the worldwide links of the islands, particularly during the war.

The Cold War

Although the end of the war allowed the lifting of restrictions on movement in the islands, military influence remained strong. Throughout the 1950s and 1960s, *Steornabhagh* airport was home to units testing military equipment, reputedly both electronic and chemical. The military presence continued there until the late 1990s, with the airport functioning as a NATO forward operating base for much of the 1970s and 1980s, until the fall of the Berlin Wall and political changes in Russia marked a decrease in international tensions.

In 1957, South Uist became the base of the Deep Sea Range, a long-range missile testing base, with its tracking station on St Kilda. Initially, this met with significant local resistance, particularly as some crofters were dispossessed of their land by the construction of the range head, and this resistance was marked by the construction of the beautiful granite statue of Our Lady of the Isles (Plate 17) by the sculptor Hew Lorimer, on the west-facing slope of the hill *Ruabhal* (Rueval) in South Uist. The rocket range, as it is locally known, is still in operation, though it is proposed at present to close it in 2028.

Modern times – the 1970s onwards

In 1975, the islands were united under one local authority area for the first time, and a new local council was created, initially called Western Isles Council, now *Comhairle nan Eilean Siar*. This had a significant impact on the landscape of the islands, which for the first time were not managed from the mainland. The priorities of the new council included improvements to the road system and housing, to slow rural depopulation, and to improve the education system, to allow children to stay at home for as long as possible before moving away for further education.

Key to the infrastructure improvements were the construction of improved causeways and bridges, and improved ferry services, to allow free movement throughout the islands. The double-track roads, reinforced causeways and bridges (Fig. 77), which allow visitors to travel from the south of Barra to the north of Lewis, are largely a result of this strategy and of national and European funding support.

New social housing was created throughout the islands and, with few exceptions, the last of the old thatched houses went out of use in the 1970s. Secondary schools were built in Barra and in Benbecula, to ensure that children did not have to leave the islands to attend school, and Lews Castle College expanded its provision to include degree teaching as part of the University of the Highlands and Islands.

Although the islands remain one of the poorer areas of Scotland

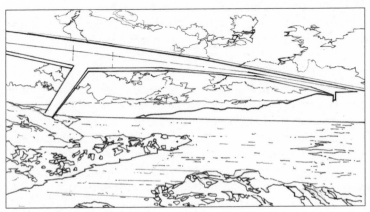

Fig. 77. *Scalpaigh* (Scalpay) Bridge

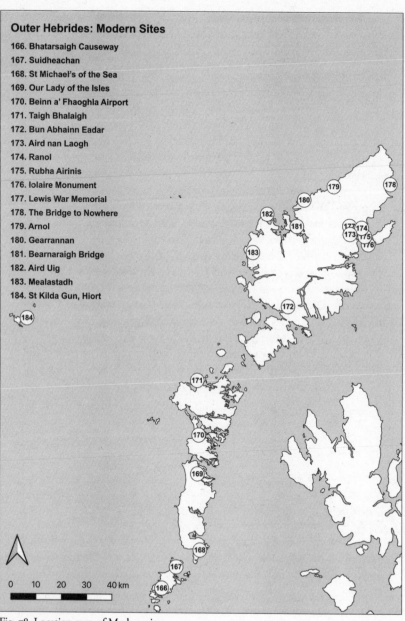

Outer Hebrides: Modern Sites

166. Bhatarsaigh Causeway
167. Suidheachan
168. St Michael's of the Sea
169. Our Lady of the Isles
170. Beinn a' Fhaoghla Airport
171. Taigh Bhalaigh
172. Bun Abhainn Eadar
173. Aird nan Laogh
174. Ranol
175. Rubha Airinis
176. Iolaire Monument
177. Lewis War Memorial
178. The Bridge to Nowhere
179. Arnol
180. Gearrannan
181. Bearnaraigh Bridge
182. Aird Uig
183. Mealastadh
184. St Kilda Gun, Hiort

0   10   20   30   40 km

Fig. 78. Location map of Modern sites

by measures such as disposable income per head, living standards are now vastly better than they were at the beginning of the 20th century. Generations of policy support for housing, education and infrastructure development have increased provision of services, access to transport, and the availability of good jobs to a level which would amaze our great-grandparents.

Every year, the islands welcome thousands of visitors from all over the world, many with family links to local people, who come to see and learn about the rich history of the community and to appreciate the beauty of the landscape.

GAZETTEER

Barraigh (Barra)

166. *Bhatarsaigh* (Vatersay) causeway   NL 6374 9759

Links the islands of Vatersay and Barra.

Construction on the Vatersay causeway began in 1989 and was completed in 1991. The population of the island of Vatersay had been falling for decades before the causeway construction was announced but turned the corner and started to rise as soon as the announcement was made. The creation of a permanent link, which allowed islanders to safely access healthcare, education and work year-round, made the small community sustainable.

167. *Suidheachan*   NF 69374 05615

Immediately to the west of the road to the airport. A private house.

This low, white house was originally built in 1935 by the author Compton MacKenzie, famous for the book *Whisky Galore*, who is buried at *Eoligearraidh* (Eoligarry) in Barra. It was later used as a factory for producing shell grit, and it was restored as a private house in 1999.

Uibhist a' Deas (South Uist)

168. St Michael's of the Sea, *Eirisgeigh* (Eriskay) NF 78656 12055

West of the main road leading through Eriskay from the ferry terminal to the causeway.

The church of St Michael's (Plate 18) was built by the islanders of Eriskay at the turn of the 20th century, using local stone, mortar made from shells, and timber salvaged from shipwrecks. The trigger for the construction of a new church was the arrival of the first priest for the island parish.

169. Our Lady of the Isles, *Ruabhal* (Rueval) NF 77635 40740

East of the A865, on the slopes of *Ruabhal*, overlooking the west coast of South Uist.

The statue of the Madonna and Child on the slopes of *Ruabhal* (Plate 17), facing out towards the Atlantic Ocean, was commissioned by local priest Canon John Morrison in the 1950s. The context of its construction was vigorous local resistance to the construction of a large missile testing range on South Uist, shortly after the end of the Second World War.

The work was designed by Hew Lorimer and is constructed of pink granite. It is located immediately downslope of the radar station, which forms part of the still-functional missile testing range.

Beinn a' Fhaoghla (Benbecula)

170. *Beinn a' Fhaoghla* (Benbecula) airport NF 78033 55338

To the north of the B892 in *Baile a' Mhanaich* (Balivanich).

The construction of the airport on Benbecula dates to just before the Second World War. It has always had a military presence, and the barracks to the north of the road and the south of the airport are on the site of an extensive Second World War military camp. The large estates of uniform housing in the southern and western part of the town were originally military housing.

Uibhist a' Tuath (North Uist)

171. *Taigh Bhalaigh* (Vallay House), *Bhalaigh*   NF 77360 75908
(Vallay)

Vallay island is tidally accessible from *Cladach Bhalaigh* on North Uist. Take local advice about crossing to the island and be extremely careful.

The largest house on Vallay is the most recent. Built in the early 1900s for Erskine Beveridge, who was a businessman from Dunfermline, it was the focus of his passions for naturalism and, particularly, archaeology. He excavated extensively on North Uist, and published *North Uist: Its Archaeology and Topography* in 1911.

The house was built in the baronial style fashionable at the time, cement-rendered, with crowstepped gables. Its scale and amenities were certainly in contrast to the other houses in use on the island at the time (Site 138). The water for the house was piped across *Traigh Bhalaigh* from a reservoir on North Uist, and tonnes of peat were cut and carted across the strand each year to heat it.

After Beveridge's death in 1920 in Dunfermline, the house was inherited by his son, who tragically drowned crossing the strand in the 1940s. The house is now entirely derelict and dangerous, so do not go into the building.

Na Hearadh (Harris)

172. *Bun Abhainn Eadar* (Bunavoneader)   NB 1310 0397
whaling station

West of the B887 road to *Huisinis*. Visible from the main A859 road heading north towards *Steornabhagh* (Stornoway).

The most noticeable surviving feature of the *Bun Abhainn Eadar* whaling station is its tall, red-brick chimney, clearly visible from the main road, particularly when travelling northward towards Stornoway. However, much of the structure of the whaling station survives, including its sea walls, jetty and flensing (skinning) platform, along with some of the buildings. It is one of the best-preserved whaling stations in the northern hemisphere.

The station was built in the early 20th century by a Norwegian company, and was acquired by Lever Brothers, the Leverhulme company, in 1922. However, it was closed in 1929 and, although it was reopened briefly in 1951 and 1952, the North Atlantic whaling industry had already passed its peak by the beginning of the 20th century, and it was not commercially viable.

173. Seaplane Slipway, *Aird nan Laogh* (Cuddy Point)

NB 4192 3281

Park at the Woodland Centre and follow the surfaced seawall path south 580m to Cuddy Point.

During the Second World War, a slipway for seaplanes, visible on aerial photographs, was constructed at Cuddy Point, as part of the wider use of Stornoway Harbour by the Fleet Air Arm. The large slipway on the northern side of Cuddy Point and the extended and resurfaced pier that presently exist are first shown on maps after this date and have developed from the wartime structures.

Wartime aerial photographs show numerous huts on the green in front of the castle, to provide accommodation, but nothing can be seen of these now. Oral tradition indicates that these were barracks for men serving on the flying boats, but they probably also provided accommodation for gunners on the battery at Ranol, and for the RAF air-sea rescue teams which operated out of Stornoway. The military also took over Lews Castle during the war.

174. Ranol Anti-aircraft Battery

NB 4194 3366

Park at the golf course and cut across the course to join the network of footpaths on the western side of the course, an uphill walk of around 650m, or park at Marybank Lodge and walk 1km along the footpath network from the west.

There is a heavy anti-aircraft battery at Ranol on *Steornabhagh* (Stornoway) Golf Course, consisting of two octagonal concrete and brick gun emplacements, two bunkers and a command position, and dating to the Second World War. One bunker is located 20m north-west of the emplacements, and the other is around 40m south-east of and in front of them. The partly demolished command position is around 30m north-west of the emplacements.

There are no known records for this installation, and it may be one of the many military structures which were rapidly constructed during the Second World War without an administrative trail. It formed a part of a network of defensive military structures established around *Steornabhagh* Harbour during the Second World War, some of which are known from oral testimony, and others of which were largely forgotten and have reappeared unexpectedly during development in recent years.

175. *Rubha Airinis* (Arnish Point) Gun Emplacement   NB 4318 3054

Park at the fabrication yard, and then follow the coastal track on foot around the eastern edge of the point for 600m before turning left onto the path to the gun emplacements. The site is also clearly visible from the ferry coming into the harbour.

This coastal battery (see Fig. 76) was a key element in the Second World War defences of *Steornabhagh* harbour. It overlooks the entrance to the harbour and was constructed and manned by the Royal Navy. It consists of two gun emplacements, an observation post and two searchlight platforms. The gun emplacements are well preserved, and still have some of their original signs forbidding smoking, and indicating which rooms were used as magazines and gun stores, along with the metal bases for the guns. To the west of the gun emplacements are the remains of the accommodation camp; several concrete hut bases can be seen.

Although the original ladder is still present in the battery observation post, it is not safe to access the upper floor of the building, and there have been problems with flooding in one of the gun emplacements.

176. *Iolaire* monument   NB 44507 30483

Park at the end of road, beside waterworks, and walk 340m south across the field following a grass path.

This monument was constructed in memory of the 201 men who were lost in the sinking of the admiralty yacht *Iolaire*, early on New Year's Day in 1919, as she returned to *Steornabhagh* (Stornoway) carrying men who had survived the First World War. The reef where the ship sank, called *Biastean Thuilm* (the 'Beasts of Holm'), is visible from the monument, close to the shore and marked with a post to ward off shipping. The wreck has recently been designated as a war grave.

177. Lewis War Memorial   NB 41712 34351

Signposted from the A859 in Stornoway, and visible on the skyline from roads approaching the town.

The Lewis War Memorial was erected after the First World War to commemorate the dead of the whole island and was located on *Cnoc nan Uan* because all four civil parishes of the island could be seen from that point. It was opened in 1924 by Lord Leverhulme, the largest single contributor to the project, who was on the point of leaving the islands, never to return, having sold the Isle of Lewis.

178. The Bridge to Nowhere, *Gearadha* (Garry)   NB 5313 5018

At the end of the B895, in the deserted township of *Gearadha*.

Lord Leverhulme intended to build a road along the eastern coast of Lewis, linking *Steornabhagh* (Stornoway) to *Nis* (Ness) and completing the circuit of roads around the island. However, this scheme, along with his wider scheme of works for the island, failed, and the handsome bridge (Fig. 79) at the end of the road is a symbol of the failure. The route north between this point and Ness can be followed as a footpath.

Fig. 79. The Bridge to Nowhere, *Gearadha* (Garry), *Leodhas* (Lewis)

179. No. 39, Arnol   NB 31044 49274

Turn north off the A859 following signs for the Arnol Blackhouse.

As croft house grants became available for building and renovating croft houses in the 20th century, increasingly the traditional thatched houses were replaced by mortared stone houses (see Fig. 75). These new houses were often called 'white houses' because of their mortared walls and larger windows, but the phrase 'white house' first occurred many centuries earlier with reference to mortared buildings, particularly churches.

This building was constructed in the 1920s to a standard design, to accommodate the family who lived in the thatched house (now roofless) to the south. It has been refurnished as a small museum to give an impression of what such a house would have looked like when in use. However, problems with damp penetration into the building are evident, and reveal some of the problems which were sometimes encountered with the modern construction methods. Typically, such a house would have been full of people and continually heated by a stove in the kitchen; in the islands' climate deterioration can be rapid when buildings are not in use.

180. Gearrannan (Garenin)   NB 1935 4419

Turn west at the northern end of *Carlabhagh* (Carloway) Bridge and follow the signs for the blackhouse village.

Most of the houses in the *Gearrannan* village are late 19th or early 20th century in date. Some of them remained occupied until the construction of the social housing at the southern end of the township in the 1970s.

One of the houses has been renovated as a museum, and it offers an interesting contrast to the thatched house at Arnol (Site 156). The house has fireplaces in the gables, rather than in the middle of the floor, and internal panelling. Box beds were still used, but the floors were covered in linoleum. Although the roofs of the buildings are now thatched, many of them were latterly covered with roofing felt, which was more waterproof.

As you leave the thatched houses and return towards Carloway, you can see the standard plan croft houses which replaced the thatched houses through the 20th century. These progress from the single-storey, two room and attic pattern, through one and a half storeys, to 1950s bungalows, succeeded by modern kit houses (see Fig. 75).

181. *Bearnaraigh Mor* (Great Bernera) bridge   NB 1648 3418

Follow signs for Great Bernera on the B8059, which crosses the bridge.

This bridge, which was built following decades of lobbying by the community on Great Bernera in 1953, was one of the earliest fixed links between the islands. It is also believed to be the earliest prestressed concrete bridge in Britain.

182. *Aird Uig* ROTOR radar station   NB 0473 3874

Turn right at the western end of the B8011 in Uig and continue to the northern end of the road, following signposts for *Aird Uig*.

This military site, still closed to the public, is the second of the two radar stations in Uig, the earlier being that at *Mealastadh* (Mealista) (see overleaf). Originally dating to the Second World War, the station was upgraded in the 1950s to a ROTOR station, part of a later network of early warning stations around the coast of the British Isles. The radar provision became increasingly obsolete in the late 1950s and 1960s.

The township of *Aird Uig* is partly made up of the remains of accommodation for staff manning the station, but the station itself remains closed to the public.

183. *Mealastadh* (Mealista) Chain Home Radar Station   NA 9914 2424

At the southern end of the road down the west coast of Uig, in the deserted township of *Mealastadh*.

In the deserted township of *Mealastadh*, on either side of the road before you reach the remains of the post-mediaeval village or the end of the road at the slipway, is a group of bunkers, concrete hut stances and a brick and concrete generator house. These are the remains of a Chain Home radar station, one of a string of coastal radar stations built before and at the beginning of the Second World War, which were strategically placed to track aircraft flying over the British Isles. The Chain Home network was the first early warning radar network in the world.

Hiort (St Kilda)

184. St Kilda Gun, *Hiort* (Hirta)   NF 10427 99028

At the eastern point of the Village on *Hiort*.

The St Kilda gun (Plate 19) was installed as a result of a German U-boat attack on the village in 1918. The U-boat gave an audible warning, and no one in the village was injured, but there was damage to the buildings and the wireless station, and it was one of very few direct attacks on the British shoreline during the First World War. As a result, the gun was installed in a tearing hurry and commissioned in October 1918. Two weeks later, Armistice was declared, and the gun was never fired.

Further Reading

Armit, I. 1996 *The Archaeology of Skye and the Western Isles*, Edinburgh University Press, Edinburgh

Ashmore, P. 2016 *Calanais Survey and Excavation 1979–88*, Historic Environment Scotland, Edinburgh

Badcock, A. 2008 *Ancient Uists: exploring the archaeology of the Outer Hebrides*, Comhairle nan Eilean Siar, Stornoway

Barrowman, C. S. 2015 *The Archaeology of Ness*, Acair, Stornoway

Barrowman, R. C. 2015 *Dun Eistean, Ness, Isle of Lewis: the excavation of a mediaeval clan stronghold*, Acair, Stornoway

Branigan, K. 2007 *Ancient Barra: exploring the archaeology of the Outer Hebrides*, Comhairle nan Eilean Siar, Stornoway

Branigan, K. 2012 *Barra: Episodes from an Island's History*, Amberley Publishing

Branigan, K. & Foster, P. 1995 *Barra: Archaeological Research on Ben Tangaval*, Sheffield University Press

Branigan, K. & Foster, P. 2000 *From Barra to Berneray: Archaeological survey and excavation in the Southern Isles of the Outer Hebrides*, Sheffield Academic Press

Branigan, K. & Foster, P. 2002 *Barra and the Bishop's Isles: Living on the Margin*, Tempus, Stroud

Burgess, C. 2008 *Ancient Lewis and Harris: Exploring the archaeology of the Outer Hebrides*, Comhairle nan Eilean Siar, Stornoway

Crawford, B. 1987 *Scandinavian Scotland*, Leicester University Press

Graham Campbell, J. & Batey, C. 1998 *Vikings in Scotland*, Edinburgh University Press

Miers, M. 2008 *The Western Seaboard: An Illustrated Architectural Guide*, Rutland Press

Parker Pearson, M. 1999 *Between Land and Sea: Excavations at Dun Vulan, South Uist*, Sheffield Academic Press

Parker Pearson, M., Sharples, N. & Symonds, J. 2004 *South Uist: Archaeology and History of a Hebridean Island*, Tempus, Stroud

Sharples, N. (ed.) 2005 *A Norse Farmstead in the Outer Hebrides: Excavations at Mound 3, Bornais, South Uist*, Cardiff Studies in Archaeology, Oxbow

Sharples, N. (ed.) 2012 *A Late Iron Age farmstead in the Outer Hebrides: Excavations at Mound 1, Bornais, South Uist*, Cardiff Studies in Archaeology, Oxbow

Sharples, N. (ed.) 2019 *A Norse Settlement in the Outer Hebrides: Excavations on Mounds 2 and 2A, Bornais, South Uist*, Oxbow

Index